Judith Stone and Felicity Taylor

A Handbook for Parents
with a Handicapped Child

Arrow Books

Arrow Books Limited
3 Fitzroy Square, London W1

An imprint of the Hutchinson Publishing Group

London Melbourne Sydney Auckland
Wellington Johannesburg and agencies
throughout the world

First published by Arrow Books 1977
© Judith Stone and Felicity Taylor 1977

Made and printed in Great Britain
by The Anchor Press Ltd
Tiptree, Essex

ISBN 0 09 914610 x

Contents

Introduction

This conversation has taken place every day for the last year:

'My name is Judith Stone (or Felicity Taylor). I am working on a handbook for parents with a handicapped child together with my partner Felicity Taylor (or Judith Stone).'

'What organization are you from?'

'None.'

'Who are you?'

'Ourselves.'

People seem to be genuinely puzzled by two people who have no links with any organization and no handicapped children of their own writing a book like this.

We see this book as our tribute, in both senses of the word, to all those families, individuals and organizations who are caring for handicapped children: we pay tribute to the work that they are doing and we offer this guide as our contribution.

There is no need for us to speak for the parents of handicapped children: we could not improve on what they have to say for themselves. In their words:

No matter how easy the child is to handle, how much it is accepted by all the family, how much it is loved, it has completely altered the way of life of a whole family. The families of the handicapped have, in the past, been conditioned into accepting whatever was offered to them in the way of support. The feeling of 'shame and blame' has effectively silenced any protests or questions which they may privately have wished to put to those in Authority regarding the appropriateness or the quality of the care offered to them. The present generation is not so meek.

We hope this book will help them in their struggle to improve the quality of life for their whole family, without what one mother of a handicapped child has called 'the lacerating pilgrimage of parents of the retarded and abnormal . . . trying to buy hope'.

HOW TO USE THE HANDBOOK

We have given the address of the head office of every organization, which in some cases is the only office. However, many of the societies have local branches – sometimes more than 300 of them – and you will probably want to find the nearest one. Whatever happens the head office of a society can tell you where to find your local branch. You will find some of them listed in your local phone book. The post office should have lists of approved organizations such as the citizens advice bureaux and the British Red Cross as well as official services. Libraries can sometimes help too.

Many small societies rely entirely on voluntary help and are run from the secretary's front room. You may need to ring at evenings and weekends to get hold of anyone. Their address may change from year to year with the office holder. If you are asking a small voluntary group to send information to you, enclose stamps (not an envelope which may be the wrong size); they probably subsidize the postage for the group out of their housekeeping.

WHAT IS IN THE BOOK

The handbook will *not* tell you what is wrong with your child and it does not describe handicaps. It is not a consumers' guide to the services offered by the organizations in it; our main source of information has to be what they tell us about themselves.

We have included every organization we could find which offered a direct service to parents of handicapped children. We also include organizations whose activities or research would be of interest to parents although they are not offering a direct service. We have not described the activities of local branches of national organizations, but we have described small, independent, local groups who are doing something that is within the scope of any family and a few friends.

We have listed publications and films only where they seemed to offer help to parents which was not easily available anywhere else. We tell you where to find comprehensive lists of books and films in chapter 3.

SCOTLAND

Scotland has the special problems of a small population in a large area. Problems which are hard to solve in thriving, well-populated and prosperous areas are harder still with shortage of resources and a scattered population. And the distances which have to be covered contribute to the disparity in provision from one area to another which is one of the most disappointing and frustrating experiences for parents throughout the UK. Parents are bound to feel some resentment when they cannot get services for their child which they know are available to families in other areas. Scotland suffers worst of all from this particular difficulty. But if you live fifty miles from the nearest day centre for the handicapped or 100 miles from the nearest large town, you cannot really criticize the local authority for not providing transport.

The one densely populated conurbation, Glasgow, suffers from all the disadvantages of urban deprivation with some of the worst housing in Europe and often totally inadequate resources to deal with its problems. When the ordinary population is severely deprived of amenities, social services and employment opportunities, the lot of the handicapped is likely to be as bad if not worse.

This is not to say that some of Scotland's provision for the handicapped, particularly in Glasgow, is not outstandingly good, or to suggest that Scottish authorities are not aware of their needs. One advantage of small numbers is greater intimacy; you tend to know most of the other individuals in the field, you are not dealing with large departments but with a few familiar faces. Hugh Stewart,

Assistant General Secretary of the Scottish Society for the Mentally Handicapped, tells the story of one paediatrician who makes a point of assessing children according to what he thinks will interest their local authority. If he knows they cater particularly well for spastics, he assesses the child as spastic; if they have a good school for mentally handicapped children, he decides that the child is mentally handicapped.

This is the first time we have included Scotland in the handbook and, while we have done our best to make sure that differences in the Scottish system have been taken into account, we cannot claim to have all the organizations and initiatives for handicapped children in Scotland.

We have not given addresses for Scottish branches of national societies which cover the whole of Great Britain.

We should like to thank the many organizations and individuals who have spent so much time in answering our questions and giving us help and encouragement ever since we prepared the first short version of this handbook for the Home and School Council in 1972.

Comments from parents would be invaluable. We want the book to be really useful and we need you to tell us what information you found helpful and what was confusing. Please write in with your suggestions and with news of any new group, activity or research experiment which other parents might want to know about.

It is difficult to avoid abbreviations when so many societies have half a dozen words to their title, but we have limited their use as much as possible. If you find some initials you don't understand, the index should direct you to the right organization. We have used the abbreviation 'he' for 'he or she' throughout the book.

All the addresses were checked in November 1976. Whenever possible, we mention when a move is being planned for 1977.

Judith Stone and Felicity Taylor   November 1976
5 Robin Grove, London N6 6PA

1 Parents with a Handicapped Child

How to find out if there is anything wrong
How parents can help their child
Parents' action groups

How to find out if there is anything wrong

The first step towards getting help for a handicapped child is for it to be recognized that a problem exists. Although some handicaps are noticeable at birth, others show up only as the child fails to grow and develop normally.

Even when a child's development seems to be different from other children of his age, this does not necessarily mean that there is anything wrong. Normal children may develop in different ways and at different rates and, of course, no one should assume that his child has any serious problem simply because he is not doing the same things at the same time as the child next door or as his older brother and sister did when they were his age. What is important is that a child is seen to be making progress as he gets older.

It is often parents who are the first to suspect when something is wrong. They may only be able to describe something which sounds minor or trivial on its own when they try to explain to the doctor why they are worried, but this is often because a whole lot of other worrying things about the child's behaviour are too elusive to pin down. Nevertheless, they reinforce the parent's intuition that something is wrong somewhere.

Parents of handicapped children often complain that they could not get anyone to take their worries seriously. Typical reactions are: 'It's because you are over-anxious that he doesn't sit up/walk/speak/read' and so on, or 'Don't worry, lots of children don't walk till they are three, talk till they are five, read till they are twelve. . . .' Too many parents of handicapped children have acquired the unfair label of 'fussy parent' at some stage before their child's handicap was recognized.

Warning signs

Professor R. S. Illingworth, University of Sheffield, in 'The development of the infant and young child, normal and abnormal' (reproduced in *The Handicapped Person in the Community*, edited by D. M. Boswell and J. M. Wingrove Open University, 1974), emphasizes the significance of 'the baby's alertness, interest in surroundings, powers of concentration, and determination – all items which are difficult to translate into scores.'

Although one child's development may vary from any other child, most children reach the same stage of development in each of the different fields at about the same time: children who are up to the average in their rate of physical development (their growth and their control of body movements) are also likely to be up to the average in co-ordination of sight and fine movements, communication, self-help and behaviour. So it is a warning signal when a child's development in one of these fields is conspicuously retarded in comparison with his rate of progress in other fields.

Normal babies acquire skills like sitting up, crawling, walking, learning bladder and bowel control at widely differing ages, but doctors seem to agree that there are some developments which occur in normal children within much narrower time limits. For instance, Professor Illingworth reports that a normal baby who was born at full-term will begin to smile between four and six weeks, and Dr Hugh Jolly, Consultant Paediatrician at Charing Cross Hospital, has suggested that a full-term baby who has had normal stimulation should be tested for brain damage if he is not smiling by the time he is ten weeks old.

Screening

In some areas a register is kept of all babies who are 'at risk'. The district community physician is responsible for any registers and there are local differences in the way in which they are compiled, but they might include children whose mothers have had illnesses in pregnancy; babies who showed some abnormal reactions at birth or immediately afterwards; babies born to families who already have a handicapped child.

If you are worried about your baby's development you should find out from your family health centre if your area has this system and, if so, confirm whether or not your baby is on the register. If he is on the register your baby will be seen regularly and any abnormality carefully checked so you should have plenty of opportunities to discuss any worries. If you are not on the register you may have to take the initiative to get advice about your child's development. The health visitor or doctor at the clinic or your GP are the obvious people to ask about your worries in the first place.

Some local authorities are now screening every baby at regular intervals. Detailed developmental records are kept of the results of tests on the baby's movement and posture, vision and hand–eye coordination, hearing and speech and social behaviour. Practice varies in different areas, but a typical pattern is to make these tests when the baby is about six weeks old, again at about six months, twelve months and eighteen months and after that at each birthday. If this system is operating efficiently in your area any difficulties should be recognized very early on.

Early recognition of handicap is obviously crucial for the best chance of effective treatment so anyone, whether or not they usually take their baby to the clinic, should not hesitate to ask the clinic to arrange for a developmental test for their baby if they are worried about any aspect of his progress.

Any GP who has his own 'baby clinic' will be able to do similar developmental tests.

Telling the parents about the handicap

'I think the doctor could have done it in a nicer way than he did, a sort of stab-in-the-back he gave me. . . .' Who is to say whether such statements are true or false or distortions of what actually took place? It is irrelevant to ask. What *is* relevant is to say that the parents came away from a consultation feeling that this is what actually did take place. Parents' reaction to their child's handicap is often conditioned by the way in which they are first told about it.

WHAT CAN BE DONE ABOUT IT?

One parents' group has suggested a few simple rules to help the medical profession be more sensitive to what is helpful to parents and what destructive at this lonely time:

1 As far as possible to tell both parents together.
2 If it is reasonably certain that there is evidence of handicap, tell parents as soon as possible.
3 In the very early days there should be someone to confide in and talk to – possibly another parent.
4 Special training for all medical and nursing staff to inhibit uninformed comment.
5 Ensure that parents, GPs and health visitors are aware of the child's condition and what this will mean. It is very difficult for parents to understand, after being told by their hospital doctor that their child is handicapped, how their GP and health visitor can be unaware of this fact.

Amongst the many doctors who are now aware of the critical importance of these early stages, one Southend medical officer has set up a scheme for bringing immediate help to parents who have just learnt that their baby is handicapped. All parents are asked if they want a visit from a doctor and a mother who could help them. Within a day or two at most, and usually within hours, if the new parents do want it, Dr Mellor then visits together with the mother of a handicapped child. The combination of doctor and mother is used particularly so that there is the opportunity for the new parents to receive professional help on the one hand and friendship on the other from someone who can say 'I know exactly how you feel for I have lived through this experience myself.' At the first visit, the main aim is to show the parents that they are not alone and to assure them that other parents are always at the other end of the telephone to help on any problem however small or to share any success.

A second visit is made a few days later to answer any of the questions which have come into the parents' minds. When the baby is under a month – often when he is only about ten days old – the parents attend their first meeting of a group of parents with Down's Syndrome babies under the age of two (it was found that these were the only babies known to be definitely mentally handicapped at such an early age). This group support continues as the child grows older. After several years, Dr Mellor was able to comment: 'We now have a new type of family in which the aggression, frustration and bitterness associated with the tragedy of a handicapped child has disappeared and been replaced with hope, insight and activity.'

Assessment

Once it has been recognized that a child has a problem, his needs must be assessed:

1 His medical needs may be assessed in hospital by doctors. Your family health centre and/or GP can refer you to any paediatrician or other consultant for assessment. One of the specialist departments at a hospital will not only be able to make an assessment, but can also undertake any treatment which is necessary.

2 Assessment of the child's educational potential and the opportunities open to him is the responsibility of the education authority and usually involves testing by educational psychologists.

3 A variety of social workers (medical social workers, psychiatric social workers, child-care officers, health visitors and so on) are involved in evaluating the social and family circumstances and the support services available so that they can suggest whether it is best for for him to live at home or in some kind of residential accommodation.

ASSESSMENT CENTRES

Assessment centres are run by local authorities, hospitals, schools, voluntary societies. The seventy regional centres which have been set up by the Regional Health Authorities help to eliminate the effect of local variations in provision by serving a wide area. All centres normally expect a child to be referred by a doctor, but some will allow parents to apply direct. The staff at a multi-disciplinary centre will include paediatricians, educational psychologists and teachers, social workers and child psychiatrists, so that every aspect of the child's future can be taken into account.

No child in hospital, or even at a day centre, can be behaving in his own normal fashion and the behaviour of young children alters significantly if they are separated from their parents for lengthy periods or in a strange situation. A recent report by Mind warns how easy it is to forget 'that the best assessment centre provides an artificial and restricted environment compared with that of the child's own home, and that the behaviour observed may well be misleading' (*Assessment of Children and their Families*, 1975, 50p plus 11p postage).

Mind Northern Office,
157 Woodhouse Lane, Leeds LS2 3EF
Tel: Leeds (0532) 453926

Misleading behaviour cannot form a basis for proper decisions about a child's future. A number of centres now encourage parents to stay with their child during assessment or like the family to move in to the assessment centre with the child for a period of time if necessary. It is worth finding out whether this is possible if you are referred to an assessment centre.

If the parents are allowed to be present there is less likelihood of their own experience and observations of the child being ignored. Dr Elizabeth Newsom of Nottingham University said 'We all think that we are so clever and know the answers but we tend to neglect the fact that parents also know a great deal about the child and have something to contribute.'

The truth of this criticism, made by a professional, is borne out not only by many parents of handicapped children, but also by the study of assessment services in *Spotlight on Physical and Mental Assessment* by Jessie Parfit (published by the National Children's Bureau, 1971, price 90p) where time after time we are told that the child's case is discussed by a panel of experts while the parents wait to be called in and told what the team have decided to do with their child.

Follow up

No decision or diagnosis concerning a child and the possibilities open to him should be presented to parents without suggesting where further advice and support can be found.

Assessment for its own sake will not necessarily help anyone. It should provide the necessary information on which a programme of treatment and education can be based which will enable parents, teachers and therapists of all kinds to help the child to reach the next stage of his development. A once-for-all interview for parents, often at the conclusion of an assessment session, is quite inadequate. Parents need time for all the implications to sink in and a chance to keep coming back whenever they want to ask something.

Ann Jones (a psychologist) wrote in *New Society*: 'By the end of the assessment the specialists should have an excellent understanding of the child's problems and the help he needs. Incredible though it may seem, however, that can often be as far as it goes. All that valuable and vital information gleaned through the experience, skill and judgement of the specialists may simply be filed away and the parents return home with their child none the wiser – not one word of advice or information having come their way.'

She suggests that when a child has been assessed, a full, written report should be compiled in straightforward non-technical language and given to the parents to read at leisure. This is what is done at her own centre and she says:

'We find that the advantages to the parents enormously outweigh any disadvantages to us in terms of the time it takes.' Yet some professionals resist this idea on the grounds that parents won't understand it or that it is somehow pandering to the parents' 'anxiety neurosis' – so-called – about their child. She concludes: 'If parents can be helped to understand and deal more constructively with the problems of their handicapped child, then at least a small part of their burden is relieved. They have enough to cope with without the added frustration of a never-ending and often hopeless fight for information. Putting it down on paper for them will not solve all their problems, but at least it seems to be a start in the right direction.'

How parents can help their child

A family may be in touch with a paediatrician, a GP, a health visitor, a teacher and a social worker and yet not with anyone who can help them to manage better:

When I had my other boy, perfectly normal, I couldn't get rid of the welfare lady . . . they kept coming round, week after week, but when I had my Kevin I never saw a soul, on my life; and that was a time I sorely needed somebody . . . we only learnt by living with him, watching him grow up . . . I was left entirely alone when he was young . . . I should have been told right from the start what to expect, all the symptoms. A booklet would have been good enough. We need one person, someone who could come to us, or we could go to him, and he'd have the time to talk to us and the knowledge we need. (Parents talking to Dr Mervyn Fox in *They Get This Training But They Don't Know How You Feel*, 1975, published by Action, price £1 including postage.)

It is now generally accepted that sympathetic support for the parents of handicapped children is one of the major needs that therapists, teachers, social workers and doctors have to provide. As Dr Ronald MacKeith, a paediatrician at Guy's Hospital, has written: ' "unreasonable" parents are anxious parents, worried because they feel uninformed and uncertain about the child's present state and his future . . . if the child and the family are to be helped, it must be done through the parents.'

But for many parents sympathy and support are not enough – they want to be fully involved in helping their child.

Who can help?

After working on a National Health Service research project in Exeter on the unmet needs of handicapped children Dr J. Rubissow reached the conclusion that: 'There are few doctors willing to advise on developmental steps to be taken, partly because they truly don't have any specific factual knowledge of use in this field.' Professor Peter Mittler points out that, for the general practitioner, diagnosis of an ailment is generally linked to treatment. But 'it is easier to diagnose mental retardation, or even a common syndrome such as mongolism, than to suggest what treatment should be provided either by the doctor, the teacher or the parent.' The same, of course, applies to those who are severely disabled. Doctors can cure or treat occasional acute illnesses; they cannot 'cure' a child who was born with spina bifida or cerebral palsy.

So parents with a handicapped child need to be realistic about the help they can expect from their GP. The mother who said: 'The doctor, he just likes to diagnose the illnesses, he won't come down to it and tell us anything to do ...' (quoted in *They Get This Training*), probably didn't realize that the average GP has less practical experience of coping with a handicapped child than she had herself. Many parents complain that their GP does not seem to be fully aware of the implications of the handicap, or know what services are available.

Parents have often experienced a similar lack of practical help and advice from social workers and health visitors. A research worker told a conference in February 1976 that Family Fund surveys had revealed that only 11 per cent of severely disabled children received regular visits from social workers, and 70 per cent rarely or never saw a social worker except for a specific purpose.

'They Can Be Helped'

National Children's Home (NCH)
85 Highbury Park, London N5 1UD
Tel: 01-226 2033

This film – based on the progress made by four multi-handicapped children attending an NCH group – aims to demonstrate practical ways of helping the children. It opens with a view of the world as seen by a child lying in a cot or pram: the ceiling, the door and an occasional glimpse of someone's feet. Then the children are introduced to stimulating activities and undergo vigorous exercises. Within six months a non-walker was walking, not perfectly but creditably; a child who had been just prone in a cot was determinedly selecting a plastic ring and placing it over a stick; the other two were clearly showing a response. The lesson which the film hopes to teach is that children need not be left to vegetate if the adults caring for them are shown what to do for them. The film is available on hire.

What advantages do parents have?

Why are parents so often discouraged from helping their child themselves? The argument seems to have two main aspects. First of all, that parents are too emotionally involved to maintain the detachment which is essential. And secondly, they lack the technical and theoretical knowledge. But the parents' commitment should be seen as an asset, not a liability; their determination to fight for their child's future could be an inspiration to everyone involved in helping the child.

Clara Claiborne Park, the mother of an autistic child, summed up in her book *The Siege* (Penguin Books, 1972) the special advantages that parents have over the most skilled and experienced professional:

1 Total familiarity with the case since birth – the child's experiences, likes and dislikes, fears and obsessions.
2 As well as a fuller knowledge of the child's past than any doctor can have, parents have a fuller knowledge

of his present. They can observe the child in the complete variety of situations to which he is exposed, not merely in the artificial setting of the consulting room.

3 Parents are there. Because they are there they can act when the child is ready. In the first years of life, more often than not, one parent or another is on hand, in actual or potential contact with the child twenty-four hours a day, fifty-two weeks a year.

4 When you are in twenty-four-hour contact, every experience can be considered for potential usefulness. And when you have known a child since birth you have as good a basis as anyone can for judging which of these experiences a child is ready to make use of and which he is not. A child's withdrawal or the edge in his voice tells parents instantly the difference between stimulation and pressure.

5 Parents are also aware of what is less obvious – of ways in which all members of their family are alike. Patterns of behaviour which might seem odd to an outsider are less so to parents who see them in their normal children and in themselves as well as in their handicapped child. Mrs Park writes: 'Elly's relative passivity was not unfamiliar to us. We all shared her physical caution, though in us it stopped short of pathology . . . long before Elly was born I had raged inwardly at three healthy children who cried "Mommy" at a resisting door that my neighbour's children would open with one energetic shove.'

6 The most important of all the parents' advantages, in Mrs Park's view, is that they know the child's language. She asks: 'Who could expect a stranger to understand a child who says "buh" for six different words from baby to fish?' Without the parents to interpret for them, professionals may quite simply get the wrong message from their patients.

7 Severely handicapped children need some kind of therapy or stimulation every day – whether or not it consists of a planned programme of treatment. Few authorities can provide this and few parents can afford to pay for it – but parents work for nothing.

8 The last advantage in Mrs Park's list is humility. Virtually all parents have a certain humility based, in part, in their consciousness that they are not professional. So, instead of running the risk of leaping to conclusions based on theories, they have learned to feel their way – not just from their experiences with their handicapped child but from their experiences with their normal children too.

Working with parents

It is not enough to give general advice along the lines of 'talk to your child, take him out to places of interest, don't give up hope.' Such advice may be sound and well-meaning, but it does not help the parent who wants guidance on ways in which she might, for instance, help the child to develop language or even to pick up and hold a spoon. Workshops have been set up so that parents and professionals can work together and learn how to influence children's development in all kinds of practical ways. One distinctive feature of the thinking underlying this kind of project is that the people running them genuinely feel that they can learn from the parents' knowledge, concern and experience of their own children as well as vice versa.

A number of organizations have been developing ways of working with parents, well-known examples being the Hester Adrian Research Centre, the Institute of Mental Subnormality and the Nottingham University psychology department. The King's Fund Centre has published a statement on collaboration between parents and professionals drawn up as a result of a series of workshop meetings. In the foreword they say:

Parents and professionals have a common objective, in the pursuit of which each brings differing skills and activities; their joint aim is to aid the development of the parents' mentally handicapped child, and to enable that child, as he grows, to lead as good a quality of life as possible. The primary task falls to the parent, day in and day out: the job of the professional is to aid the parent in the performance of that basic task. Without genuine collaboration between them, service to the mentally handicapped person will inevitably be diminished (*Mental Handicap Paper No. 9*, 1976, from King's Fund Centre, 126 Albert Street, London NW1 7NE; price 25p).

These projects are undertaken in the belief that parents can learn to play a bigger part in the treatment of their own children, and that specialists such as doctors and teachers should learn not merely to take parents into their confidence but to enlist their active cooperation in the process of treatment. They believe that many parents are eager for detailed information and guidance.

Devon County Council has run at least two weekend conferences for parents of children with a specific handicap to meet teachers, doctors and Devon County officials from the education, health and social services departments who were involved in one way or another with handicapped children. The object of the three-day courses was to enable parents and officials to meet in an informal atmosphere to exchange ideas and discuss their problems.

Three or four years ago a PhD student from Nottingham University invited two groups of families with severely mentally or multiply handicapped children to undertake a behaviour modification course. There were eight or nine families in each group divided according to the children's stage of development. They met once a week and in the first place were taught the theory. Then they started to try it out for themselves. Each week a different family took home the video-tape recorder and filmed their family's activities so that their experiences could be shared with the group. Every child in the group was visited at home by the leader of the project at least once a month. When that particular project came to an end, the video-tape recorder – essential for monitoring their progress – belonged to the University. So a Round Table group in Derby raised £700 or so for the parents to buy one of their own. The Association came into being simply to solve the problem of finding a proper owner for the video-tape camera and recorder. However, once they had a separate identity they began to draw in 'outsiders', people who were not directly involved in the University projects. They meet once a fortnight and have started organizing some social projects, such as a Christmas party with all the food prepared by the children. Six post-graduate students from Nottingham University, together with Dr Elizabeth Newsom, took six children on holiday so that the students could experience for themselves what it was like to look after a severely handicapped child for twenty-four hours a day. Students taking a course on teaching mentally handicapped children at a local college of education each visit a child in his home every week. They become involved with that one child – playing with him, taking him swimming and so on – and learn to see from a parent's point of view. It is everyone's hope that these experiences will help to put theoretical studies into perspective and that projects like this will give professionals some of the know-how about the practical day-to-day difficulties of looking after a handicapped child which is too often conspicuously lacking.

Derbyshire Association for Parents of Mentally Handicapped Children
3 Acres Road, Lower Pilsley, Chesterfield, Derbyshire
Tel: Chesterfield (0246) 851349

It doesn't matter how few of you there are. Once a project gets going, no matter how modest in scope, it can generate all kinds of new ideas and activities. In Staffordshire, a social worker who had been in touch with a number of families of handicapped children at a playgroup set up a regular coffee morning. With the support of the voluntary services officer, the group developed a whole range of projects and activities including a holiday play scheme and a handbook for parents of handicapped children in North Staffordshire.

Voluntary Services Officer
Area Social Services Office
12 Croft Street, Newcastle, Staffs. ST5 2BA
Tel: Newcastle (0782) 611411

One group grew out of a babysitting service offered on market day in Worksop by a teacher at a local further education college to parents of mentally handicapped children under five years old. Mothers came, but found the chance to meet one another and talk over similar problems was more valuable than the actual babysitting. So they decided to form their own committee and run a mothers' group and playgroup, for both physically and mentally handicapped children. A regular Wednesday playgroup has been running for over a year, together with fund-raising activities, social evenings, outings, etc. 'It is a solid and happy band of parents who are determined to help and encourage these children, who never asked for their handicaps.'

Toddlecap.
2 Forest Lane, Manton, Worksop, Notts.
Tel: Worksop (0909) 85332

Parents' action groups

The pioneers of the nineteenth century were the great philanthropists like Dr Barnardo and Lord Shaftesbury, who devoted their lives to other people's deprived children. The pioneers of the twentieth century were the parents of children with particular handicaps who set out together to revolutionize their own children's prospects. The societies which exist now – with large central organizations and many departments, permanent offices, professional staff, regional offices, local groups throughout the country – must be beyond the wildest dreams of their founders.

It may not be all pure gain. Iain McMurray, General Secretary of the Scottish Society for the Mentally Handi-capped, had this to say at an international congress of societies for the mentally handicapped:

Every success gained contained its own seeds of failure. Meet the child's needs and the parent is contented. And contentment is a cancer. Many of us know of voluntary organisations which did remarkable pioneering work in their early years. Their membership acknowledged this success in terms of contentment and today the organisations are composed of professionals who arrange conferences for each other, who meet to consider what their function should be and in whose close-knit brotherhood, pressure is quite out of place. These organisations have lost their soul, their purpose in life. A consumer's group without a consumer.

It is not enough to pretend that the problem does not exist – that parents' groups are as rebellious as they once were. Nor is it enough to pretend that policy now dictates a more professional approach – that our primary objects are to exert political and legislative influence or whatever. These activities are misguided unless they reflect accurately the needs of the handicapped and *not* the needs of those who serve them.

And so we have a paradox. On the one hand the parent-centred organisation is vital, and yet improvements in services result in less parent involvement.

Parents' action groups are the latest development, emerging to meet the new situation. They are not necessarily identified with one handicap, but what mainly distinguishes them is that, along with the mutual support and comfort parents of handicapped children can find from one another, they see themselves as pressure groups campaigning actively and sometimes aggressively for a better life for families with handicapped children.

There has been talk of a federation, but in the meantime they are separate, independent, local groups campaigning mainly on local issues.

ASSOCIATION OF PARENTS OF HANDICAPPED CHILDREN

The Secretary
Association of Parents of Handicapped Children
42 Rugby Road, Cubbington, Leamington
Tel: Leamington (0926) 22537

A small, local, independent group whose activities are focused on helping parents through mutual support and providing information. About a dozen families meet very informally every month, sometimes for cheese and wine, sometimes for a speaker from a section of the social services department or the Rowntree Trust, for instance. They have the impression that the official-sounding name of the association has proved helpful in getting problems sorted out with the local authority over questions such as a school place for an individual child. They have occasional activities for children such as Christmas parties and summer outings.

BRADFORD METROPOLITAN DISTRICT ACTION GROUP FOR MENTALLY HANDICAPPED PEOPLE

Mrs N. Newton (Secretary)
Bradford Action Group
5 Beacon Brow, Bradford 6
Tel: Bradford (0274) 74601

The Bradford Action Group, set up in 1975, is not prepared to wait for the authorities to change the future of the mentally handicapped in Bradford. It feels that parents of the mentally handicapped have been passive long enough; they must now stand up and fight for society's joint responsibility towards the mentally handicapped to be accepted. They hold that it is thoroughly unacceptable for parents to be expected to cope alone with a mentally handicapped person, without relief, for every hour of every day for the rest of his life. The home should be the axis on which the life of the mentally handicapped person turns, but not in any circumstances should the home be the capsule in which the handicapped person is imprisoned.

The Group is campaigning for full-time education in school up to the age of nineteen for all handicapped people, admission into school at the age of two where this would be helpful, short-term relief (not in hospital) for parents and full day care for all on educational principles after school-leaving age.

It is asking for a working party representing the council, parents and all the professions to plan the future for mentally handicapped people; parents must be allowed to participate in the planning decisions upon which they may be dependent for the rest of their lives.

The first task is to compile a register of all mentally handicapped people in the Bradford district and a review of current facilities.

The Action Group charges a subscription of 50p per family for which members receive any help the group can give, any action that can be taken on their behalf and a regular newsletter three times a year.

HAMMERSMITH PETER PAN SOCIETY

Mrs Ettie Crawford (Chairman)
Peter Pan Society
104 Cleverly Estate, Shepherd's Bush, London W12
Tel: 01-743 4866

All the efforts of this group are concentrated on trying to get a unit in their own area for the short-term care of the most severely subnormal children. After a vigorous campaign, master-minded by their chairman who has an inside knowledge of the workings of the social services committee, they succeeded in getting a pilot scheme catering for ten children. In contrast to the hospital right outside London in Watford which was all that could be offered before, this unit is within easy reach of every parent in the borough whose child might go there. With the additional problem of cuts in local government spending to contend with, they now have to find a way of converting the pilot scheme into a permanent – and slightly larger – establishment with permanent full-time staff. Most of the families in this group are parents of children who attend a special care unit in the annexe of a school for severely subnormal children. The group is acutely conscious of the many other things which need to be done, but cannot afford to dissipate their energies until the unit is safely established. A guide to services for handicapped children in Hammersmith is in the pipeline.

KITH AND KIDS

Maurice Collins, Kith and Kids
58 The Avenue, London N10
Tel: 01-883 8762

This family group is outstanding for its creative thinking

and practical resourcefulness. Its first modest project was for a few families with handicapped children to prepare and eat Sunday lunch together and spend an enjoyable afternoon with handicapped and normal children and adults all joining in the activities. Since then its projects have proliferated. There are regular parents' evening discussion meetings. The summer holiday project is not a playscheme – it is an attempt to develop the social abilities of the children with each child individually programmed to move on to the next stage. This might be anything from making eye-contact with another person to crossing a road on their own. The project is run by young volunteers (two volunteers to one handicapped child) – many of them from fifth and sixth years of local schools – with professional support. A secondary, but by no means less important, aim of the scheme is to accustom the group of volunteers to the idea that handicapped people are not to be feared but are individuals with varying problems who, with a little understanding and tolerance, can be valued members of the community. (See chapter 4, **Social skills**, page 223.)

It has undertaken major projects such as running a large inter-disciplinary day conference (attended by the Secretary of State for Social Services of the day) and conducting a radio phone-in programme.

All its ideas have now come to focus on the aim of full social integration of the handicapped into the community. It has formulated an impressive thirty-one-point practical programme of legislation and public education to bring this about and, whilst continuing with its family activities, it has emerged as an authoritative, forceful and effective pressure group known nationally by all those – parent and professional – who are concerned with the welfare of handicapped children.

Maurice and Doreen Collins, founder members of the group, have written a book called *Kith and Kids – Self-help for Families of the Handicapped* about their own experiences and the experiences of the group (Souvenir Press, 1976; price £2.50).

TOTNES ACTION GROUP FOR HANDICAPPED CHILDREN

Judy Ellis
Totnes Action Group
Follets, Ringmore, Nr Kingsbridge, South Devon
Tel. Bigbury-on-Sea (054–881) 521

This is a militant group of parents who have children with all types of handicap. Its aim is to create change in the attitudes of the caring professions towards handicapped children and their families as well as to fight for more resources. It has an active publications department and runs a parents' journal whose content would do credit to any national organization. In addition to informative articles, it expresses outspoken ideas and criticism of what is being done to help. It runs holiday playschemes, has obtained the use of a council house for use by handicapped adults, is completing a survey of local needs and is hoping to run a 'two-to-one' scheme in the summer (see KITH AND KIDS).

Membership is open to anyone interested, with the emphasis on parents with handicapped children. Subscription £1 a year.

2 Specific Handicaps

Directory of services and organizations

For most parents, this chapter will be the starting point in using the *Handbook for Parents with a Handicapped Child*. And the first entry you turn to will probably be the name of your own child's handicap. Here you will find a list of organizations whose main concern is with that handicap and perhaps the details of some journals, books or films about it. Many of the large national organizations have such a comprehensive range of activities that we could not possibly do full justice to them here. We have told you where to find them; the rest is up to you.

Services which are described in other chapters – aids or genetic counselling (chapter 3), holidays (chapter 8) or schools (chapter 5) and so on – may well also be among the services provided by these societies. We have not necessarily listed them all twice. If you have joined a specialist society, it's always worth asking them for advice and help before looking for a particular service elsewhere.

We do not describe or discuss the nature of the handicaps listed.

General

There are two organizations which belong in this chapter but whose interests cover too wide a field to fit conveniently under the name of any one handicap or disability, so we have put them at the beginning.

INVALID CHILDREN'S AID ASSOCIATION (ICAA)

ICAA
126 Buckingham Palace Road, London SW1W 9SB
Tel: 01-730 9891

The ICAA has always been concerned with helping handicapped children living at home with their families. Its aim is to support the family so that it can go on coping with the problem of looking after a handicapped child. The ICAA has therefore developed an individual casework service for parents, operating in parts of London, Kent and Surrey. Amongst its other activities it runs preschool playgroups, a parents' discussion group and discussion groups for handicapped teenagers. Its residential schools specialize in the care and education of children with asthma and those with speech and language difficulties. The information service sees itself as a kind of citizens advice bureau solely related to children's handicaps and providing a sympathetic ear as well as a useful service and information. The ICAA is essentially a pioneering body and it helps new voluntary societies to get under way if there is a handicap without a society working for it. A film has been produced about its work called 'I Want to Be', distributed by Town and Country Productions Ltd.

Town and Country Productions Ltd
21 Cheyne Row, London SW3 5HP
Tel: 01-352 7950

UNION OF THE PHYSICALLY IMPAIRED AGAINST
SEGREGATION

P. G. Hunt
Union of the Physically Impaired against Segregation
c/o Flat 2, St Giles Court, Dane Road, Ealing, London W13
Tel: 01-579 9679

'First and foremost, we are *people* not "patients", "cases", "spastics", "the deaf", "the blind" or "the sick". The Union rejects entirely any idea of medical or other experts having the right to tell us how we should live, or withold information from us or take decisions behind our backs.' The Union's aim is to get rid of all segregated arrangements for physically impaired people and replace them by arrangements for them to participate fully in society. To do this it sees it as essential for disabled people to do more to help themselves. It welcomes contact with young handicapped people, parents and other sympathizers who are interested in the Union's commitment to full integration. People under eighteen may apply for junior membership. The Union has a regular open newsletter, holds meetings and discussion groups and hopes to set up special-interest groups within the Union on aspects like residents' rights in institutions, housing alternatives, employment.

Aphasia See **Speech and language disorders**

Arthritis See **Rheumatism and arthritis**

Asthma

ASTHMA RESEARCH COUNCIL

Asthma Research Council
12 Pembridge Square, London W2 4EH
Tel: 01-229 1149

The Council exists solely to raise funds for research programmes on asthma; it does not undertake any welfare work. The Friends of the Asthma Research Council have published a booklet called *Coming to Terms with Asthma* by Dr Paul Buisseret (1975). This costs 25p post free and includes sections on what asthma means, allergic asthma, other forms of asthma, the treatment of the disease and research into it. The publication is intended to provide general background information that will be of help in giving asthma sufferers or parents of an asthmatic child a better understanding of what asthma really is, what causes it and what is being done about it. Asthma sufferers can help themselves by learning to breathe properly and *Breathing Control for Asthma and Emphysema* (1974) by

Dr J. L. Livingstone and Jocelyn Reed is the tenth edition of a manual of exercises for general breathing and relaxation, children's exercises and graded exercises towards athletic fitness. It costs 70p post free.

The Child with Asthma: Social, Emotional and Educational Adjustment. An Annotated Bibliography by Doria Pilling (National Children's Bureau, 1975, price £1.65)

Available from:
National Foundation for Educational Research
Book Division
2 Jennings Buildings, Thames Avenue, Windsor, Berks SL4 1QS
or:
National Children's Bureau
8 Wakley Street, London EC1V 7QE
Tel: 01-278 9441

Mrs Pilling, research officer of the National Children's Bureau, has produced a review of research and sources covering the period 1958 to 1973 on the subject of children with asthma. The literature is divided into three sections: (1) emotional and social adjustment; (2) family adjustment; and (3) educational attainment. It is reviewed in some detail. There are also abstracts of research findings. In her 'overview of research' Mrs Pilling concludes that: 'the evidence now available indicates that the emotional adjustment of the general population of asthmatic children differs little from that of non-handicapped children'. She points out the significance of the fact that unlike many other illnesses, in which the child is usually taken to hospital during an acute episode, children usually remain at home during asthmatic attacks, and the parents are intimately involved in the child's care at this time. Research on another chronic disorder (diabetes) has shown that parents who do not fully understand the procedures of management of the condition are the most anxious. Mrs Pilling therefore concludes that precise information to parents about how to cope with an asthmatic attack would seem to be essential. She suggests that they also need an explanation of the illness, advice on how to take any necessary precautions without being unduly restrictive, and the opportunity to express their feelings about having an asthmatic child.

Your Child with Asthma – Some Advice for Parents and Others by Simon Godfrey MD (Heinemann Health Books Ltd, 1975, £1.25)

The publishers make it clear that this book is not intended to be a 'do it yourself' book on asthma for parents; but Dr Simon Godfrey, Consultant Paediatrician at the Brompton and Hammersmith Hospitals for a number of years, attempts to answer the very common questions which parents ask. As well as a simple account of the way in which the lungs are affected by asthma, the medical section includes what the *Times Educational Supplement* called: 'a useful myth-dispelling section on the role of allergy and emotional factors'. There is a description of the various kinds of treatment which are available for the asthmatic child. A terse list of rules tells parents how to avoid or deal with the dangerous situations which can occasionally arise.

See also **Chest and heart**

Autism

NATIONAL SOCIETY FOR AUTISTIC CHILDREN

National Society for Autistic Children
1a Golders Green Road, London NW11 8EA
Tel: 01-458 4375

The National Society is the main source of information about every kind of help for parents with an autistic child. Its publications include a list which is revised annually of all schools and units for autistic children. A newsletter and a quarterly journal are sent to everyone who joins as a member of the National Society. There are also more than twenty affiliated local groups which organize their own programmes of projects, meetings and so on. A major part of the Society's activities, both locally and nationally, has been the establishment of its own day centres for the care and education of autistic children – there are eleven which have been set up by local groups jointly with the National Society.

The Society is acutely aware of the stresses to which parents of autistic children are subject. Although head-quarters staff, committee members, local societies and individual parents do their best, support and counselling are not always available at the right time to everyone who needs them. The Society is now actively discussing how it can establish a workable scheme for volunteers to act as counsellors and share with parents the experience of coping with an exceptionally trying situation.

SCOTTISH SOCIETY FOR AUTISTIC CHILDREN

Scottish Society for Autistic Children
12 Hope Street, Charlotte Square, Edinburgh EH2 4DD
Tel: 031-226 4241

Affiliated to the National Society for Autistic Children, the Scottish Society is particularly concerned with the children's education. It is opening its own school for autistic children who will be mostly weekly boarders with a few day pupils. The Society holds small meetings for parent members to give them an opportunity to discuss problems generally with a psychiatrist. It also holds more formal public meetings with professional speakers.

Blindness

ROYAL NATIONAL INSTITUTE FOR THE BLIND (RNIB)

RNIB
224 Great Portland Street, London W1N 6AA
Tel: 01-388 1266

There is scarcely any aspect of the lives of blind people at every age which is not touched by the activities of the

RNIB. It runs schools and libraries, holiday homes and housing trusts, the world's second largest braille publishing house and is the almost exclusive supplier of special aids to blind people. Recent reforms in its constitution now mean that one third of its Council members are themselves blind. The Institute offers an Education Advisory Service on a regional basis for parents of blind children. It maintains schools for blind children of all ages from nursery upwards as well as schools for blind children with additional handicaps. It has an adolescent assessment centre. RNIB publications include pamphlets and books dealing with its services for blind children and a catalogue of aids, apparatus and games for the blind.

ASSOCIATION OF BLIND AND PARTIALLY SIGHTED TEACHERS AND STUDENTS (ABAPSTAS)

ABAPSTAS, *Terry Moody*
Department of Political Economy
University of Glasgow, Glasgow G12 8RT
Tel: 041-339 8855 Ext. 559

This Association acts as a pressure group to improve facilities, offers consultation and advice, and provides a check list of information for students. It campaigns for the right of blind people to manage their own affairs. As the editor of its newsletter, J. Peter Salt, wrote in October 1974: 'We are not trying to get rid of sighted people who work for the visually handicapped, neither are we seeking to relegate them to a permanent position on the back seat, but a small minority of them must accept that they must share the driving seat with us.' ABAPSTAS works closely with the National Federation of the Blind of the UK and they are currently engaged on a campaign for the integration of visually handicapped children into ordinary schools. It has a seven-point programme for technological development designed to improve braille equipment and to gain for blind people the full benefit of advances in electronic communications.

BRITISH RETINITIS PIGMENTOSA SOCIETY

Mrs Lynda Drummond-Walker (Secretary)
British Retinitis Pigmentosa Society
12 Ridge Green, South Nutfield, Nr Redhill, Surrey RH1 5RN
Tel: Nutfield Ridge 3416

This is the 'youngest' society in this book. It was formed in 1976 to help families suffering from retinitis pigmentosa which is the third highest cause of blindness. The response to a membership call on the Radio 4 'In Touch' programme was overwhelming and within a few months membership had reached 500 families. Like its American counterpart, the Society aims to be both a self-help group for patients and their families and a link between all concerned with treatment and research in this disease. The first urgent need was for information and, with the help of medical advisers, it has produced an information pamphlet explaining the basic ways in which the disease is transmitted and some of the genetic implications. There is a quarterly newsletter. Within the first few months four branches were established which have a normal programme of local activities, including fund-raising. The Secretary, who has had the disease herself for the last four years, has already involved MPs and others in a much needed campaign for research into cause, treatment and cure.

NATIONAL FEDERATION OF THE BLIND OF THE
UNITED KINGDOM

National Federation of the Blind of the United Kingdom
20 Cannon Close, Raynes Park, London SW20 9HA

The Federation sees itself as a pressure group bringing the collective view of blind and partially sighted people to bear on those responsible for providing services for them. However, it will always do whatever it can to give advice and help to individuals. It is currently running a vigorous

campaign to bring about a substantial shift in education
policy towards integration of the visually handicapped in
ordinary schools, with the support of special units. With
ABAPSTAS it has published an authoritative critique
of the Vernon Report, *Educational Provision for the
Visually Handicapped*, 1973, obtainable from the Secretary
(price £1).

RESEARCH CENTRE FOR THE EDUCATION OF THE VISUALLY HANDICAPPED

Research Centre for the Education of the Visually Handicapped
Department of Special Education, Faculty of Education
50 Wellington Road, Edgbaston, Birmingham B15 2EP
Tel: 021-440 2450

The Centre has direct links with schools for the visually
handicapped. Currently it is working on a Schools Council
project on visual perception training and is also doing
research into the educational needs of multi-handicapped,
blind children.

The Centre publishes research results, articles and
lectures including a register of European research projects
on non-medical aspects of blindness.

SCOTTISH NATIONAL FEDERATION FOR THE WELFARE OF THE BLIND

Scottish National Federation for the Welfare of the Blind
39 St Andrews Street, Dundee DD1 2EU
Tel: Dundee (0382) 27101

The Federation coordinates the views of the various
organizations for the blind and partially sighted in Scotland
and promotes the interests of the blind through these
organizations. It publishes a leaflet on services for the
blind and partially sighted outlining the facilities available
and details of who provides them.

WALES COUNCIL FOR THE BLIND

Hywel H. John
Wales Council for the Blind
Penfro lon-y-coed, Brecon, Powys LD3 7NA
Tel: Brecon (0874) 2881

> The Council is newly reconstituted and its activities and services are under review. However, it will act as an advisory and consultative body in all matter affecting the welfare of the blind and partially sighted in Wales, and cooperate with local authorities and voluntary groups to provide and develop welfare services.

WARWICK UNIVERSITY RESEARCH UNIT FOR THE BLIND

Dr John Gill
Warwick University Research Unit for the Blind
University of Warwick, Coventry CV4 7AL
Tel: Coventry (0203) 24011

> The Unit provides embossed maps and diagrams for the blind, a computerized braille document service, braille bank statements and braille transcription of ordinary needs such as recipes, knitting patterns and working instructions. It also designs gadgets such as timing devices for cookers and audio clocks. The problem is to bridge the gap between research prototype and mass production. Unfortunately the Unit's future is uncertain because of lack of funds.

'Growing Up Without Sight'

Concord Films Council Ltd
201 Felixstowe Road, Ipswich, Suffolk
Tel: Ipswich (0473) 76012

> This film is based on the nursery school for blind children run by Anna Freud at the Hampstead Child Therapy Clinic. The film shows the pioneering work of the school and demonstrates how lack of vision affects every aspect of the development of young children.

Services for blind people

REGISTRATION

In order to qualify for the many special welfare services for the blind, a person must be registered as blind. Registration is voluntary. To be on the register a person must have such limited vision that he cannot perform any work for which eyesight is essential. A form has to be filled in by a consultant ophthalmologist who is a doctor. The hospital or the social services department should make the necessary arrangements. There is a similar register of the partially sighted. Where registration is refused an appeal can be made to the Ophthalmic Referee Service.

CONCESSIONS

Registered blind people can get special concessions. TV licences at a reduced price can be obtained from the local post office on production of a certificate of blindness from the local authority. All registered blind people are eligible for a free radio set under the terms of the British Wireless for the Blind Fund. Your local authority can help you get this. Braille letters, books and papers, etc., can be sent post free to or from a blind person if they are clearly marked 'Articles for the blind', as can special tapes and cassettes, but not ordinary letters. The RNIB can provide a leaflet about postal concessions, available free.

RNIB
224 Great Portland Street, London W1N 6AA
Tel: 01-388 1266

'In Touch'

A lively radio programme specially for blind listeners, broadcast every Sunday afternoon on Radio 4. It does its best to respond to ideas and suggestions from listeners. A BBC publications directory of aids and services for blind and partially sighted people (also called *In Touch*) was produced in conjunction with the programme (1973, price 60p, plus 17p for postage).

BBC Publications
PO Box 234, London SE1 3TH
Tel: 01-407 6961

TALKING NEWSPAPER ASSOCIATION OF THE UK (TNAUK)

Philip Brew (Honorary Secretary)
TNAUK
Department of Language and Linguistics
University of Essex, Colchester CO4 3SQ
Tel: Colchester (0206) 44144

This Association aims to help any group which is publishing or wants to publish a talking newspaper. Talking newspapers can help to keep visually handicapped people in touch with their own local community by providing them with a source of local news. Any small group can set up a newspaper; the Association suggests a minimum of six people but the actual number depends on the scale of the project. The TNAUK produces a useful set of notes to help any group wanting to start a newspaper. The Association also offers two starter packs: one includes a talking newspaper directory, notes about charity status, sample canvassing and appeal letters, and a copy of its current newsletter. The other consists of a sample cassette with extracts from seven existing talking newspapers and magazines and a specially designed postal pack. These cost £1 each. The Association can always put potential subscribers in touch with their nearest newspaper.

TRAVEL CONCESSIONS

A blind person and guide may travel on British Rail paying one fare only on any journey connected with work, training, hospital visit or specialist, and from home to a centre for training, education, etc. A voucher has to be issued by the local social services department, or its agent, and is presented at the booking office when the ticket is bought. Similar concessions may also be available for flights on domestic airlines.

Bone-marrow disease

VOLUNTEER BONE-MARROW REGISTER

Volunteer Bone-Marrow Register
St Mary Abbots Hospital, Marloes Road, London W8

This is a register of volunteers willing to donate bone marrow to any patient, child or adult, with a bone-marrow disease which can be treated only by a marrow transplant. It is estimated that there may be at least 500 patients (including 200–300 children) in the UK alone who require such treatment.

The Register, started in September 1974, now has over 3000 names and was made possible by financial assistance from the Anthony Nolan Appeal Fund which provides funds for the special laboratory, its staff, equipment and running expenses necessary for testing (tissue-typing) the volunteers. Anthony Nolan is a five-year-old boy with a rare marrow disease, the only treatment for which is bone-marrow transplantation.

Because the chances of finding a suitable donor for him are about one in 50 000 and since no funds were available from the National Health Service, Anthony's mother, Mrs Shirley Nolan, launched a personal appeal for funds in the press and on the radio and TV. Her campaign continues.

The special tissue-typing laboratory is administered by Dr D. C. O. James, Consultant Pathologist and Director of the Blood Transfusion Unit at Westminster Hospital.

Brain damage

ASSOCIATION FOR THE TREATMENT OF BRAIN-DAMAGED
CHILDREN

Mrs D. T. Llewellyn
Association for the Treatment of Brain-Damaged Children
21 Rowington Close, Coventry CV6 1PR
Tel: Coventry (0203) 591837

The Association was formed in December 1969 when a group of parents of young brain-damaged children got together because of their concern at the lack of specialized physiotherapy facilities for their children. Many parents did not realize the vital necessity of early diagnosis and treatment, so it was decided to raise enough money to establish and finance a domiciliary service for preschool-age, brain-damaged children in and around the Coventry area. There are now about 100 members with more than forty children, mainly of preschool age, who have all types of severe mental or physical handicap. The Association employs three physiotherapists and a speech therapist who treat children at home or at their playgroup from as young as six weeks. There is no charge to parents for this treatment. A minivan has been given by the local Round Table and is used to take three children each week into Leamington Spa for hydrotherapy. A home nurse will spend up to two hours looking after children in their own home to give the mother a break – a small charge is made for this (30p per hour in 1975) and the balance is made up by the Association. The Association is completely self-supporting with no grants from any source and it raises money in any way that is legal. Its next major aim is to set up short-stay facilities for under-fives. It says: 'The necessity for our service has been proved over and over again, and we would hope to extend our area even more in future, as sadly there will always be children in need of our help. We hope that parents in other areas will be encouraged by our efforts and start groups of their own.'

Brittle bones (osteo genesis imperfecta)

BRITTLE BONE SOCIETY

Mrs Margaret Grant, Brittle Bone Society
63 Byron Crescent, Dundee DD3 6SS
Tel: Dundee (0382) 87130

The Society was formed in 1972 with the object of raising funds for research into the causes of osteo genesis imperfecta and similar disorders. It aims to give support and friendship to patients and their families and to provide information and advice on subjects such as genetic counselling, welfare benefits and sources of help.

Cancer

MALCOLM SARGENT CANCER FUND FOR CHILDREN

Malcolm Sargent Cancer Fund for Children
56 Redcliffe Square, London SW10
Tel: 01-352 6884

The Fund will help children suffering from cancer, leukaemia or Hodgkin's disease, either in their homes or in hospital. All requests for help must be sponsored by a doctor, medical social worker or district nurse, one of whom completes the application for grant form with the child's parents. The Fund expects to respond with the minimum of fuss and the maximum of speed. Grants are paid for every possible need for the child and his family, including travelling expenses for visiting a child in hospital.

See also **Leukaemia**

Cerebral palsy

See **Spastic**

Chest disorders

CHILDREN'S CHEST CIRCLE (CCC)

Welfare Secretary
Chest and Heart Association, Children's Chest Circle
Tavistock House North, Tavistock Square, London WC1
Tel: 01-387 3012

This is now incorporated in *Hope*, the quarterly magazine for people of all ages suffering from chest and heart diseases. The CCC was formed to encourage, support and give information to the parents of 'chesty' children and the magazine pages consist of an authoritative medical article arising from members' letters and a page of news and views. Parents organize an 'in touch' correspondence scheme for children themselves. Subscription to *Hope* costs £1 a year. This includes membership of the circle and the 'in touch' scheme.

See also **Asthma** and **Heart disorders**

Club feet

INFORMATION TAPE

Mr W. Welford, Nursing Officer
St James's Hospital, Leeds LS9 7TF
Tel: Leeds (0532) 33144

St James's Hospital has produced a short cassette tape for mothers explaining the condition of club foot and how it develops. It outlines in simple friendly terms how treatment will proceed. The Hospital can supply copies of the tape but other consultants may not follow exactly the same programme of treatment as the one described.

The ICAA and the Lady Hoare Trust may be able to help children with this condition (see **Physical handicap**).

Coeliac disease

COELIAC SOCIETY

Hon. Secretary, Coeliac Society
PO Box 181, London NW2 2Q7

The secretary is very anxious to stress that children with coeliac disease are not handicapped; they may live a normal life apart from their strict diet. The Coeliac Society issues a newsletter and a handbook which includes food lists and recipes.

Cystic fibrosis

CYSTIC FIBROSIS RESEARCH TRUST

Cystic Fibrosis Research Trust
5 Blyth Road, Bromley, Kent BR1 3RS
Tel: 01-464 7211

The Trust was founded in 1964 to finance research to find a complete cure for cystic fibrosis and to improve current methods of treatment. Over 200 branches and groups have been established throughout the UK to help and advise parents with everyday problems of caring for a child with cystic fibrosis. Group secretaries or welfare officers may visit families and organize meetings. There is a regional network which may also organize meetings with specialist speakers. A newsletter, *Cystic Fibrosis News*, is circulated to all parents known to the Trust. There are fund-raising committees in all areas which welcome volunteers who will help in raising money for research.

Deafness

NATIONAL DEAF CHILDREN'S SOCIETY (NDCS)

NDCS, 31 Gloucester Place, London W1H 4EA
Tel: 01-486 3251

The NDCS is devoted to the whole emotional and social development of deaf and partially hearing children. When parents learn that their child is deaf, it is often the first source of help to which they turn. The welfare department directs parents to the appropriate experts as well as trying to help with problems. Mothers have formed regional groups of 'dogsbodies' who are willing to tackle any job which is needed to relieve the pressure on other parents with a deaf child. They work voluntarily through the education or social services department in their area. The Society makes sure that government departments are supplied with factual information about the needs of deaf children. The annual report of the NDCS is a mine of information, not only about its own activities but also the whole field of deafness. It has a register of every other organization catering for the deaf.

BREAKTHROUGH TRUST

Mr A. Kenyon, Breakthrough Trust
103 Ridgeway Drive, Bromley, Kent BR1 5DB
Tel: 01-857 4170
(Many of the active workers are deaf so it would be appreciated if you would write rather than telephone except in an emergency.)

This group is run by deaf and hearing people who seek to provide opportunities for the integration of deaf and hearing people into one community: deaf and hearing children of all ages, families as a whole, deaf and hearing adults. Its work is based in members' own homes. Children need adults with whom they can identify; by having a friendly working relationship with deaf adults who are active in deaf–hearing society and who set an example of initiative and responsibility, deaf children learn not to underrate their own potential. There are ten active groups in different areas and they organize a wide variety of self-help projects.

BRITISH DEAF ASSOCIATION

British Deaf Association
38 Victoria Place, Carlisle CA1 1HU
Tel: Carlisle (0228) 20188

This is the representative organization of the adult deaf. It has 160 branches. The majority of its council members are deaf. It has a further education officer who organizes courses for deaf school-leavers. It has also produced a working party report on *Training Facilities and Employment Opportunities for Deaf School Leavers*. The Deaf Mountain Venture is administered from the head office. The NDCS has contributed to the expenses of children joining its expeditions.

KIDS NATIONAL CENTRE FOR CUED SPEECH

Kids National Centre for Cued Speech
17 Sedlescombe Road, London SW6 1RE
Tel: 01-381 0335

Dr R. Orin Cornett, who invented cued speech in 1966 in America, describes it as 'an oral method of communication that is manually supported'. That is to say, every sound of speech and every lip movement is reinforced by the hand in one of eight hand shapes. The hand cues are made in four positions very close to the lips. The deaf child is, therefore, enabled to 'see' the *sounds* which he can neither hear nor lip-read. When he speaks and cues simultaneously, each cue that he makes reminds him to articulate the sound indicated by the cue. This helps him to clarify his speech. Cued speech enables the deaf child not only to understand but to be understood. The National Centre for Cued Speech has been set up to help children with a hearing impairment by the support of the cued speech method; to train and advise parents, teachers, schools and centres in the use of the method; to maintain a national register of teachers with a diploma in cued speech; to encourage research and readily make available the results to individuals, statutory and voluntary bodies; to supply lecturers in the method; to encourage discussion amongst those using it and to make available books and articles on the subject. The work of the centre is backed by the RNID and the NDCS.

NATIONAL COUNCIL OF SOCIAL WORKERS WITH DEAF PEOPLE

National Council of Social Workers with Deaf People
Revd H. J. Clarke
Leicester County Mission for the Deaf
135 Welford Place, Leicester LE2 6BE

A professional body whose members are all engaged full time in working with deaf people. Many members work in clubs and institutes for the deaf. They are inevitably involved when deaf teenagers get into some kind of trouble but that is only part of their work and they are also available to offer help to deaf teenagers who are having to make the difficult transition from school to the outside world.

ROYAL ASSOCIATION IN AID OF THE DEAF AND DUMB (RADD)

RADD, 7 Armstrong Road, London W3 7JL
Tel: 01-743 6187

A Christian organization working in the south-east to improve the social, general and spiritual welfare of deaf people. The staff gives a dedicated service and the handbook is full of stories of genuine practical help to deaf people in every kind of situation. RADD has social clubs and churches for all age groups and their chaplains and social workers specialize in work among those deaf who have additional handicaps and those who are emotionally disturbed or have psychiatric illnesses. Although it does little direct work for deaf children while they are still at school, the Information Officer, Reverend D. H. Bozon, has a special interest in all children with communication difficulties and is always happy to answer inquiries on any aspect of deafness, including education, career prospects, communication problems, welfare and so on, and to help in any way he can.

Information Officer, RADD
101 Horn Lane, Woodford Green, Essex IG8 9AE
Tel: 01-504 8159

ROYAL NATIONAL INSTITUTE FOR THE DEAF (RNID)

RNID, 105 Gower Street, London WC1E 6AH
Tel: 01-387 8033

The RNID is the protective association for all deaf, deaf-blind and hard-of-hearing people in the UK and is the only national body dealing with every aspect of deafness. The Council consists of professional workers for the deaf in social services, medicine, education and other disciplines. The RNID offers a full range of services including a library covering every aspect of deafness, an information service, a social services department, a hearing aid advisory service and technical laboratories in both London and Glasgow. It publishes an illustrated magazine, *Hearing*, and a full range of brochures and leaflets dealing with deafness and the means of alleviating or coming to terms with the handicap.

SCOTTISH ASSOCIATION FOR THE DEAF

Scottish Association for the Deaf
Moray House, Edinburgh EH8 8AQ
Tel: 031-556 8137

The Association is responsible for promoting the interests and welfare of the deaf in Scotland. It is affiliated to the RNID. It is responsible for coordinating methods and activities designed to provide guidance and help for deaf people of all ages in Scotland. Membership includes organizations and individuals interested in any way in the welfare of the deaf and hearing impaired.

SCOTTISH CENTRE FOR THE EDUCATION OF THE DEAF

Centre for the Education of the Deaf
Moray House, Edinburgh EH8 8AQ
Tel: 031-556 8137

Scotland is justifiably proud of the fact that the first school for the deaf in the whole of the UK was opened in Edinburgh in 1769. Two hundred years later the Scottish Centre for the Education of the Deaf was established in the same district of Edinburgh, to act as a resource and training centre for all kinds of help for children and adults who are deaf. One of its first projects was a complete appraisal of the education of deaf people in Scotland, from early infancy to adult education. The Centre works to satisfy the educational needs of deaf children intellectually socially and morally, working with schools, speech therapists, technical experts and parents – particularly members of the Scottish region of the National Deaf Children's Society.

Services for deaf people

RADIO LINK

Cubex Hearing Centre, 324 Grays Inn Road, London WC1X 8DH
Tel: 01-837 6127

Radio Link is specifically designed for hearing-impaired children, particularly in school. It is a form of radio in which a special hearing aid worn by the child is the receiver and both the transmitter and the miniature microphone are simply and inconspicuously worn by the teacher. This system gives the child and the teacher complete freedom of movement both indoors and out. It enables a class of hearing-impaired and hearing-perfect children to be taught together in the same way. Radio Link can be used to replace conventional individual or group speech-training systems and can be used in rooms which have not been acoustically treated.

TELEVISION

RNID, 105 Gower Street, London WC1E 6AH
Tel: 01-387 8033

> Every month in collaboration with the BBC the RNID print a simple explanation of six or eight TV plays – including plays for children – and mail them free to any deaf person who asks to be put on the mailing list.

'Vision On'

> This BBC TV children's programme is designed to be a totally visual experience. It was planned as a programme primarily for deaf children and the little speech which is used is not essential for understanding what is going on.

Deaf/Blind

NATIONAL ASSOCIATION FOR DEAF/BLIND AND RUBELLA HANDICAPPED

Mr J. Price Owen
National Association for Deaf/Blind and Rubella Handicapped
164 Cromwell Lane, Coventry CV4 8AP
Tel: Coventry (0203) 462579
or c/o Deaf Centre, Hertford Place, Coventry
Tel: Coventry (0203) 29680

> The Association offers practical help and information for parents on every aspect of caring for a deaf/blind child. It is campaigning for a national policy for the deaf/blind. It has recently amended its constitution to enable it to extend help and care to the congenitally deaf/blind regardless of age. There are seven regional groups and the particular causes for which they are working and the level of activity differs from one to another.

Diabetes

BRITISH DIABETIC ASSOCIATION

British Diabetic Association
3–6 Alfred Place, London WC1E 7EE
Tel: 01-636 7355

H. G. Wells – a diabetic – was one of the Association's founders in 1934. Now over 120 branches hold meetings and the Association provides free guidance and help on social, welfare and diabetic questions. It does not discuss individual treatment or prescribe diets for diabetics – that is the job of the doctor and dietician. Its newspaper, *Balance*, published six times a year, includes *Young Balance* for children, and has articles on diet and recipes as well as reports on medical progress and practical hints on day-to-day problems. Its information leaflets on diabetes include *The Diabetic at School* and *Childhood and Adolescence*. The Association runs holiday camps for diabetic children and cruises and holidays abroad for teenagers. It has close links with three hostels for diabetic children who cannot be cared for in their own homes.

Down's Syndrome

See **Mental handicap;** see also chapter 4, **Treatment,** DOWN'S CHILDREN'S ASSOCIATION, page 228

Dyslexia

BRITISH DYSLEXIA ASSOCIATION

British Dyslexia Association
18 The Circus, Bath BA1 2ET
Tel: Bath (0225) 28880/20554

Regional groups concerned with specific reading, spelling and writing difficulties campaign for better facilities for treatment and offer advice and information to parents. The North Surrey group produces an excellent journal which is distributed to members of all groups. While professionals use different terminology to describe a whole range of writing, reading and spelling difficulties from severe to mild, there is general agreement that better methods of identifying children with difficulties and better remedial techniques are badly needed. Many parents feel that the right approach is to campaign for better local education authority provision rather than setting up and supporting private enterprise.

SCOTTISH ASSOCIATION FOR THE STUDY OF DYSLEXIA LTD

Scottish Association for the Study of Dyslexia Ltd
3 Coltbridge Avenue, Edinburgh EH12 6AF
Tel: 031-337 3292

This Association covers the whole of Scotland. It provides direct help to children through its own remedial teaching unit at the same address as the office. It also advises on possible teaching approaches to parents or teachers who do not attend the unit. Members of the Scottish Association are automatically members of the British Dyslexia Association and receive copies of its publications.

Dyslexia – The Case for Action (1976)

North London Dyslexia Association
78 Whitehall Park, London N19 3TN
Tel: 01-272 1331

This is a short paper which looks at the various diagnostic terms currently in use and at treatment. It ends with some hard-hitting recommendations for administrative action. Price 15p post free.

A Dyslexic Child in the Family (1976)

This lecture, by Dr A. F. Cheyne, is a psychiatrist's sensitive and helpful consideration of the emotional tightrope to be negotiated by parents. It is one of two lectures given at a conference of the North London Dyslexia Association in March 1976. Both transcripts are bound together at a cost of 70p including postage.

See also page 241.

The Assessment and Teaching of Dyslexic Children (1970)

ICAA, 126 Buckingham Palace Road, London SW1
Tel: 01-730 9891

> This publication is available direct from the ICAA which has always taken a particular interest in the needs of children with speech and language difficulties and acted as sponsors in the launching of the British Dyslexia Association.

Eczema

NATIONAL ECZEMA SOCIETY

Honorary Secretary, National Eczema Society
27 Doyle Gardens, London NW10 3DB
Tel: 01-969 2691

> The Society concerns itself with the needs of eczema sufferers and their families. It was first formed in July 1975 and within a year more than twenty-five local mutual help groups had been set up. The Society's eventual aim is for a self-help group in every major town. The Society holds regular national meetings as well as local activities. Promising research ventures are being considered for support in the long-term hope that medical treatment of eczema may become even more effective, with perhaps one day the discovery of cause and cure. By acting as a clearing house for lay and professional information on the condition, the Society helps members and others to understand eczema both as a physical and social condition. In collaboration with medical specialists, it has produced a layman's guide to the condition and its treatment called *What is Eczema?* It has a lively, well-planned quarterly journal with each issue focusing on a special theme.

Epilepsy

BRITISH EPILEPSY ASSOCIATION (BEA)

British Epilepsy Association
3–6 Alfred Place, London WC1E 7ED
Tel: 01-580 2704

It is estimated that there are at least 100 000 children in this country who suffer from one of the forms of epilepsy. Around 60 000 of these children are at ordinary schools. An important part of the Association's work is to improve public understanding about epilepsy. It produces a leaflet called *A Teachers' Guide to Epilepsy* which in our opinion should be in every school. As well as a brief explanation of epilepsy, it includes nine rules for classroom first aid and hints on classroom common sense. If you have an epileptic child in an ordinary school, make sure that your child's teacher has seen this leaflet and give him a copy if he hasn't. The Association has an advice service, run by social workers, which can provide information by letter, phone call or interview. Helpful publications on holidays and social activities are also available. There is a twice-yearly tabloid newspaper for members. As a result of a study conference, special protective headgear has been developed in the form of a helmet disguised as a wig that can be individually fitted.

SCOTTISH EPILEPSY ASSOCIATION

Scottish Epilepsy Association, 48 Govan Road, Glasgow G51 1JL
Tel: 041-427 4911

The Association has similar aims to the BEA and employs social workers to give advice and help to people suffering from epilepsy and their families. It runs a sheltered workshop and a social club in Glasgow and organizes an annual two weeks' holiday. It promotes parents' and friends' groups and maintains contacts with other organizations in Britain and abroad.

Help for the Epileptic Child – a Handbook for Parents, Nurses and Teachers by Jorge C. Lagos MD (Macdonald & Jane's, £3.95)

> Dr Lagos is a paediatric neurologist at the Children's Memorial Hospital in Oklahoma City, USA. His book was edited to fit the British situation by Dr Euan Ross who is a paediatric specialist at the Department of Child Health of the Central Middlesex Hospital Medical School. The British Epilepsy Association gave help and advice. In each of the chapters practical, simple questions are asked and answered: for instance in Chapter 1, 'Is there any difference in meaning between the word "seizure" and the word "convulsion"? '; Chapter 2, 'Is there a way to predict how babies who have had seizures during the first few days of life will eventually develop?'; Chapter 3, 'When do children "outgrow" breath-holding spells?'; 'Can children consciously or subconsciously fake an epileptic seizure?'; Chapter 7, 'How do children with epilepsy compare in intelligence with non-epileptic children?' The answers are in a conversational style but are not patronizing in tone or content.

Familial Dysautononia (Riley–Day Syndrome)

DYSAUTONONIA FOUNDATION

Dysautononia Foundation
370 Lexington Avenue, Suite 1508, New York, NY 10016, USA

> It may seem extraordinary to be giving a New York address, but there is no English organization specifically able to give support, advice and information on this rare disorder. The foundation publishes information leaflets with practical advice for parents on how best to cope with the nursing and care of a child.
>
> One English mother who has sent for their publications would be happy to make local contacts.

Mrs Sandra Posner
50 The Grove, Edgware, Middlesex
Tel: 01-958 4530

Friedreich's Ataxia

FRIEDREICH'S ATAXIA GROUP

Friedreich's Ataxia Group
Bolsover House, 5–6 Clipstone Street, London W1
Tel: 01-636 2042

The group's hard work in fund-raising has expanded the amount of research into the treatment and causes of this rare disease from one small laboratory in a London hospital to several research projects in London, a special research laboratory in Bristol and a research fellowship at Newcastle. It is also a social group for people with the disease and their families and friends. It publishes a regular newsletter and a helpful booklet of advice. There is a number of local branches, including one in Scotland.

Haemophilia

HAEMOPHILIA SOCIETY

Haemophilia Society
PO Box 9, 16 Trinity Street, London SE1 1DE
Tel: 01-407 1010

The Society provides a great deal of help for parents. It gives advice on all aspects of concern, from diagnosis and treatment, to education, holidays and treatment centres. It gives such practical help as grants and loans. Advice and help are also available through the Society's social worker. There are local groups in many parts of the country and inquiries from interested people are always welcomed.

Heart disorders

ASSOCIATION FOR CHILDREN WITH HEART DISORDERS

Association for Children with Heart Disorders
John Whitehead
536 Colne Road, Reedley, Nr Burnley, Lancs.
Tel: Burnley (0282) 27500

The Association was formed at the end of 1973 and now has about eleven branches in Lancashire and Cheshire, coordinated by a governing council which makes sure that they are all aiming in the same direction. It has concentrated on trying to improve facilities in two ways: first of all by putting pressure on the authorities and secondly, by raising money. Its success as a pressure group has dramatically reduced the waiting lists for heart operations in Liverpool. Its fund-raising efforts have produced over £12 000. It has sponsored a research technician to assist the cardiac work at Liverpool Hospital and undertaken to pay two years' salary in the hope that the National Health Service will take over the commitment after that. It has also set up a 'heart valve bank' at Liverpool Hospital. The Association is a registered charity run entirely by voluntary effort with no office or paid staff.

BRITISH HEART FOUNDATION

British Heart Foundation
57 Gloucester Place, London WC1H 4DH
Tel: 01–935 0185

Although the Foundation has no direct welfare activities' it encourages Heart Circles who can give encouragement and practical help to parents of children with cardiac conditions. The Foundation acts as a clearing house and can put parents in touch with reliable contacts. Its principal function is financing and sponsoring research into the causes, prevention and treatment of diseases of the heart and circulation.

See also **Chest disorders**

Huntington's Chorea

ASSOCIATION TO COMBAT HUNTINGTON'S CHOREA

Maureen Hart-Jones, Association to Combat Huntington's Chorea
Lyndhurst, Lower Hampton Road, Sunbury-on-Thames,
Middx TW16 5PR
Tel: 01–979 5055

Although this disease strikes mainly those of middle age,

the children and families of sufferers are often traumatically affected by it because of its hereditary character. The Association, formed in 1971, is run by HC families for HC families. It intends to sponsor research into the condition, to give help and support for families and provide advice and information to them and to the general public. The Association has published two booklets discussing the disease, one for families, one for professional workers.

Hydrocephalus

See **Spina bifida and hydrocephalus**

Kidney disease

BRITISH KIDNEY PATIENT ASSOCIATION

Mrs Elizabeth Ward, British Kidney Patient Association
Bordon, Hants
Tel: Bordon (042–03) 2021/2

Elizabeth Ward, the mother of a twenty-two-year-old son with kidney failure, says that there is a small band of almost forgotten people, nearly 900 in fact, in this country who depend for their very existence on renal dialysis. Nearly all of them are aged between ten and thirty-five, and their lives, though being maintained, are drastically restricted by their treatment. She began the Silver Lining appeal to support the work of the National Kidney Research Fund. But the Fund exists solely to raise money for pure research into kidney disease and is unable to offer any assistance to parents which might be termed 'welfare'. It says that, sadly, it frequently has to turn down requests for help from distressed parents. So Mrs Ward broke away from the Fund and formed the British Kidney Patient Association as a campaigning organization to look after the interests and welfare of all renal patients. The Silver Lining Appeal is now committed to raising money for publicity to recruit donors for transplant kidneys, holiday facilities for patients on dialysis, portable kidney machines, up-to-date dialysis equipment, and help to patients for costly diets and the travel expenses incurred for their treatment.

Mrs Ward claims that renal patients, many of them young, will die this year, not because treatment is not known but because no treatment is available for them. She says: 'The problems are immense but not insurmountable. With a helpful press, a caring public, and a Department of Health aware of its responsibilities, we will see the day in the not too distant future when our patients and those who care for them, can look with confidence for the help they so desperately need and have the right to expect and we will not rest until that day is here.'

Leukaemia

LEUKAEMIA SOCIETY

Mrs Joan Williams, Leukaemia Society
45 Craigmoor Avenue, Queens Park, Bournemouth
Tel: Bournemouth (0202) 37459

Parents of children with leukaemia or any of the related cancers of the blood or lymph system need a listening ear – someone to help them bear their anxieties – and also someone to answer their questions. The Leukaemia Society is a group of parents who have felt all this themselves and know from their own experience the kind of help other parents really need and want. In contrast, well-meaning relatives and friends may either hang back because they are unsure about what is wanted or intrude by doing all the wrong things. Each member of the national committee acts as area secretary for a region, so that the network of contacts and services can reach parents anywhere in the country. They organize practical help such as holiday caravans, babysitting, care of other children, help with transport and hospital visiting. They arrange programmes where expert speakers discuss with parents questions they cannot always ask their own child's doctor. Many of the members have seen their children successfully treated and members' combined experience of all types of treatment enables them to advise on what is available and where and how to get it.

LEUKAEMIA RESEARCH FUND

Leukaemia Research Fund
43 Great Ormond Street, London WC1N 3JJ
Tel: 01-405 0101

The Fund exists to encourage, promote and assist research into leukaemia and related blood diseases. It relies largely on local branches for raising over £300 000 a year to support research programmes at hospitals and medical centres throughout Britain. Its annual report gives full details, including technical information, about the progress of the various research projects.

Limb deficiency

LADY HOARE TRUST FOR PHYSICALLY DISABLED CHILDREN

The Trust offers help to families of children suffering from any form of limb-deficiency irrespective of the cause.

See **Physical handicap**

Mental handicap

NATIONAL SOCIETY FOR MENTALLY HANDICAPPED CHILDREN (NSMHC)

NSMHC, Pembridge Hall, 17 Pembridge Square, London W2 4EP
Tel: 01-229 8941/01-727 0536

Forty thousand parents of mentally and multiply handicapped children belong to the NSMHC. Through its network of local societies, regional offices and the central office it can offer friendship and support to parents in distress. As well as regular meetings for parents, some local societies run preschool playgroups, social clubs, holiday activities and residential hostels. The regional offices have considerable flexibility and devise their own special projects to meet the particular needs and interests of their areas. The national organization finances research, runs three training establishments, has facilities for emergency short-term care, provides a friendly and efficient information service, organizes a wide variety of courses, conferences and information-exchange sessions for parents and professionals. Publications include two quarterlies – a specialist journal and *Parents' Voice* (subscription £1 per year) for parents and general readers. A comprehensive list of publications on mental handicap is available from the Society's own bookshop, which also has a mail-order service. It publishes a directory of residential accommodation for mentally handicapped people and a paperback series, *Subnormality in the Seventies*. An important part of the work of the NSMHC is increasing public awareness and understanding of mental handicap so that better provision is made for the special care and education of mentally handicapped children.

Trusteeship Scheme. To allay some of the anxiety of parents about who will care for the child when they die, the NSMHC has devised a scheme which provides for a specially appointed visitor to keep in close touch with each child and to watch over his affairs as closely as necessary. The name of the scheme is rather misleading – the service offered is befriending rather than trusteeship in the legal sense (see chapter 3, **Property**, page 160). This would include remembering birthdays and Christmas, cooperation with the various authorities involved, regular visits and friendship. The entry fee to the scheme is £750 from 1 January 1976 and the Society has arranged an insurance plan whereby small contributions can be paid monthly if this is preferred. Full details are set out in an explanatory leaflet.

SCOTTISH SOCIETY FOR MENTALLY HANDICAPPED

Scottish Society for Mentally Handicapped
69 West Regent Street, Glasgow G2 2AN
Tel: 041-331 1551/2

The Society, one of the liveliest in Scotland, is very much a parent-centred organization. Its aims are to promote the welfare of the mentally handicapped. It fosters closer cooperation between parents and others responsible for the welfare of mentally handicapped people as well as mutual help and support among parents and relatives. It encourages research. The Society helps to establish and maintain day centres, sheltered workshops and residential hostels and has set up its own short-stay homes for emergencies and other relief to parents. It has pioneered a scheme to cooperate with local authorities in providing hostels for the mentally handicapped.

ASSOCIATION OF PROFESSIONS FOR THE MENTALLY HANDICAPPED (APMH)

APMH, 126 Albert Street, London NW1 7NF
Tel: 01-267 6111

The aim of the Association is to encourage high standards of care and development of mentally handicapped people by facilitating cooperation and the sharing of knowledge among all professionals working for or with the mentally handicapped, by offering a unified professional view on the strategies of mental handicap, and by educating the public to accept, understand and respect mentally handicapped people. The Association developed as a result of a spontaneous movement among professional workers to unite their efforts across professional and service demarcation lines. Parents can join as associate members – individuals who are interested in furthering the work of the Association – at a subscription of £1 a year.

CAMPAIGN FOR THE MENTALLY HANDICAPPED

Campaign for the Mentally Handicapped
96 Portland Place, London W1N 4EX
Tel: 01-636 5020

The Campaign is an informal but highly effective pressure group, including parents and professionals, fighting for the integration of mentally handicapped people into their local communities with the right to have a say in their own lives. They claim that integration should mean handicapped people using the normal range of health, educational and welfare services with special help when they need it. It also means the provision of effective counselling and support for handicapped people and their families from birth throughout their life. They want to see residential facilities for small groups of people, no matter how handicapped, near their friends and neighbours. They argue that real community care of this kind will lead to the closure of all the remote and unsatisfactory institutions which exist today.

There is no formal committee or organization of which one can become a member. A small national policy group meets every six weeks to decide on areas of concern where some action should be taken. Anyone who is interested in their work can ask to be sent the newsletter (three or four times a year) and can also be sent minutes of meetings, details of issues on which evidence is to be submitted to government departments and so on. Every three or four months there is an open meeting, usually out of London, which is a talking rather than a policy-making session. Their policies are authoritatively set out in a series of publications. In two areas – Bristol and Cardiff – area groups have been set up and have, among other things, produced local guides to services.

CENTRE AT SUNLEY HOUSE

Centre at Sunley House, Gunthorpe Street, London E1
Tel: 01-247 1416

This is an experimental centre for mentally handicapped people and their families at Toynbee Hall, which began at the end of 1974, financed by a grant from the King's Fund. The aim is to provide a base for local families with a mentally handicapped member where they can get practical help and the opportunity to take part in all kinds of activities, including a youth club, adult evening club, Saturday morning club for hyperactive and non-communicating children, holiday activities and so on. The Centre has links with all the local statutory and voluntary services.

Other services available to anyone with a handicapped child, whether or not they live locally, include a counselling service, social and educational meetings for parents, workshop and discussion groups, information leaflets, links with manufacturers, cooperation with others in the field. A telephone information service is available from 10 a.m. till 5 p.m. Monday to Friday; Tuesday and Thursday till 7 p.m. The involvement of parents and the local community is crucial to the success of the project.

HESTER ADRIAN RESEARCH CENTRE

Professor Peter Mittler, Hester Adrian Research Centre
The University, Manchester M13 9PL
Tel: 061-273 3333

This is a full-time university research centre for the study of learning processes in the mentally handicapped. It makes its research both relevant and accessible to parents. Many of its projects have aimed to help parents cope with practical problems and provide guidance about stimulating the child's development. It is now carrying out a major investigation into means by which parents can be involved: games to play which develop cognitive skills, and ways of disseminating the information to professional workers who come into regular contact with parents. Another project studies the very early development of Down's Syndrome babies and ways of intervening in an attempt to improve attainment. These are only two of a variety of projects to help mentally handicapped children from an exceptionally sympathetic and committed team of researchers who are always concerned to persuade professionals of the importance of the parent's role in helping a handicapped child.

INSTITUTE OF MENTAL SUBNORMALITY

Institute of Mental Subnormality
Wolverhampton Road, Kidderminster, Worcestershire DY10 3PP
Tel: Kidderminster (0562) 850251

The Institute is an independent charity offering a full education and training programme for parents, voluntary workers and all categories of staff involved with those who are mentally handicapped. Its activities for parents include 'The Parents' Programme', a training and advisory service for parents and professional workers who are directly involved with families. The programme includes courses, discussion groups and talks, many held at a three-bed-roomed house in Kidderminster, rented by the Institute and furnished as far as possible as an ordinary home. Training programmes for individual children are devised and carried out there in a domestic environment. Children in residential care are introduced to an ordinary home life, in small groups, with the hope that many of them will eventually be able to live at home. The doctor in charge said: 'It's much more convincing for a mother to have seen a child get over its problem in a house setting than in a ward situation, which can be unreal.' Because of the Institute's concern about the lack of provision for children with language problems, it has established a special unit at Lea Castle Hospital which is concerned with the assessment of language problems and provision of programmes of treatment by parents, teachers and others involved with the children. The Institute publishes a quarterly journal, *Apex*, subscription £1.20 a year, free to members. Anyone interested in subnormality may join the Institute as an individual member, subscription £1 a year.

IN TOUCH

Mrs Ann Worthington, In Touch
10 Norman Road, Sale, Cheshire M33 3DF
Tel: 061-962 4441

Ann Worthington pioneered correspondence magazines which put parents in touch with other families whose children have similar handicaps, all of whom have some kind of mental handicap as well. Membership is now almost 800 families. They tell each other about their children's everyday problems and achievements, just as families with normal children chat about them with their friends. Many families who first made friends through the post have later arranged to meet one another. There are several 'round robin' magazines circulating within groups which have up to ten members. Each member contributes a letter and sends it on to the next family on the list; when the bundle of letters completes the circle back round to them again a few weeks later, they take out their old letter, put in a new one and have new ones to read from all the other members before sending it on again. A general newsletter is published several times a year, gives helpful advice and information and asks for contacts for parents whose children have rare conditions. Mrs Worthington has also assembled sets of information sheets from a number of different sources.

KING'S FUND CENTRE

King's Fund Centre, 126 Albert Street, London NW1 7NF
Tel: 01-267 6111

The Centre is a forum for the discussion of current problems, and to help accelerate the introduction of good ideas and practice in the health service. The Mental Handicap Project publishes a quarterly *Bulletin* (annual subscription £2) on mental handicap which is, in fact, an imaginative and generous pack of material of interest to everyone with a concern for mental handicap, written or reproduced from a wide range of international sources. It also runs multi-disciplinary meetings and courses, all of which are advertised in the *Bulletin*. For example, with the APMH and the IMS it sponsored a two-day workshop of parents and professionals which produced a statement of about 'the kind of service for mentally handicapped children towards which we should be striving and which identifies what can be done, in practical terms, during the next five years' (*Mental Handicap Papers No. 10,* 1976;

available from the King's Fund Centre, price 40p). Non-professionals are welcomed to meetings provided that they come to discuss general issues and not their own specific problems. Some idea of its activities can be gained from the 1975 programme which included a residential seminar on collaboration between parents and professionals, and 'Fun and Games at Mea House' in Newcastle, a special session of the King's Fund exhibition on play and toys for the mentally handicapped together with workshop sessions.

MENTAL WELFARE COMMISSION FOR SCOTLAND

Mental Welfare Commission
22 Melville Street, Edinburgh EH3 7NS
Tel: 031-225 7034

This is a permanent organization created by the Mental Health (Scotland) Act 1960. It is independent of the National Health Service, and has eleven commissioners; three of them must be doctors, one a lawyer and at least one a woman. Its duties are to investigate allegations of ill-treatment, including poor standards of care, to visit regularly patients detained in hospital or under guardianship in the community, and to report to the appropriate authority any problems that need to be solved to 'secure the welfare' of a mentally disturbed person. Although its activities (described in its report *No Place to Go*, HMSO, 1975) rely on persuasion rather than legal force it has become in the words of Bill Kenny, in *New Psychiatry* (6 November 1975): 'a force to be reckoned with when things need to be done to safeguard the care of mentally disordered people.'

MIND (NATIONAL ASSOCIATION FOR MENTAL HEALTH)

Mind, 22 Harley Street, London W1N 2ED
Tel: 01-637 0741

Mind is a charity concerned with those suffering from any form of mental illness or severe stress, including children and young people who are maladjusted, emotionally disturbed or mentally handicapped to any degree. It wants to see that proper help is provided either by taking action itself or by pressing for official action. It believes that spreading knowledge about the true facts of mental disorder will help to overcome the stigma still attached to it. Mind runs homes, schools and hostels for disturbed children and acts as coordinator for over 100 affiliated local associations. It runs a lively public information service answering queries about any aspect of mental disorder. *Mind Out* is a bi-monthly magazine on mental health topics (subscription £1.50 for six issues). *Mind Information Bulletin* is a monthly digest of news, parliamentary reports, research reports, films, books, pamphlet articles and diary of events from the mental health field (annual subscription £3). These two publications have to be ordered from head office. Otherwise its mail order and bookshop service is run from Mind Northern Office and its book list includes *Children Apart – Autistic Children and their Families, Parents and Mentally Handicapped Children* (price 50p) and *Your Mongol Baby*. A book of simple hymns designed to be used by mentally handicapped people is also available.

Mind Northern Office, 157 Woodhouse Lane, Leeds LS2 3EF
Tel: Leeds (0532) 453926

NATIONAL DEVELOPMENT GROUP FOR THE MENTALLY HANDICAPPED

Department of Health and Social Security
Alexander Fleming House, Elephant and Castle, London SE1
Tel: 01-407 5522

Mrs Barbara Castle, as Secretary of State for Social Services, announced the formation of this group at a conference of the NSMHC in February 1975. At that time she said that it would be vital for the group to play a very active role, initiating and developing ideas and not merely responding to ideas put to it. The Group advises the Secretaries of State for Social Services and for Wales on the development of government policy for the mentally handicapped and the strategy for implementing it. Professor Peter Mittler of the Hester Adrian Research Centre is the Chairman and has direct access to Ministers. Other members of the group include people from medicine, nursing, social services, education and administration. Many people have expressed their disappointment – publicly and privately – that parents were not represented on the group.

In its second bulletin, issued in July 1976, the Group reported that for the time being it would be concentrating on four main areas of work, each of which would be discussed in detail by a specialist sub-group. These were:

1 adult training centres and day services for adults;
2 services for mentally handicapped children;
3 short-term residential care;
4 the mental handicap hospital.

The Group's first major publication was a pamphlet on joint planning to improve local standards in mental handicap services: *Mental Handicap Planning Together*, Pamphlet No. 1, July 1976.

At the same time a multi-disciplinary development team was created as a back-up to the Group to assist health and local authorities in the preparation of local plans for the development of services for the mentally handicapped. This team provides specialist information about the current state of development of mental handicap services within the National Health Service and local authority personal social services. The Director is Dr G. B. Simon, well known for his work at Lea Castle Hospital and the Institute of Mental Subnormality.

Before the team started work there were criticisms from voluntary organizations in the field of mental handicap of its terms of reference and planned methods of working. The Campaign for the Mentally Handicapped was particularly concerned that the team can visit only by invitation from local authorities. It felt that all areas should be visited and all parents' organizations or community health councils should have the right to request a visit.

The Campaign hoped that the experience, views and wishes of groups who have in the past been ignored would be taken into account – those who are themselves mentally handicapped and their parents. Experience during the team's first year of work has reinforced the view that staff working in local services and local parents should be able to ask the team to visit their area, and that parents should be directly represented on the National Development Group. Mind felt that the initial composition of the team reflected too much emphasis on hospital care, neglecting the 80 per cent of mentally handicapped people living at home. They were also concerned about secrecy and lack of public accountability. In October 1976 Mind still believed that it was essential for there to be more parent and pressure group representation.

NATIONAL ELFRIDA RATHBONE SOCIETY

National Elfrida Rathbone Society
83 Mosley Street, Manchester M2 3OG
Tel: 061–236 5358

A national organization concerned with promoting voluntary community social work on behalf of educationally handicapped children through local groups. Local committees organize case work and operate preschool playgroups, clubs and holiday playschemes.

SCOTTISH ASSOCIATION FOR MENTAL HEALTH

Scottish Association for Mental Health
11 St Colme Street, Edinburgh EH3 6AG
Tel: 031-225 4606

The aim of the Association is to foster a wider understanding of the importance of mental health, to undertake the practical provision of services and facilities for those who are mentally ill or mentally handicapped, to befriend patients in hospital, to provide an advisory service and to produce publications on every aspect of the subject.

Better Services for the Mentally Handicapped (HMSO, 1971)

HMSO, Mail Order Dept
PO Box 569, London SE1
Tel: 01-928 6977
or local HMSO offices. It can be ordered through booksellers.

Command Paper 4683, published by the government in June 1971, discussed every aspect of this subject: mentally handicapped people and their families, existing services and provision for the future, descriptions of voluntary services and research projects in the field. It laid down lines of guidance as to how the government wished services to develop. Five years later it is still being used as the yardstick by which to measure whether or not the standard of provision for mentally handicapped people – both quantity and quality – is adequate. The Association of Professions for the Mentally Handicapped have produced a substantial booklet called *Better Services – the Realities* (1974, price 50p) based on the proceedings of their first annual conference. The British Association of Social Workers (BASW) set up a working party to produce an informed response to the government's proposals and help to stimulate discussion. Its report, *Better Services for the Mentally Handicapped: Report of the Working Party on the Government White Paper (Cmnd 4683),* including at least forty recommendations for the action needed to improve services, costs 65p. It introduces these recommendations with the comment: 'Mentally handicapped children like all children, can bring joy, satisfaction and other positive features to family life, a fact not mentioned in the White Paper.'

BASW, 16 Kent Street, Birmingham B5 6RD
Tel: 021-622 3911

Metabolic storage disorders

See TAY–SACHS DISEASE for the following rare metabolic storage disorders: Batten's disease, Fabry's disease, generalized gangliosidosis, Gaucher's disease, glycogen storage disease, Hunter's Syndrome, Hurler's Syndrome, Krabbe's disease, Maroteaux–Lamy Syndrome, metachromatic leucodystrophy, Morquio's disease, the mucopolysaccharidoses, Sanfilippo Syndrome, Wolman's disease and related disorders.

Mongolism (Down's Syndrome)

See **Mental Handicap;** see also chapter 4, **Treatment,** DOWN'S CHILDREN'S ASSOCIATION, page 228

Multiple sclerosis

CRACK – MULTIPLE SCLEROSIS SOCIETY

Crack, Multiple Sclerosis Society
4 Tachbrook Street, London SW1V 1SJ
Tel: 01-834 8231

Crack is the young arm of the Multiple Sclerosis Society. Membership is open to anyone with multiple sclerosis, their relatives, or indeed anyone interested in the Society's activities and objectives. Anyone joining Crack automatically becomes a member of the Multiple Sclerosis Society and receives the support of a nationwide organization plus regular copies of its journal. Crack speaks of itself as a crusade and aims to create a true fighting spirit not only among young people with MS but also amongst the people around them – families, friends, social workers and doctors – who can influence them and help them to attack the disease.

Muscular dystrophy

MUSCULAR DYSTROPHY GROUP OF GREAT BRITAIN

Muscular Dystrophy Group of Great Britain
Nattrass House, 35 Macaulay Road, Clapham, London SW4 0QP
Tel: 01-720 8055

The main concern of this group and its local branches is to raise money for research to find a cure, both for muscular dystrophy and for other neuro-muscular diseases such as myasthenia gravis and muscular atrophy. The group also publishes helpful pamphlets and a quarterly journal in the form of a newspaper covering news, events and activities in the branches as well as general information. Advice on welfare matters can be given by the head office.

Myasthenia gravis

Myasthenia Gravis Council
Muscular Dystrophy Group of Great Britain
Nattrass House, 35 Macaulay Road, Clapham
London SW4 0QP
Tel: 01–720 8055

There is now a Myasthenia Gravis Council within the Muscular Dystrophy Group.

Osteo genesis imperfecta

See **Brittle bones**

Paget's disease

NATIONAL ASSOCIATION FOR THE RELIEF OF PAGET'S DISEASE

Mrs A. Stansfield
National Association for the Relief of Paget's Disease
413 Middleton Road, Middleton, Manchester M24 4QZ
Tel: 061-643 1998

This is mainly a disease of older people, but there is a junior form that occurs, rarely, in children. The Association was formed in 1973 to raise funds for research into the causes and treatment of the disease and to alleviate the distress caused to the sufferers.

Paraplegic

See **Spinal injuries**

Partial sight

PARTIALLY SIGHTED SOCIETY

Partially Sighted Society
40 Wordsworth Street, Hove, Sussex
Tel: (0273) 736053

The Society was formed in 1973 mainly as a result of pressure from the parents of partially sighted children. Since then it has become an organization with over 8000 members – partially sighted people of all ages and parents, ophthalmologists, teachers and lawyers. Its aim is to make sure that the interest and needs of partially sighted people are represented at all levels wherever it seems necessary. More than thirty groups are now established throughout the country. Projects in careers and employment and in the field of education are already under way. Booklets on vision and common defects are published, as well as a monthly magazine, *Oculus*, and a quarterly journal, *Eyepiece*. Membership of the Society is free and open to all. The organization has a special national education committee which can answer queries on education. It looks at questions about the education of partially sighted children from a consumer's and layman's point of view as well as from the professional angle.

Education Committee Chairman, J. R. Andrews
29 Bushey Way, Beckenham, Kent BR3 2TA
Tel: 01-650 8427

DISABLED LIVING FOUNDATION

Disabled Living Foundation
346 Kensington High Street, London W14 8NS
Tel: 01-602 2491

The Foundation has a project to consider the problems faced by partially sighted people, including very young partially sighted children. The information collected is being fed into the Foundation's information service and the aids centre will have details about suitable aids.

OPTICAL INFORMATION COUNCIL

Optical Information Council
Walter House, 418–422, The Strand, London WC2 0PB
Tel: 01–836 2323

> The Council produces a large-print leaflet, *So You're Partially Sighted*, available post free.

> See also **Blindness** – many organizations for blind people also have much to offer to those who are partially sighted.

Physical handicap

ACTION RESEARCH FOR THE CRIPPLED CHILD

National Fund for Research into Crippling Diseases
1 Springfield Road, Horsham, Sussex RH12 2PN
Tel: Horsham (0403) 64101

> Action Research for the Crippled Child raises money to discover through research how to prevent crippling diseases and help those disabled by them. The fund is not linked to any specific disease, so the money can be spent where and when it is most needed. A quarterly journal, *Action*, with news and discussion of ideas in the field is available, annual subscription £1.50. *Integrating the Disabled*, the report of a working party under Lord Snowdon, was published in 1976 (price £2.50). In the foreword, Lord Snowdon writes: 'Need disabled people still be put in herds – in schools, buses, homes – and labelled as such? Can they not instead have the equal opportunity, so commonly enjoyed, to go where they want, how they want, and when they want?''

CENTRAL COUNCIL FOR THE DISABLED

Central Council for the Disabled
34 Eccleston Square, London SW1V 1PE
Tel: 01-821 1871

> The Council is a national action group for all physically disabled people, and a coordinating body of voluntary organizations. It brings pressure to bear on central and

local government to improve the environment for all disabled people. It concentrates on access, housing, holidays and legal parliamentary matters. The monthly information bulletin (subscription £1 a year) has a useful survey of parliamentary, international, local government and other news. The Council runs an information bureau and has a useful list of publications. Changes in the Council are envisaged in 1977, including a move within the London area.

LADY HOARE TRUST FOR PHYSICALLY DISABLED CHILDREN

Lady Hoare Trust for Physically Disabled Children
7 North Street, Midhurst, West Sussex GU29 9DJ
Tel: Midhurst (073-081) 3696

After the success of the fight for compensation for the thalidomide children, the Trust turned its attention to the many other physically handicapped children in need of help. The Trust finances and organizes a comprehensive welfare service to give every kind of support and help – personal, financial and practical – to the family. Professional social workers make sure that families get the help they need and will contact schools, the Red Cross or anywhere where help is available on their behalf. The Trust can make gifts of electronic typewriters, electrically operated cars to make children mobile, or financial help for whatever aids will fill a particular need. It has holiday homes, two for families, two for children only. The Trust also carries out research into the needs of the physically handicapped; for instance, a special survey on writing in education for the physically handicapped.

WALES COUNCIL FOR THE DISABLED

Wales Council for the Disabled
Crescent Road, Caerphilly, Mid Glamorgan
Tel: Caerphilly (0222) 869 224

The Council is a new organization which aims to integrate physically disabled people into the living community of

Wales and improve the opportunities for them to participate in everyday life. It is bringing together all the organizations – disabled action groups, voluntary welfare organizations, professional bodies and statutory authorities. The Council's activities cover the whole of Wales and it can give advice and assistance on all aspects of disability and disabled living. Contacts can be made through its many local groups and affiliated bodies. Currently it has working parties active in the fields of education, mobility, accessibility, day and residential care, employment and holidays.

The Secondary Education of Physically Handicapped Children

This report, by a committee of inquiry into the needs of physically handicapped children in Scotland, covers careers opportunities and training as well as education, and stresses the need for the development of aids and adaptations to give physically handicapped children more independence, mobility and employment opportunities. It was published in 1975 and is available from HMSO, price 86p.

PKU

NATIONAL SOCIETY FOR PHENYLKETONURIA AND ALLIED DISORDERS

B. Talbot
National Society for Phenylketonuria and Allied Disorders
26 Towngate Grove, Mirfield, West Yorkshire
Tel: Mirfield (0924) 492873

This is a society begun in 1973 for PKU patients and their families to work for their medical, educational and social welfare. It publishes a quarterly magazine, News and Views, giving information about PKU dietary treatment, recipes, parents' contributions, etc. It holds regional day conferences and an annual holiday conference weekend for PKU families. Future plans include social and medical research.

See also **Mental Handicap** for the NSMHC who publish *The Child with PKU*, by Linda Tyfield and John Holton (1974).

Polio

BRITISH POLIO FELLOWSHIP

Mr D. Powell, British Polio Fellowship
Bell Close, West End Road, Ruislip, Middx HA4 6LP
Tel: Ruislip 75515

The Fellowship can offer a professional advice service for parents as well as a personal welfare service for polio sufferers to encourage their rehabilitation. It runs a sheltered workshop and hostel. Financial aid is sometimes possible. Local branches run many leisure and holiday activities.

Renal disease

See **Kidney disease**

Restricted growth

ASSOCIATION FOR RESEARCH INTO RESTRICTED GROWTH

Mr C. Pocock
Association for Research into Restricted Growth
4 Laburnum Avenue, Wickford, Essex
Tel: Wickford (037-44) 3132

This group has taken the initiative by setting up a programme for research into the causes and the treatment of conditions of restricted growth – an area which was totally neglected before. It claims that nine out of ten GPs will never meet a single case of restricted growth in the whole of their medical career. So the tenth, when he or she does have a case, has no case studies or experience to refer to. The Association has therefore set up a medical sub-committee under a coordinator who is a GP and himself a person of restricted growth. This committee provides a referral service both for patients and for doctors, to put them in touch with experts in the field of restricted growth in their own area. They will, of course, observe proper medical etiquette. The medical sub-committee has published *A Layman's Guide to Restricted Growth* (price 25p, including postage). There is a children's committee for parents of children with restricted growth for mutual counselling and self-help, with additional outside support when this is needed. The Association has a clothing information officer. There is an ambitious and varied programme of every kind of activity so that members can enjoy a normal social life.

Rheumatism and arthritis

ARTHRITIS AND RHEUMATISM COUNCIL FOR RESEARCH

Arthritis and Rheumatism Council for Research
Faraday House, 8–10 Charing Cross Road, London WC2H 0HN
Tel: 01-240 0871

The Council has been financing research into arthritis and all rheumatic diseases since 1936. It has found that six children in every 10 000 are affected with one of the many different types of rheumatic disease. Its research has shown that 70 per cent of the children who get arthritis early in life can make a good recovery. The Council campaigns to improve the services to help the rheumatic sufferer now in the light of present knowledge ahead of the day when a completely effective treatment is discovered. It has over 500 local branches which organize social and fund-raising events, show films on the subject and distribute leaflets as well as its informative magazine, published three times a year. You can also take out a subscription to this direct from the Council for 50p a year.

BRITISH RHEUMATISM AND ARTHRITIS ASSOCIATION

Group 130, British Rheumatism and Arthritis Association
1 Devonshire Place, London W1N 2BD
Tel: 01-935 9905

A small group of young people with various forms of arthritis have formed the 130 Group as a branch of the British Rheumatism and Arthritis Association. The Group caters for people aged fifteen to thirty-nine. The branch does not serve one area; it is intended to be nationwide. Its committee consists solely of young arthritic people who tend to have different problems from those of older people. Most of them are not lonely, as many members of the parent organization are. On the contrary, they seek desperately to be independent, to find ways of living the sort of life they want. They face lack of understanding from employers, insurance companies, social workers and many others who consider arthritis to be a disease of old age. The 130 Group hopes to help its members by enabling them to share these frustrations and, perhaps, make them more widely understood. It offers help and advice and an opportunity to share common problems. A friendly, informal monthly newsletter contains tips and factual information intended to be useful to members in their daily lives. It also helps them to keep in touch with one another and to exchange views. The 130 Group also arranges club holidays in specially adapted hotels and centres in Britain and abroad. The subscription, which includes full membership of the British Rheumatism and Arthritis Association, costs £1 per year. The Association is moving in 1977 to 6–7 Grosvenor Crescent, London SW1X 7EH.

Riley–Day Syndrome

See **Familial Dysautononia**

Sickle cell anameia

ORGANIZATION FOR SICKLE CELL ANAEMIA RESEARCH
(OSCAR)

Oscar, 200a High Road, Wood Green, London N22 4HH
Tel: 01–889 4844

> OSCAR was set up to raise funds for research and to raise
> the level of awareness about sickle cell anaemia and its
> implications among those at highest risk – people whose
> origins are in areas where malaria has been endemic.

Spastic

SPASTICS SOCIETY

Spastics Society, 12 Park Crescent, London W1N 4EQ
Tel: 01-636 5020

> The doyen of voluntary societies, the Spastics Society
> celebrated its twenty-first anniversary on 5 January 1973.
> Started, like many other voluntary societies, by a small
> group of parents, with capital of £5, its guide to services
> is now sixty pages long. A family services and assessment
> centre at 16 Fitzroy Square, London, is the base for a
> variety of advisory and counselling services. There is
> accommodation for up to twenty-five people, mostly
> arranged in family suites. Parents can bring the other
> children in the family along when a spastic child or
> adolescent is to be assessed. There are four family-help
> units operated nationally. They are designed to provide
> short-term care. This may mean a holiday for parents or
> even just a shopping trip or else a chance to have some
> time alone with an able-bodied child. Some units also
> organize a home babysitting service. The Society has
> established over forty schools, centres, workshops, resi-
> dential homes, clinics, hostels, training centres and holiday
> hotels. It has its own staff training centre, Castle Priory
> College. A major function of the Society is to promote
> research into the causes, prevention and treatment of
> cerebral palsy and it finances a £2 million medical research
> programme at Guy's Hospital. It has also guaranteed a

Chair in Child Development at the University of London. More than 130 local voluntary groups affiliated to the Spastics Society each organize their own programme of activities.

SCOTTISH COUNCIL FOR SPASTICS

Scottish Council for Spastics
Rhuemore, 22 Corstorphine Road, Edinburgh EH12 6HP
Tel: 031-337 2804/2616

The Council was set up in 1946. With the cooperation of statutory and local authorities, it manages schools, day centres, sheltered workshops, residential homes and hostels. It runs its own therapeutic services including a mobile therapy unit. The Council arranges visits and leisure activities and organizes the Scottish Spastic Games.

Speech and language disorders

ASSOCIATION FOR ALL SPEECH-IMPAIRED CHILDREN (AFASIC)

AFASIC
Room 14, Toynbee Hall, 28 Commercial Street, London E1 6LS
Tel: 01-247 1497

AFASIC exists because children who are of average intelligence but suffer from speech and language disorders are so few, and their special problems therefore tend to be neglected. It is an association of parents whose children suffer from speech and language difficulties, together with professionals and anyone else concerned with these problems. It provides an information and advisory service for parents, including help in finding the most suitable place for diagnosis. There is no accepted screening procedure for recognizing children who fail to develop understanding of language and/or normal speech, so many of them do not get suitable speech therapy and education at an early enough age. AFASIC campaigns to change this. The society plans a programme of research and education to tackle every aspect of the problems and campaigns to improve and coordinate health, social and educational services. There are regional groups throughout the UK and the Association has an area register so that parents who wish may be put in touch with others living near by. It also organizes special holidays for children suffering from speech and language disorders with young helpers on a one-to-one basis.

INVALID CHILDREN'S AID ASSOCIATION (ICAA)

ICAA, 126 Buckingham Palace Road, London SW1 9SB
Tel: 01-730 9891

The ICAA administers three residential special schools for children with language disorders. It has developed highly structured language-teaching schemes and makes extensive use of the Paget–Gorman Sign System as a means of giving children a soundly based method of communication leading to development of spoken and written language. Simple material published for language stimulation work can be used by parents with some guidance.

Spina bifida and hydrocephalus

ASSOCIATION FOR SPINA BIFIDA AND HYDROCEPHALUS (ASBAH)

ASBAH, 30 Devonshire Street, London W1N 2EB
Tel: 01-935 9060/01-486 6100

ASBAH is the association which works and cares for children born with spina bifida and hydrocephalus ('water on the brain'). It encourages and supports their families so that the children can live at home, attending local schools wherever possible, growing up in the community. The Association recognizes that the care of a disabled child is much less daunting if expert help and advice is readily available and in some areas it has specially trained social workers who provide a shoulder to lean on to ease the strain. It has provision for short-term care, either to tide the family over a crisis or give them a much-needed breathing space. It can also give children with nowhere to go during school holidays a corner they can call home which welcomes them as each school holiday comes round. Their Samaritan Fund provides grants towards some of the special needs of spina bifida children: either those which cause real financial hardship, such as the cost of hospital visits or of special appliances not available from statutory sources; or those which cause frustration, such as lack of facilities for recreation or holidays to give new and productive experiences away from the sometimes over-protective atmosphere of home.

A full-time education and training officer has been appointed to the staff at headquarters, qualified to give expert help in finding rewarding work or occupation.

The appliances department makes sure that information about a wide range of aids reaches all who can benefit, and at the same time encourages the production of improved equipment and appliances and investigates the cause of delays and errors in the supply of them.

The Association wants to promote research into causes and treatment and genetic advice. There are seventy local associations and a regular magazine, *Link*, with a circulation of 9000 (subscription 75p).

SCOTTISH SPINA BIFIDA ASSOCIATION

Scottish Spina Bifida Association
190 Queensferry Road, Edinburgh EH4 2BW
Tel: 031-332 0743

As well as acting as a channel for passing information and advice to parents, the Association tries to arrange practical help. Physiotherapy groups and playgroups are held in centres where there are no other preschool facilities. The Association provides a number of aids which are not available on the National Health Service. The Association has local branches which organize parents' meetings and are affiliated to ASBAH.

Spina Bifida: The Treatment and Care of Spina Bifida Children

A practical and sympathetic guide written by Nancy Allum, a journalist (published by Allen & Unwin, 1975, £4.75 hardback, £2.50 paperback).

Spinal injuries

SPINAL INJURIES ASSOCIATION (SIA)

Spinal Injuries Association
126 Albert Street, London NW1 7NF
Tel: 01-267 6111

The Association's overall aim is to promote the welfare of all those suffering from spinal-cord injury. The programme for doing this is by collecting and disseminating information, promoting cooperation between statutory and voluntary organizations, promoting research surveys and development projects, arranging conferences, training courses, exhibitions and other activities aimed at helping paraplegics, tetraplegics and those caring for them. Full membership is open only to those with spinal-cord injuries. Those under sixteen suffering from spinal-cord injury can become junior members, free of charge. Associate membership is open to all. The SIA intends to issue regular bulletins of useful information – the second of these being devoted entirely to the problems of housing. Its first major publication is a readable, frank, practical guide for newly paralysed people covering every aspect of their new way of life. *So You're Paralysed* by Bernadette Fallon, attractively illustrated by Liz McQuiston, is available from the Association (1975, price £2, plus 30p postage).

SCOTTISH PARAPLEGIC (SPINAL INJURY) ASSOCIATION

Jean Stone, Scottish Paraplegic (Spinal Injury) Association
3 Cargil Terrace, Edinburgh EH5 3ND
Tel: 031-552 8459

The voice of Scottish paraplegics, this Association is concerned with welfare, housing and employment as well as sport and recreation. It tries to help the general public understand some of the problems of disability and to enable its members to take their part in the life of the community. It runs a very lively and informative magazine. Full membership is available only to people with spinal injuries; non-paraplegic people may join as associate members. Subscriptions for both are 50p a year.

There are also national paraplegic associations for England, Wales and Northern Ireland which are concerned mainly with sport for people with spinal injuries. Addresses can be obtained from the British Sports Association for the Disabled.

BSAD
Stoke Mandeville Stadium, Harvey Road, Aylesbury, Bucks
Tel: Aylesbury (0296) 84848

Tay–Sachs disease

BRITISH TAY–SACHS FOUNDATION

British Tay–Sachs Foundation
The Hospital for Sick Children
Great Ormond Street, London WC1N 3JH
Tel: 01-405 9200 Ext. 313

A very rare genetic disorder produces Tay–Sachs disease only where both parents are carriers. It is a hundred times as common among Jews whose family origins were in Eastern Europe than in any other group in the population. The Foundation aims to screen those couples most at risk to find the carriers. They can then take a pre-natal test during pregnancy which will tell whether or not the baby will be normal. The Foundation provides specialist genetic counselling for families affected by a wide range of other metabolic storage disorders, and pre-natal testing where possible. It is keeping a central register of families affected by all these conditions throughout the country and aims to keep in contact with them. Any family can always approach the Foundation for personal advice and support.

Thalassaemia

UNITED KINGDOM THALASSAEMIA SOCIETY

United Kingdom Thalassaemia Society
c/o University College Hospital, Paediatric Department
Huntley Street, London WC1E 6AU
Tel: 01–387 9300 Ext. 155

> The society has been set up to work within the communities which are most at risk – those of Mediterranean, Arabic, Indian and Far Eastern origin. Its activities cover ante-natal screening; raising funds so that advances in prevention and treatment can be put into effect; a full programme of activities for mutual support and information including a disco run by Thalassaemic teenagers and a multi-language newsletter.

Thalidomide

THALIDOMIDE CHILDREN'S TRUST

Thalidomide Children's Trust
The Shrubbery, Church Street, St Neots, Huntingdon, Cambs.
PE19 2BU
Tel: Huntingdon (0480) 74074

> The Trust was established on 10 August 1973 as a result of the successful campaign for compensation for victims of thalidomide. Its objects are: 'The care, welfare, treatment and education of, or otherwise in any way for the relief of, the disabilities of, or to meet the needs of, children suffering from congenital disability due to thalidomide.'

Tuberous sclerosis

TUBEROUS SCLEROSIS GROUP

Mrs E. Galbraith, Tuberous Sclerosis Group
11 Deveron Road, Bearsden, Glasgow G61 1LJ
Tel: 041-942 6664

> Set up in January 1975 and still very much in its infancy, this is an informal group run by parents for parents of children with tuberous sclerosis and the aim of the group

is to put parents in touch with one another. At present there are correspondence magazines circulating among the twenty-four members which they hope to develop into a newsletter. They want to gather information on all aspects of the disease, welfare benefits, aids, etc. They hope to help in any research undertaken into the condition and its early detection where parents are at risk. They have close links with the National Tuberous Sclerosis Association of the USA.

Vaccine damage

ASSOCIATION OF PARENTS OF VACCINE-DAMAGED
CHILDREN

Mrs R. Fox
Association of Parents of Vaccine-Damaged Children
2 Church Street, Shipston-on-Stour, Warwickshire CV36 4AP
Tel: Shipston-on-Stour (0608) 61595

Although it is not against vaccination, which has obviously saved many thousands of lives, the Association wants to see public recognition of the risks in order that the national vaccination programme can be monitored to discover the safest methods. It is negotiating at present for compensation for a small group of carefully checked cases of children, all of whom were definitely normal at birth. It has looked at what other European countries are doing to protect their immunization schemes by insurance and hopes to make proposals for the British government to take up some form of similar protection, if necessary by taking a case to the European Court of Human Rights.

3 Help

Common law requires authorities to act fairly and in accordance with natural justice whether or not there are Acts of Parliament or local authority regulations explicitly covering the sphere of activity. The General Assembly of the United Nations has made a declaration on social progress and development proclaiming the necessity of protecting the rights and assuring the welfare and re-habilitation of the physically and mentally disadvantaged. In December 1971 they also issued a declaration on the rights of mentally retarded persons. These declarations provide a useful frame of reference for people anxious to ensure that handicapped people enjoy the same rights as other human beings.

These fundamental principles may seem less in evidence when decisions are made than the pressing problems of sharing out scarce resources or a hankering after adminis-trative tidiness. But parents need not feel that they are helpless and at the mercy of the powers-that-be; they have rights and the means of exercising them if they know how to go about it.

The first thing you need to know is who is making the decisions on a day-to-day basis; who decides whether the local authority can supply special fittings for the toilet or can send transport to take a child to a special club. Most routine decisions are taken by officers employed by local or central government. If they have made a decision which you want to dispute, you will have to do so on the facts of the case. It is no use trying to convince them that the policy is wrong; their job is to carry it out to the best of their ability whether they agree with it or not. If the authority's policy is to give grants for boarding-school places only when home circumstances are exceptionally difficult, don't waste time arguing that there are other good reasons why a handicapped child may need to go to boarding school; get on with proving how difficult your home circumstances actually are.

If you really cannot get what you need without a change in policy, your argument is with the policy-makers, who are the politicians – local councillors or MPs. We have tried throughout this book to tell you when there are laws or regulations from central government giving you positive rights and when the matter has been left to the discretion of the local authority. Generally, it is easier to convince a local authority, which is providing personal services direct to people, that it ought to take a different line over a discretionary power or to make an exception for a special case, than to get the law changed. However, financial stringency may make local authorities more strong-minded in resisting special pleadings. It is usually a long and gruelling task to achieve a change in the law nationally, although many of the most effective pressure groups are to be found campaigning on behalf of handicapped children.

If you think that your local authority has refused you something to which you are legally entitled or that a wrong decision has been taken – a place offered at an unsuitable school, for instance, or an application for a ramp to the front door turned down for a family who have a child in a wheelchair – there are several courses of action you can take.

It is always worth starting by trying to enlist the personal support of your local councillor and your MP. A persistent and enthusiastic politician can often cut right through the red tape and sort out problems surprisingly quickly.

The Secretary of State with overall responsibility for the service involved will often 'persuade' a local authority which is behaving unreasonably to change its mind even if he does not choose to exercise any formal powers over local authorities which may be given to him by Acts of Parliament. You can always appeal to the Secretary of State quite informally by writing to him at the department or at the House of Commons. It is best if you can refer to the clause of the Act of Parliament or circular which you think the authority is acting contrary to. We have given references which should help you to do this wherever possible.

The local ombudsman can put moral pressure on a local authority and the parliamentary ombudsman can put moral pressure on a government department if there seems to be a question of maladministration. In both cases there are procedures to be followed in appealing to the respective ombudsman and these are set out in leaflets available from their offices and also from citizens advice bureaux and libraries.

Commission for Local Administration in England
21 Queen Anne's Gate, London SW1H 9BU
Tel: 01-930 3333
and
Micklegate House, Micklegate, York
Tel: York (0904) 30151

Commission for Local Administration in Wales
Portland House, 22 Newport Road, Cardiff CF2 1DB
Tel: Cardiff (0222) 371073

Commission for Local Administration in Scotland
125 Princes Street, Edinburgh EH2 4AD
Tel: 031-226 2823

Parliamentary Commissioner
Church House, Great Smith Street, London SW1 P3 BW
Tel: 01-212 6271

A number of organizations listed in this chapter will give guidance and help in making any appeal. In particular, see **Law**, page 155.

Chronically Sick and Disabled Persons Act 1970 (Scotland 1972)

This Act made the first serious effort to see that handicapped people had a right as citizens to a standard of living equal to that of other members of the community, and equal access to facilities provided by the community. It gave local authorities the duty to help substantially and permanently handicapped people with practical help and adaptation in their homes: radio, television, libraries and recreational facilities at home and outside the home; transport, travel, holidays; meals; a telephone and any special equipment needed to use it. They also had to see that any buildings open to the public must make practical provision for the disabled. Local authorities can make their own definition of need. But once they have decided that someone comes within that definition, they have a statutory duty under the Act to meet that need. *Circular 12/70*, however, said that authorities could consider needs 'in the light of resources' so in times of financial stringency the services provided under the Act have inevitably failed to live up to the intentions of its sponsors. In February 1976 a complaint was made to the ombudsman that the qualification introduced by the circular constituted mal-administration because it appeared to mislead local authorities into believing that if they didn't want to pay for something that they could change their mind and claim that the need no longer existed. Four years after the passing of the Act, Alfred Morris, Minister for the Disabled, said: 'There is still much to do if we are to raise the general standard of local services up to that of the existing best. Our task in the year ahead is to reduce the disparities in local provision. For the quality of help severely disabled people receive should not have to depend on the local authority area in which they live.' Unfortunately, worthy sentiments don't add up to legal rights.

OUTSET

Outset, 30 Craven Street, London WC2
Tel: 01-930 4255

This is a charity which mobilizes volunteers to undertake projects. They have been actively involved in large-scale projects in nineteen local authorities in which their volunteer helpers did door-to-door surveys to discover people

who may be eligible for help under the Chronically Sick
and Disabled Persons Act 1970. As a result of this experience they have built up considerable information and
expertise about the Act and have become concerned with
promoting good practice by local authorities both in
identifying needs and in discharging their duty under the
Act by meeting those needs. Outset would be interested to
hear from parents who feel that their own authority is
failing in either of these respects.

General

DEPARTMENT OF HEALTH AND SOCIAL SECURITY (DHSS)

DHSS, Alexander Fleming House, London SE1 6BY
Tel: 01-407 5522

Welsh Office
Cathays Park, Cardiff CF1 3NQ
Tel: Cardiff (0222) 44101

Scottish Home and Health Department
St Andrew's House, Edinburgh EH1 3DE
Tel: 031-556 8501

Under the direction of the Secretary of State for Social
Services, the DHSS is responsible for all personal health
and welfare services in England, and for the entire social
security system in Great Britain. One of the Parliamentary
Under-Secretaries of State, Alfred Morris, was appointed
to have special responsibility for the welfare of the disabled. The Welsh Office under the Secretary of State for
Wales and the Scottish Home and Health Department
under the Secretary of State for Scotland look after their
health and welfare services. Local authorities provide most
of the welfare services under the guidance and regulations
of the Secretary of State. The DHSS is responsible, for
example, for seeing that the provisions of the Chronically
Sick and Disabled Persons Act 1970 are carried out. All
three departments publish annual reports on their work,
which often contain valuable statistical and technical
information. Booklet HB1, *Help for Handicapped People*,

gives general guidance on services for handicapped people by both national and local authorities in England and Wales, and how to apply for them. It should be available from social security offices or social services departments of local authorities. *Help for Handicapped People in Scotland*, issued by the Scottish Office, gives similar advice.

PERSONAL SOCIAL SERVICES COUNCIL

Personal Social Services Council
Brook House, 2–16 Torrington Place, London WC1E 7HN
Tel: 01-323 4757

This Council, chaired by Lord James of Rusholme, has been established to advise Ministers on all aspects of the personal social services and to provide information and advice to everyone concerned with them. Two of their sub-committees may be of interest to parents of handicapped children.

The terms of reference of the Children and Family Life Group are to 'Keep under continual review all matters affecting the needs of children and their families'. Although the group will be more concerned with policy than with practical help, the needs of handicapped children will certainly be much in mind. The group will be available for consultation with any interested organization or group and will have power to co-opt members to serve on specific projects and study groups.

The Consumer Participation Group has the responsibility of representing the views of *consumers* of the social services. It is intended to keep their interests under review and to make sure that appropriate organizations are consulted in policy making. Members of the group include representatives of consumer organizations and professional bodies. Both these groups are new, their methods of working are still being developed, but they are anxious to base their recommendations on the real practical knowledge and experience of those involved. They could be used as an effective lever on the statutory system to bring about changes and improvements.

A.H.F.P.—D

LOCAL AUTHORITY SOCIAL SERVICES DEPARTMENT

Your town hall or your local library will tell you how to reach the social services department.

The social services department (social work department in Scotland) is the chief source of help from your local council, especially if anyone in the family is handicapped or disabled. In fact, Section 2 of the Chronically Sick and Disabled Persons Act 1970 states that the local authority should take the initiative in finding out about the numbers and needs of handicapped people and in taking steps to meet them (see **Registers**, page 163). The social services department has responsibility for implementing the Act and it is well worth contacting it to make sure that it is aware of your problems and that you are getting all the help available. It may be able to provide (possibly on long-term loan) a range of aids for communication, dressing, feeding, mobility, safety equipment, toilet facilities. Some of the different services which may be provided by the social services department are listed later in this chapter by name (e.g. **Aids, Home helps** and **Transport,** etc.). If you contact it, it will send a social worker – sooner or later depending on how hard-pressed or efficient the organization of the department – to discuss your needs. The social services department normally has teams of social workers based at area offices to serve each neighbourhood. As Phyllis Willmott put it in her classic *Consumer's Guide to the British Social Services* (Penguin Books, 3rd edn, 1973): 'Almost everywhere community care is at present more of a humane idea than a practical reality. Even though great progress in developing services is in general being made, it is still true that some authorities lean over backwards to do all they can, whereas others do the absolute minimum.'

In 1975 it was reported that only 40 per cent of social workers were qualified at all and that the percentage among residential workers was even smaller. The Central Council for Education and Training in Social Work (CCETSW) was set up in an attempt to rationalize the extraordinary diversity of courses for people who wanted to qualify as social workers. A report entitled *Social Work: People with Handicaps Need Better Trained Workers* was published by CCETSW in October 1974. The considerable public and professional discussion about the need for a training which equips the social worker to deal with all their clients' needs stresses that, although every social worker must have a common base of general knowledge, some expertise is essential. Families with a handicapped child will have contacts with social workers if they want the help which the social services department should be able to offer them. They need to recognize that the social worker may have no special training in the needs of handicapped children and so may not be fully informed about what services are available. Some social workers see their role as some kind of therapist or personal counsellor in helping families to understand their problems rather than as a source of practical help and information in finding solutions to them.

Central Council for Education and Training in Social Work
Central Office, Derbyshire House, St Chad's Street
London WC1H 8AE
Tel: 01–278 2455

COUNCILS OF SOCIAL SERVICE

National Council of Social Service
Community Work Division, 26 Bedford Square
London WC1B 3HU
Tel: 01-636 4066

There is a local council of social service in many areas which acts as an umbrella organization to coordinate the work of local voluntary groups. Their membership includes representatives of all the groups in the area and they encourage member organizations to work together to build up services and to make good any gaps. A local council ought to be able to put individuals in touch with any local organization for the handicapped, and give support and advice to parents' groups. For example, they might be able to give advice on how to obtain grants, accommodation, volunteer help and babysitting for any project. The National Council of Social Service holds a register of local councils.

FAMILY SERVICE UNITS (FSU)

FSU, 207 Old Marylebone Road, London NW1 5QP
Tel: 01-402 5175/6

In the past twenty-four years FSU has pioneered case-work methods of helping families under such severe stress that they were at risk of breaking up. Families with multiple problems may be quite unable to care for a handicapped child without sensitive support. A success story from Manchester in an annual report describes how the FSU social worker was able to help one family to such good effect that the happy ending included the parents dealing with their own problems effectively, one handicapped child beginning to attend an adult training centre regularly and another able to return home after living in hospital for five years. There are more than 100 social workers based at twenty-two units. The FSU family caseworker works intensively with a limited number of families and caseloads are kept to a reasonable number in a way which is not possible for social workers in local authority departments.

VOLUNTARY COUNCIL FOR HANDICAPPED CHILDREN

Voluntary Council for Handicapped Children
8 Wakley Street, Islington, London EC1V 7QE
Tel: 01-278 9441/7

The establishment of the Council was recommended by the National Children's Bureau working party which produced the report, *Living with Handicap*, in 1970. It was set up in 1975 as an independently elected body forming part of the National Children's Bureau to promote cooperation between all the voluntary and statutory organizations interested in the well-being of handicapped children. It will provide comprehensive information about available services and sources of help, and will attempt to identify gaps and overlaps in services, and arrange consultation with interested parties to remedy these. It will not duplicate work that is already being done elsewhere, but work for the best use of all resources. Although it cannot offer a case-work service for parents, it will be able to assist them to find the best source of help. The senior officer is herself the mother of a handicapped child.

She has compiled a very useful pocket-sized booklet, *Help Starts Here*, to explain to parents of children with special needs how to find out about help, professional advice and support. It is available free from the Council.

Access

ACCESS FOR THE DISABLED

Central Council for the Disabled
34 Eccleston Square, London SW1V 1PE
Tel: 01-821 1871

The Central Council masterminds this pressure group and information service on the problems faced by the physically handicapped in gaining access to buildings open to the public, such as theatres and libraries, shops and restaurants and to all kinds of travel facilities. There is a national project to support local guides on access for the disabled – around 100 have been published so far. Full information on existing local projects or how to undertake one for your own area can be obtained from the Council, including step-by-step instructions and standard forms for measuring and describing buildings.

One of its own guides covers access to public conveniences throughout the country, price 23p.

The Council sponsored *London for the Disabled* by Freda Bruce Lockhart (Ward Lock, 1971). This book costs 50p and is available from the Council if you can't get it at your local bookshop.

See also **Travel**

Adaptations

It is possible to have your home adapted to make life easier for a handicapped person and everyone looking after him. An adaptation is anything that involves structural alterations to your house: things like ramps, lifts, rails, special lavatories. For instance, even a simple alteration like rehanging a door so that it opens the other way may make it much easier to cope. The social services department can arrange for this to be done, or can pay all or part of the cost of having it done. It should be prepared to arrange for an occupational therapist or social worker to call and discuss what adaptations could help you. It may get in touch with the hospital which your child attends and ask the consultant or occupational therapist there for advice. However, these are discretionary powers, and some authorities are more willing than others to devote resources to this kind of help. There may be a long wait involved in going through all the stages of approval and planning before the work is carried out.

See also **Aids**

Adoption

ADOPTION RESOURCE EXCHANGE (ARE)

Adoption Resource Exchange
40 Brunswick Square, London WC1 4A2
Tel: 01-837 0496/7

Registered adoption agencies in most parts of the UK cooperate through the Adoption Resource Exchange to improve adoption opportunities for children with special needs, such as older children, children of mixed racial parentage or those with medical problems. Through the exchange a child may find adoptive parents even if they live in a different part of the country. Prospective parents can apply direct to the ARE who will be able to suggest which of its member organizations may be able to help.

ASSOCIATION OF BRITISH ADOPTION AND FOSTERING AGENCIES (ABAFA)

ABAFA, 4 Southampton Row, London WC1B 4AA
Tel: 01-242 8951

The ABAFA can give general information about adoption services in Great Britain. Publications include *Opening New Doors* (1975, price 60p, post free) based on talks about finding families for older and handicapped children.

PARENTS FOR CHILDREN

Parents for Children
222 Camden High Street, London NW1
Tel: 01-485 7526

This is a new, specialized adoption agency. Its main efforts will be directed at the child with major disabilities and handicaps, including older children. It will try to find new sources of adoptive parents; for example, single parents will be considered and far less attention than usual given to the age of the prospective adopters. The agency will attempt to make sure that continuing support is given after adoption. Because it is to be concerned only with the needs of this specific group of children, it hopes to be able to concentrate skills and knowledge and evaluate the experience of its own and other groups trying to arrange adoption for 'difficult' children.

PARENT-TO-PARENT INFORMATION ON ADOPTION SERVICES (PPIAS)

PPIAS, 26 Belsize Grove, London NW3
Tel: 01-722 5328

The group tries to help families wishing to adopt children by arranging contacts with parents of adopted children and by giving them information about societies and agencies for adoption. It could, for example, put prospective adoptive parents of a handicapped child in touch with other families who have already adopted a child with similar handicaps, and can arrange for parents with similar problems to contact one another.

'Difficult to Place'

Town and Country Productions Ltd
21 Cheyne Row, Chelsea, London SW3 5HP
Tel: 01-352 7950

This film by the Church of England Children's Society, which has done a lot of work in placing handicapped children for adoption, describes the plight of young children who are unlikely to be adopted because they are mentally or physically handicapped. While explaining the enormous problems that face families who do adopt these children, the film encourages those who feel they have the aptitude and ability to undertake their care.

Aids

However trivial or overwhelming the practical problems a parent of a handicapped child is coping with, someone may well have produced an aid to help solve them. It may be a question of improvising with a home-made attachment or installing a large piece of sophisticated equipment. Don't struggle on when something gets difficult, like lifting your child in and out of the bath. It is always worth asking the organizations listed here to tell you what is available. If nothing seems to fit the bill, look at the list under the heading **Design projects** – maybe someone can design something specially for you.

Your GP has lists of aids which may be prescribed under the National Health scheme (*Surgical Appliances Contract, Provision of Medical and Surgical Appliances, NH Drug Tariff*). Small items such as hypodermics, elastic hosiery are usually supplied by your local chemist on prescription. Larger items, such as wheelchairs, and specialized equipment, such as artificial limbs, walking aids, etc., supplied on hospital consultant's recommendation, are available free or on long-term loan from your regional Department of Health and Social Security Artificial Limb and Appliance Centre (see below).

A doctor can also recommend to the Department of Health that larger items should be supplied by the health service even if they are not on the regular list. For example, families have been supplied with the large size or the double 'buggy' pushchair and with special tricycles in this way (see chapter 7, **Cycling,** page 330).

Aids may also be supplied by social services departments. If it looks as if none of the authorities are prepared to pay, look under **Grants** or **Help** for some other possibilities.

ARTIFICIAL LIMB AND APPLIANCE SERVICE

This service is the responsibility of the Department of Health and Social Security and is provided through artificial limb and appliance centres serving all regions in England and Wales. The service is provided through the hospital service in Scotland. Centres are staffed with specially trained doctors who can prescribe aids and arrange training for patients referred to them by consultants and family doctors. They provide a full range of artificial limbs and appliances, including powered wheelchairs and artificial eyes. There may be some delays, particularly for more expensive equipment like a Possum machine.

Although aids are available only on a doctor's recommendation, advice and servicing can be obtained direct from the centres. A full list of addresses is given in *Help for Handicapped People* (see above under **General,** DEPARTMENT OF HEALTH AND SOCIAL SECURITY, page 96.

Because of the special problems of children, a children's prosthetic unit has been established at Roehampton where occupational therapists trained and experienced in this work can teach children how to use powered limbs. Parents are encouraged to join their children in the unit so that they can learn about the equipment. There is also a biochemical research and development unit for the investigation of all aspects of artifical limbs and development. There are similar facilities on a smaller scale at hospitals in Liverpool, Oxford and Edinburgh and a unit at the Chailey Heritage, a voluntary body for the care of physically handicapped children.

Children's Prosthetic Unit
Queen Mary's Hospital, Roehampton, London SW15 5PR
Tel: 01-789 6611

BRITISH RED CROSS SOCIETY

Staff Officer
Services for the Handicapped, Branch Affairs
British Red Cross Society, 9 Grosvenor Crescent
London SW1X 7EJ
Tel: 01-235 5454

Local branches of the Red Cross often have stocks of home nursing aids – bedpans, bed boards, fracture cages, plastic sheets and so on – which can be hired for a nominal sum or loaned free for short periods. A variety of aids may be seen (by appointment) at national headquarters in London and advice is always available.

The Society's publications include the following useful guides and pamphlets:

List of Aids for the Disabled, H/4 (price 8p, plus postage)

Illustrated Catalogue of Aids for Handicapped People (price 40p, plus postage)

Home-made Aids for Handicapped People – an illustrated booklet of instructions and diagrammatic drawings for making over fifty simple aids. It includes a section on 'Toys for Handicapped Children' (price 50p, plus postage).

HEARING-AID DISTRIBUTION CENTRES

Hearing aids are supplied and maintained free of charge by the National Health Service. They are fitted by specially trained technicians at hearing-aid distribution centres.

The standard range of NHS aids have been of the type which are worn on the body. In November 1974 the NHS began a five-year programme of issuing a new, light-weight aid which is worn behind the ear. They expect to supply about one million of these over the course of the programme. As well as the aids which are manufactured for the NHS, there are commercially produced and marketed aids which can be supplied free of charge through the NHS for children who cannot benefit from one of the standard ones.

Aids centres

We have listed here some of the places where you can go and look at the aids which are available to see whether there are any that will help you and your child. They do not supply the aids but will be able to tell you where to get them.

DISABLED LIVING FOUNDATION

Disabled Living Foundation
346 Kensington High Street, London W14 8NS
Tel: 01-602 2491

This is an essential source for anyone concerned about equipment. It has an aids centre which is a permanent exhibition with a separate section showing children's aids. It can also provide many sets of notes and its information service will give you other leads to follow up.

DISABLED LIVING CENTRE

Disabled Living Centre
84 Suffolk Street, Birmingham B1 1TA
Tel: 021-643 0980

This is the newest of the aids centres and was opened by Alfred Morris, the Minister for the Disabled, in February 1976. It was set up by the social services department and, under the supervision of an occupational therapist, it will be responsible for assessments. It will be open, by appointment, from 9 a.m. to 5 p.m. every weekday. Disabled people will reach the centre from a stairlift.

MERSEYSIDE AIDS CENTRE

Merseyside Aids Centre
Youens Way, East Prescot Road, Liverpool 14
Tel: 051-228 9221/2

> This Centre is entirely financed by and integrated into the Liverpool social services department. The supervisor is a senior occupational therapist and the Centre aims to provide assessment of how far people are able to benefit from the use of all kinds of aids. People will normally be referred by a hospital, GP or the social services department, but individuals or voluntary organizations can ask for an appointment to visit. The social services department is hoping that the Centre will be used as a base for research projects, study days and so on.

NEWCASTLE UPON TYNE COUNCIL FOR THE DISABLED – AIDS CENTRE

Newcastle Upon Tyne Aids Centre
Mea House, Ellison Place, Newcastle Upon Tyne NE1 8XS
Tel: Newcastle (0632) 23617

> This Centre is sponsored and founded by voluntary effort. It is normally open five days a week but arrangements will be made during an evening or on a Saturday when families are available and parking is easier for disabled people. All visits are by appointment. The staff are professionally qualified but they do not undertake assessment of individual cases. The section for disabled children is very well used. They have visits from doctors, therapists, nurses and social workers with specific children in mind as well as those with a general interest in paediatrics. Also parents bring their children to try chairs and aids. Special projects have included a 'Fun and Games' week in cooperation with the King's Fund.

NAIDEX

Central Council for the Disabled
34 Eccleston Square, London SW1V 1PE
Tel: 01-821 1871

> An annual trade fair for manufacturers of all kinds of equipment for the disabled. The exhibition is always combined with a residential conference.

VISITING AIDS CENTRE

VAC Department, Spastics Society
12 Park Crescent, London W1N 4EQ
Tel: 01-636 5020

> The Spastics Society has a mobile information and aids exhibition housed in a purpose-built trailer which has a tail-lift for wheelchairs. The trailer tours around twenty centres a year and tries to contact all the relevant local organizations beforehand by distributing circulars and advertising widely. The Visiting Aid Centre provides a service for all disabilities, not just spastics.

TRAVELLING EXHIBITION OF AIDS

The Administrator, Central Council for the Disabled
34 Eccleston Square, London SW1V 1PE
Tel: 01-821 1871

> This consists of 400 articles which are transported by van. Suitable buildings have to be made available and also facilities for display. This may simply be sixteen six-foot trestle tables although some authorities have taken the trouble to devise room lay-outs and to borrow additional large items such as hoists, wheelchairs and so on which are too large for the travelling exhibition to carry around. An occupational therapist is in charge of the exhibition which is primarily intended for professionals caring for the disabled. However the hosts to the exhibition are urged to find a building with access for wheelchairs and

they try to arrange one evening session up to 8 p.m. so that disabled people and their families can visit it.

'Equipment for the Disabled'

Orders to:
Equipment for the Disabled
2 Foredown Drive, Portslade, Sussex BN4 2BB
Tel: Brighton (0273) 419327

This is a series of comprehensive illustrated booklets on aids, equipment, including do-it-yourself items covering different aspects of disabled living. It is compiled at the Nuffield Orthopaedic Centre at Mary Marlborough Lodge in Oxford, and is intended for use by those professionally concerned with selecting equipment for handicapped people. The compiler stresses that it is not written directly for patients and their families but one parents' group especially recommended it as the best guide it has found. Items included have been assessed in use and there is a brief description of relevant points, together with illustrations, details of manufacturers and suppliers and an indication of price range. Titles include *The Disabled Child, Leisure and Gardening, Wheelchairs and Outdoor Transport.* The fourth edition is being published from 1975 onwards over four years; third editions will still be available until superseded. Each booklet costs £1.50, plus postage. The series can be found in some reference libraries.

Attendance allowance

Addresses of social security offices should be displayed in main post offices.

The attendance allowance is a tax-free allowance for adults and children over the age of two who are severely disabled, either physically or mentally. It is not subject to a means test, and not taken into account when other benefits are assessed; nor do you have to have national insurance contributions to qualify. In order to qualify, the handicapped person must need help from another person very frequently throughout the day. This may either be in coping with going to the lavatory, being fed, etc., or because continual supervision is necessary to prevent the child doing serious harm to himself or to anyone else. Or you may qualify because the child needs prolonged or repeated attention during the night for the same reasons. Any family could say the same about every normal, very young child, so you can claim the attendance allowance for a child only if the attention and supervision is very much greater than normal. There are two levels of benefit, the higher rate was £12.20 a week and the lower rate £8.15 in 1976. The higher rate applies where the child needs looking after both day and night (night has been defined as beginning when a child has been settled down for the night). The lower rate applies when *either* day *or* night care is needed.

You may apply for the grant for a child on Form DS 2C, available from any social security office. Part of the form must be filled in by a doctor, either your GP or hospital consultant. A consultant's recommendation seems to be more effective in getting a claim accepted. The Department of Health and Social Security may arrange for a medical examination if they think it is necessary. The Attendance Allowance Board will decide whether or not you are entitled to the allowance. It is well worth appealing if your claim is refused or you are awarded the lower rate as in the early operation of the scheme over 50 per cent of cases who appealed were successful. To ask for a review you must write to the Attendance Allowance Board within three months. Set out your case in as much detail as possible, and try to include evidence from your doctor, social worker, etc. Legal advice (see **Law**) may be useful in composing the letter. You should receive a copy of the doctor's report and should comment on this if you disagree with anything. If your appeal fails, you have to wait another year for a second try. You could appeal to the National Insurance Commissioner on a point of law, but would need expert help to do this. (This advice is based on that given in the Child Poverty Action Group's

National Welfare Benefits Handbook, edited by Ruth Lister, published annually, price 50p). Foster parents of handicapped children are not eligible to claim the allowance. Details of attendance allowances are given in leaflet NI 205, available from any social security office.

See **Fostering**

Babysitting

See **Help** and **Volunteers** for people who may be able to help with babysitting. For example, one parent wrote to describe the help given to handicapped children in Bristol by local medical students who make a regular commitment to look after handicapped children, free of charge, either at home, or on weekend holidays or camps. Some social services departments run a 'good neighbour' scheme where people, often retired, offer regular neighbourly help and support and can sometimes babysit, usually during the day.

Bedding

Disabled Living Foundation
346 Kensington High Street, London W14 8NS
Tel: 01-602 2491

The Disabled Living Foundation can advise on beds and bedding and has a list of beds, mattresses, pillows, sheets, waterproof covers, etc. You may be entitled to assistance towards the cost of bedding if you are eligible for supplementary benefit.

See **Incontinence**

Benefits

SOCIAL SECURITY

The Department of Health and Social Security is responsible for paying the benefits which come under the heading of national insurance – in other words, benefits to which you are entitled without any means test, although some of them depend on your contributions to the scheme. They are also responsible for all the benefits which come under the heading of supplementary benefit – the old national assistance. You have to undergo a means test to decide if you qualify for supplementary benefit. Inquiries about individual cases must be addressed to your local social security office; it is essential to go to the right one for your own area. The address should be in every local post office.

The DHSS issues a booklet, *Family Benefits and Pensions*, which tells you about the conditions for granting all social security benefits including local authority grants. This is available only from the Leaflets Unit.

DHSS Leaflets Unit, Block 4
Government Buildings, Honeypot Lane, Stanmore, Middlesex
HA7 1AY

Supplementary benefit. Supplementary benefit is intended to help people who are not in full-time work and whose income, whether from benefits or from other sources, is not enough to meet their needs. The amount of supplementary benefit is worked out through a means test (see leaflet SB1 which should be available at post offices, citizens advice bureaux, etc.). If you do not understand how your benefit has been calculated or why you have been refused benefit, you are entitled to ask for a written explanation, called a 'notice of assessment'. If you are receiving supplementary benefit and have a handicapped child or other handicapped member of the family, you can ask the Supplementary Benefits Commission for an extra allowance to help with the continuing expenses of abnormally heavy wear and tear on clothing and shoes caused by the disability. You may be given extra help for other special expenses for special diets, extra heating, laundry expenses, fares for regular visits to a relative in hospital. These are only examples. If your request for a discretionary addition is refused wholly or in part, you should appeal (See **Information services**, CITIZENS ADVICE BUREAUX, page 149).

Any handicapped child over sixteen years who has left school may be entitled to a supplementary benefit allowance if he is not in full-time paid employment, regardless of family circumstances

Invalidity care allowance. A new allowance to be introduced in 1976–7 will provide a weekly allowance for people who cannot go out to work because they have to look after a severely disabled relative who is receiving an attendance allowance. It will not apply to married women who are supported by their husbands.

See also **Attendance allowance**; **Mobility**, MOBILITY ALLOWANCE

CHILD POVERTY ACTION GROUP (CPAG)

CPAG, 1 Macklin Street, London WC2B 5NH
Tel: 01-242 3225/9149

The Group was formed in 1965 to campaign for resources for the many families living at or below the official poverty line in this country. Its research into all aspects of family poverty has made it a leading authority in the field. There are branches of CPAG in many parts of the UK which campaign for a more understanding attitude to family poverty, as well as helping low-income families to obtain their welfare rights. Branches also act as watch dogs over public services used by these families.

National Welfare Benefits Handbook, edited by Ruth Lister, is published annually. The citizens rights office, associated with CPAG, advises on every aspect of social security benefits, particularly on appeals.

DISABILITY ALLIANCE

Disability Alliance
96 Portland Place, London W1N 4EX
Tel: 01-794 1536

The Disability Alliance is an alliance of over thirty organizations and fifty specialists in the field of disability. In the words of one of its members, the organizations were 'united in fury at the poverty' of the proposals contained in the long-awaited review set out in the White Paper, *Social Security Provision for Chronically Sick and Disabled Persons* (HMSO, July 1974). The aim of the Alliance is to secure the payment of an income as of right and on equitable principles to all disabled persons, whatever their age, cause, type or place of disablement, or working capacity, in order to eliminate their poverty or financial hardship. The second of its publications was *The Financial Needs of Disabled Children*, by Jonathan Bradshaw (1975, price 60p). Although it does not offer a specific service to parents with a handicapped child, the Alliance is very interested in hearing from families, and especially from those who might be willing to outline their personal experiences of financial hardship – anonymously if they prefer – for use when dealing with the media or with government departments.

Bereavement

COMPASSIONATE FRIENDS

Compassionate Friends
50 Woodwaye, Watford, Herts WD1 4NW
Tel: Watford 24279

This society was founded in 1969 by the Reverend Simon Stephens. The members are themselves bereaved parents who know from experience that, when people suffer the loss of a child, it can be helpful to talk to someone else who really knows what it is like to go through this. They have a very sensitive and unobtrusive approach to parents, not dependent on religious belief. Their aims are simple: to relieve the mental and physical distress, to give financial support to medical projects concerned with reducing the number of deaths among children and to promote education on death 'because we are victims of a society in which death, the last taboo subject of our time, is swept under the carpet and ignored'.

Books

Most of the organizations we describe produce book lists relating to their special interests and you can often order the books from them direct. The National Society for Mentally Handicapped Children has a bookshop which is open from 9.30 to 5.30 from Monday to Friday. It stocks an enormous range of books to do with children with every kind of handicap, although there is naturally a bias towards mental handicap. It also runs a mail order service. It publishes a forty-page booklist which costs 15p. It is worth asking for recently published books even if they are not yet listed.

NSMHC Sales Ltd
Pembridge Hall, 17 Pembridge Square, London W2 4EP
Tel: 01-229 8941

REFERENCE BOOKS

The *Social Services Yearbook* includes details of local authority social service officers, senior social workers and committee members and lists special schools, day centres, residential homes and so on. There are other directories and yearbooks covering the whole organization of education, health and social services. These will be found in any good reference library.

RESEARCH PUBLICATIONS SERVICES LTD

Research Publications Services Ltd
Victoria Hall, Fingal Street, London SE10 0RF
Tel: 01-858 7768/1717

This is a centre for the distribution of the publications of a number of institutes and centres whose interests are relevant to handicapped children, including the King's Fund and the National Council of Social Service. These are publications which are not normally handled by commercial organizations. Their catalogue is free.

Catholic services

BISHOPS' CONFERENCE OF ENGLAND AND WALES

Archbishop's House, Westminster, London SW1P 1QJ
Tel: 01-834 3144

The Bishops' Conference has a number of committees with responsibility for different fields. There is one for education and another for social welfare which, in turn, has sub-committees with a special interest in child care and the welfare of the handicapped. Each committee has at least one episcopal member as well as clergy, religious and lay members, appointed individually or to represent a particular organization. They can call on the services of expert 'consultors'. These committees advise the Bishops' Conference and provide information and research material. The Conference is involved in official consultations with governmental and voluntary bodies. They might be prepared to support individual cases of principle for people who approached them direct or through their parish priest.

There is also a Bishops' Conference for Scotland:

Social Welfare Commission
89 Muiryfauld Drive, Glasgow G31 5RU
Tel: 041-554 2942

CATHOLIC HANDICAPPED CHILDREN'S FELLOWSHIP

Miss M. Donnelly, Catholic Handicapped Children's Fellowship
2 The Villas, Hare Law, Stanley, Co. Durham DH9 8DQ
Tel: Stanley (020–73) 4379

Most of the Roman Catholic Dioceses of England have a diocesan fellowship working independently in their own area. They offer practical and moral help to parents who are trying to cope with the spiritual as well as the mental and physical needs of handicapped children.

Children's societies

BARNARDO'S

Dr Barnardo's
Tanners Lane, Barkingside, Ilford, Essex IG6 1QG
Tel: 01-550 8822

A voluntary Christian society which exists to care for children in need and their families. Barnardo's pioneering residential work has been modified in the light of modern theories of child care. It has twenty-one special homes and schools for physically handicapped children and those with educational or emotional problems. It is now turning its efforts to providing support services for families in densely populated areas where child care needs are greatest and the existing services are most hard pressed. So Barnardo's has rapidly expanded its provision of day-care centres linked with support from social workers for families in need. Mentally and physically handicapped children may be placed by Barnardo's with foster parents who provide loving care and a normal home background. In some places, Barnardo's can offer practical help to families with a handicapped child, such as babysitters, day-care, short or longer periods of residential care or holidays.

CHURCH OF ENGLAND CHILDREN'S SOCIETY

Church of England Children's Society
Old Town Hall, Kennington Road, London SE11 4QD
Tel: 01-735 2441

The Society aims to provide a coordinated system of child care to meet the individual needs of any child in real need, within a Christian framework. Many of the handicapped children in the Society's care have parents who are keenly interested in their progress and the staff encourage them to participate in every way. It has two residential nurseries for under sevens and there is a unit for handicapped children at its nursery in Matlock. There is a school for handicapped girls in London and a family home for children with severe educational problems in Derbyshire. Children with less severe handicaps are helped in the Society's family homes and nurseries or may be found long-term foster homes. It is setting up family-grouped homes in some of which handicapped and normal children will be integrated, in place of the old-style children's homes. It can also provide short-term care to tide families over a difficult period. The Society is establishing day centres where children and their families can be helped when they are in difficulty without necessarily coming into residential care.

NATIONAL CHILDREN'S HOME (NCH)

NCH, 85 Highbury Park, London N5 1UD
Tel: 01-226 2033

Set up in the great tradition of Victorian philanthropy, the NCH has always been run on a family system with small groups of children living in separate houses. NCH is a voluntary Christian organization focusing on work with families in need. It owns houses and flats which can be used as temporary accommodation by homeless and one-parent families. It has special schools for both physically and mentally handicapped children who are placed there by local education authorities. Its family aid can take many forms from practical help to legal advice. Day care is based on family centres, open fifty-two weeks a year, involving the whole family. It is sometimes possible for NCH to find foster homes for handicapped children.

SHAFTESBURY SOCIETY

Shaftesbury Society
Shaftesbury House, 112 Regency Street, London SW1P 4AX
Tel: 01-834 2656

For over 130 years this Christian society has provided special care for disabled children. It runs five residential schools for children with all kinds of physical disabilities and four residential centres where young men who cannot live at home can live with others of the same age with similar severe disabilities. Muscular dystrophy is the most common handicap catered for in this way. Its holiday centre at Whitstable provides holidays for physically and mentally handicapped children as well as older disabled people. They have help from able-bodied volunteers.

In the London area the Society provides advisory services and has clubs for those who are physically handicapped. It has its own housing association to provide purpose-built homes for physically handicapped and elderly people.

Clothes

DISABLED LIVING FOUNDATION

Disabled Living Foundation
346 Kensington High Street, London W14 8NS
Tel: 01-602 2491

The Disabled Living Foundation has had a clothing advisory panel since 1963; a leaflet, *Clothing*, describes the publications and other services and information available, which include a book on *Clothing for the Handicapped Child* (1971, price £1.20, including postage). There are demonstration clothing collections which can be used in local exhibitions and fashion shows. The Foundation has prepared an audio-tape on 'How to adapt clothing for handicapped children', which shows a series of clothes, usually available in local shops, which can be simply adapted for handicapped children. The tape runs for twenty-nine minutes and can be hired from the Medical Recording Service Foundation.

Medical Recording Service Foundation
PO Box 99, Chelmsford CM1 5HL
Tel: Chelmsford (0245) 421475

KING'S FUND CENTRE

A revised and updated catalogue of garments for the handicapped and disabled has now been published in two loose-leaf volumes, price £5.50, obtainable from Research Publications Services Ltd. Many of these clothes can be bought only by bulk order.

Research Publications Services Ltd
Victoria Hall, Fingal Street, Greenwich, London SE10 0RF
Tel: 01-858 1717/7768

SHIRLEY INSTITUTE

Miss E. Clulow, Shirley Institute
Didsbury, Manchester M20 8RX
Tel: 061-445 8141

Comfortable Clothes is a free, mail-order catalogue of easy-to-wear garments for those with special needs which can be ordered singly through the Institute from the manufacturers.

Looking Your Best

NSMHC, Pembridge Hall, Pembridge Square, London W2 4EP
Tel: 01-229 8941/01-727 0536

This cheerful pull-out supplement in September 1974 to *Parents' Voice*, the journal of the National Society for Mentally Handicapped Children, is full of ideas to help handicapped young people take a pride in their appearance and dress. It is available, price 5p plus postage, from the Society's bookshop.

GRANTS

There are a number of grants for uniforms or 'necessitous' clothing to which school-age children may be entitled. Your education welfare office (see chapter 5, **Education**

welfare service, page 272) or school will be able to tell you if they can help you.

See also **Benefits**

Day care

For parents who would like to be able to look after their handicapped child at home, the deciding factor may be the kind of day care they can rely on for their child before he reaches school age and in the school holidays.

In some areas an attempt to meet this need is made by the social services department in day nurseries and other centres; in others a hospital department or voluntary society such as Barnardo's, the National Children's Home or the Spastics Society may set up its own day centres. The social services department ought to know what is available irrespective of who is providing it. A survey of full-time centres in 1972 showed that nine out of thirteen in the sample were developed because of local pressure and voluntary effort (*Spotlight on Services for the Young Handicapped Child,* by Jessie Parfit).

We give two examples of exciting projects – one voluntary, the other official – to show what is possible.

Hornsey Handicapped Children's Centre
26a Dukes Avenue, London N10 2PT
Tel: 01-444 7241

This Centre, an independent local venture, is an outstanding example of what can be done by private initiative and enterprise. The Centre, built and maintained by the Hornsey Trust for Handicapped Children, provides:

1 A nursery school with qualified teaching staff, to receive very young children as soon as their handicaps have been discovered and educate them to the full extent of their capabilities.
2 Parent relief, providing properly supervised facilities where parents can regularly bring and leave their

children and enjoy a few carefree hours; children
of all ages, including young adults are accepted.

3 A treatment centre, where physically handicapped
children can be given treatment, including physiotherapy, occupational and speech therapy, under the
direction of well-known consultants.

4 A meeting-place for the 'Roundabouts Club' that
meets weekly to provide a social evening for mentally
handicapped children and young adults.

5 A recreational centre and meeting-place for handicapped children and their parents.

Over fifty children with all kinds of handicap regularly
attend the Centre for education and treatment, and thirty
more come in for physiotherapy. The Centre also carries
out research into the techniques of teaching severely
mentally handicapped children, with the cooperation of
parents.

Honeylands, Pinhoe Road, Exeter
Tel: Exeter (0392) 67171

The same survey of day centres includes the comment: 'It is
unfortunate that in many cases there seems to be insufficient
encouragement and support from the statutory services
who may, nevertheless, be failing to provide similar services
in sufficient numbers themselves.' Although there are far
too few day-care facilities it is possible for a statutory
authority to meet the need with a humane and sensitive
service. A family support and treatment unit for young
handicapped children living at home with their families,
Honeylands is part of the National Health Service although you might find it hard to believe this if you visit it.
No one wears a uniform so that parents, nurses, speech
therapists, psychologists, social workers, doctors and
voluntary helpers are indistinguishable. All sorts of
children attend, brothers and sisters, helpers' children and
every type of handicapped child.

There is an infant unit where mothers can stay whilst
they learn how to handle their handicapped baby. Many
infants also come in for a day whilst parents are out

shopping and so on or for short residential periods (weekends or up to two weeks) to give their parents some relief. These arrangements are very flexible and are made at the parents' convenience. In school holidays many children who attend special schools in term time come to Honeylands either daily or for a short residential period. The hospital transport service is freely available. There is a full therapeutic programme based on two principles: first, parents as partners, with coffee mornings, evening meetings and discussion groups for parents. Second, the individual treatment programme of each child takes the form of play activity which incorporates the various physiotherapy, speech therapy, social training and medical needs. There is also a hospital primary school.

A hundred and fifty children, aged from infancy up to twelve years, are in contact with Honeylands at any particular time. They can sleep thirty with a bit of a squeeze. There is an adventure playground. The indoor hydrotherapy and swimming pool is under construction. They own a beach hut at Dawlish Warren and a minibus to get them there.

'Exeter Project for Handicapped Children', by F. S. W. Brimblecombe, the Consultant Paediatrician in charge of Honeylands, was published in the *British Medical Journal* for 21 December 1974.

A film, 'Before the Bough Breaks . . .', has been made about Honeylands. The film is available for sale or on loan (£5 loan charge) together with a booklet of background information. Available from:

Film Services Library
Glaxo-Farley Foods Ltd, Torr Lane, Plymouth, Devon PL3 5UA

Design projects

ACTIVE

Deborah Jaffe, c/o Toy Libraries Association
Sunley House, Gunthorpe Street, London E1 7RW
Tel: 01-247 1386

An informal group of therapists and engineers began
meeting at regular intervals throughout 1975 at various
centres for handicapped children. They found that there is
a great deal of scope for cooperation between technicians
and engineers on the one hand and teachers, parents and
therapists who face day-to-day problems in trying to help
severely handicapped children on the other. They want to
work together in constructing and adapting toys, games
and simple teaching machines for handicapped children,
particularly those who are non-communicating or mentally
handicapped. They hope to identify unmet needs and that
the result will be further development in the design of such
equipment. An open workshop day – 'Play and Communication for Severely Handicapped Children' – was
held in January 1976.

CENTRE ON ENVIRONMENT FOR THE HANDICAPPED

Centre on Environment for the Handicapped
126 Albert Street, London NW1 7NF
Tel: 01-267 6111

A centre providing advice and information on design of
the environment for handicapped people. In this context,
'environment' means everything from regional and city
planning to interior fittings and equipment – the full range
of facilities. There is a reference library of publications,
plans, photographs, etc. Advice may be given by consultant architects to all those engaged in planning or
designing buildings. The Centre publishes a quarterly
newsletter of general interest.

REHABILITATION ENGINEERING MOVEMENT ADVISORY PANELS (REMAP)

N. Breatley (National Organizer)
REMAP, Thames House North, Millbank, London SW1P 4QG
Tel: 01-834 4444 Ext. 4112

The idea behind REMAP began in Teesside in 1964. An engineer said: 'There are many engineers here. If only a few of them gave a little of their spare time to designing and having made those special items of equipment which handicapped people need, and are not available commercially, how useful it would be.' A small group was formed and the scheme worked. There are now twenty-six panels in different parts of Great Britain, each of them autonomous and self-supporting. The small central organization helps with information and advice and in setting up new panels. It is a registered charity sponsored by REHAB (British Council for Rehabilitation of the Disabled). Engineer volunteers cooperate with the handicapped individual's own medical advisers and social service departments, in a wide range of jobs, from devising a special car door handle, to a variety of difficult hoisting installations.

COLLEGES

A number of schools and colleges have undertaken projects in the design of toys and equipment for handicapped children. Some projects have developed out of the personal experience of a disabled designer, some out of a 'community help' project, others out of a request for help from an individual parent of a handicapped child. This list gives brief details of some departments who have done this kind of work. It is also worth approaching a local comprehensive school if you have a practical problem which needs solving. They may be inspired to launch the kind of imaginative and extensive 'aid for the disabled' scheme pioneered at Wanstead High School in Redbridge, London, described in *The Handicapped Person in the Community* (edited by D. M. Boswell and J. M. Wingrove, Open University, 1974).

Hertfordshire College of Art and Design
Design Research Group, Hatfield Road, St Albans, Herts AL1 3RS
Tel: St Albans 64414

The Design Research Group works in cooperation with hospitals and special schools on the design of equipment to improve motor and conceptual skills of the handicapped. Current work includes the development of prototype aids for use in hydrotherapy and the design and preparation of teaching material and aids for use with handicapped children.

The Eccentric Playform, a therapeutic play apparatus evolved by the Design Research Unit in consultation with medical experts, is currently in production. It is intended to assist motor coordination and at the same time be fun to play with. Further details may be obtained from the manufacturers:

The Hospital Division
Price Brothers & Co. Ltd, Wellington, Somerset

London College of Furniture
41–71 Commercial Road, London E1 1LA
Tel: 01-247 1953

The College runs a two-year sandwich course for the Higher Diploma, Play Equipment (Design and Manufacture). Students have a special interest in the play problems of handicapped children. Design and prototype projects have been carried out with a number of organizations such as the Toy Libraries Associations and clinics and hospitals.

Information sheets on these projects are available from the research assistant of the department at the College. The department welcomes inquiries from individuals and organizations. The College hopes to be able to run an evening course for parents, therapists and teachers on making toys for the handicapped.

Middlesex Polytechnic at Hornsey
Advanced Studies/Design, Crouch End Hill, London N8 8DG
Tel: 01-348 2402

Penny Thrift started by designing a walking frame for her own use, called the Pennyweight. She went on to raise the funds needed to form the Disabilities Design Research Group. Since then they have designed the Bin Chair which gives all round upholstered support and enables handicapped children to sit up in comfort. The chair was a finalist in the Design for Living Award Competition 1974. The chair, with pot and play tray as optional extras, can be obtained from:

Rowen (Onllwyn) Ltd
Seven Sisters, Nr Neath, West Glamorgan, South Wales
Tel: Seven Sisters (063-976) 308

Mr W. F. McCain
Paisley College of Technology
High Street, Paisley, Strathclyde PA1 2BE
Tel: 041-887 1241

The current work of the Department of Mechanical and Production Engineering is concerned with long-term research on the multiple design criteria required of equipment intended for the severely mentally handicapped. As well as the need for safety, strength, proper acoustic properties, suitability of number of parts, it wants to design equipment which will fulfil such needs as verbal recognition, ways of controlling the difficulty of the task. It has completed the design of a type of play brick for use by mentally handicapped children lacking in hand-dexterity. The department has been able to make practical suggestions to parents who have written asking for help with particular problems. One mother of a hyperactive nine-year-old boy wrote to Paisley after she read about its work in an earlier version of this book. Her son developed the habit of banging his bedroom windows very hard. The College was able to suggest a design solution.

Royal College of Art, Kensington Gore, London SW7 2EU
Tel: 01-584 5020

Department of Design Research. One of the functions of this department is to carry out professional research projects under contract with the aim of finding a solution to practical problems. The cost of a project can range from more than £50 000 a year down to perhaps a single fee of £500, according to the scope and staffing. Some of its specially designed bathrooms and toilets for spina bifida children are in use. A project on play equipment for handicapped children has been completed. Lists of completed and current work are available free from the department. A brochure giving a detailed brief for therapeutic equipment and toys for handicapped children based on an exhibition of prototypes held some time ago still sells well at 50p.

School of Industrial Design. Students in this school may undertake special design projects as part of their course. Three students won the Melchett Award from British Steel for their design of an adjustable desk and chair for physically handicapped children.

Part of the problem about producing highly specialized equipment for disabled people is that the market is so small that it is not profitable for factory production. However, committed individuals may set up workshops which can cater for special needs. We give two examples; one was recommended by the parent of a handicapped child.

FDTS Ltd, Highfield Works
West Byfleet Corner, West Byfleet, Surrey KT14 6LP
Tel: Byfleet 42043

Mr W. H. Davis deals personally with any inquiries from people with a handicap – both children and adults. He specializes in producing nylon safety harnesses and straps for helping people in wheelchairs, car chairs and so on.

There are no standard harnesses as customers are treated individually to suit the disability and use for which the harness is needed.

Toby Churchill Ltd, 20 Panton Street, Cambridge CB2 1HP

Toby Churchill was a twenty-one-year-old university student when a mysterious virus disease left him badly paralysed, speechless and confined to a wheelchair. After much research he has produced his first invention, the Lightwriter, a portable typewriter keyboard with an electronic display board. It is light enough to be held on the lap and has an easy touch. As each key is pressed, the character appears on the luminous display board – messages move leftwards and disappear at the left-hand end. The display panel, which holds thirty-two characters, is mounted behind the keyboard and can be reversed to be read by people facing the user or removed altogether so that it can be placed on a table. A buzzer mounted at the side attracts attention.

Developmental guides

One of the difficulties often facing parents of handicapped children is that they have no norm by which to judge their individual child's development. The kind of standardized test which compares an individual with the rest of the population (the basis of many of the tests used in assessment procedures) is useless for parents of a handicapped child who want to know how their child is getting on.

A divisional children's officer for Dr Barnardo's, who is himself the father of a mentally handicapped child, told a conference held by the Institute of Mental Subnormality in February 1976: 'Parents of a handicapped child soon get lost when there is a breakdown of the normal framework of development. They have nothing by which to measure their child. . . .'

The experimental development guides produced by the National Children's Bureau ought to help parents – and anyone else who looks after a child for all, or a large part of, every day – to keep a basic, continuous record of the major and minor developmental milestones in their child's progress. A parent using these guides would get a clear idea for himself of the precise areas in which his child was progressing or failing to progress. This should also be an invaluable source of systematic information for any professional in his dealing with a child and enable areas of specific retardation, delay or difficulty to be detected at the earliest possible stage.

Each guide is divided into five sections, printed on different colour paper. Section A is physical development. It deals with some of the most obvious stages of a child's physical growth and control of body movements. For example, sitting, crawling and walking, many of which take place in the first year, and more complex movements which develop later, such as running, jumping and climbing. Section B deals with coordination of sight with fine movements. In the very early stages this includes learning to grasp and reach for things. The guide lists significant stages such as when a child can put lids on pots and pans, turn the pages of a book, scribble, match shapes, copy shapes and so on. Section C covers the steps involved in acquiring speech and understanding of language. Section D – self help – covers the practical skills which help a child achieve independence, such as feeding, dressing, washing, toilet training and so on. Section E is concerned with the child's relationships with adults and other children: does he show curiosity about toys, things or persons? does he stop crying when picked up and spoken to? does he do what the other children do when he is in a group?

Copies of the handbook and of the developmental guides (*Part 1: 0–3 years; Part 2: 2–5 years*) are available from:

Developmental Records Project
National Children's Bureau, 8 Wakley Street, London EC1

Emigration

The NSHMC says that there are countries which will not accept as immigrants families with a handicapped child.

It suggests that parents should make full inquiries from the High Commissioner or embassy of the country concerned before they make any plans to emigrate.

Escorts

TRANS-CARE INTERNATIONAL

Trans-Care Ltd, Group House, Woodlands Avenue, Acton London W3
Tel: 01-992 5077

This is a twenty-four-hour medical escort service. It consists of a network of doctors and state-registered nurses throughout Britain and most of Europe who are available to escort a patient – including children of any age – anywhere throughout the world. This is a commercial service.

VOLUNTARY SERVICES

The WRVS has a comprehensive service providing escorts throughout the country. This would be available to handicapped children – or their families – to help them get to hospitals or clinics, training centres, clubs, riding lessons and so on. Often the same person will regularly escort the same child. This also applies to much longer journeys to escort a handicapped child going to and from a residential school. Most requests for this service are made through hospitals, social services departments, and so on, who defray the costs. But individuals who cannot afford to pay for a taxi or hire car may certainly approach their local WRVS office for help.

WRVS, 17 Old Park Lane, London W1Y 4AJ
Tel: 01-499 6040

Local branches of the British Red Cross Society and the St John Ambulance Association may run similar escort services. You should contact the local organizer for details.

See also **Transport**, page 182.

Films and filmstrips

Almost every organization or society has produced at least one film on its work, either for fund-raising purposes, or for advice and information to the parents they are trying to help. Some, like the Spastics Society, have their own film library. It would be impossible to mention every film here, but many of the films are included in the National Children's Bureau catalogue. We have also listed some of the main distributors of specialist films who cover the field of handicap.

NATIONAL CHILDREN'S BUREAU (NCB)

NCB, 8 Wakley Street, London EC1V 7QE
Tel: 01-278 9441

The information service has collected together a comprehensive index of films available for hire concerned with children. Over 450 titles are classified under various subject headings, including a précis of each film's content, its running time and source of supply. Price £1.23.

CAMERA TALKS LTD

Camera Talks Ltd, 31 North Row, London W1R 2EN
Tel: 01-493 2761

This firm's catalogue of audio-visual aids includes 35-mm film strips, taped commentaries, slide sets, and 8-mm film strips, as well as 16-mm films, on many different aspects of health and welfare, including mother and child health, mental health, education, and social services. Subjects include 'Music Therapy for Handicapped Children' and 'Further Education for the Mentally Handicapped'. Many of the items are for sale only. They also sell audio-visual equipment.

CONCORD FILMS COUNCIL

Concord Films Council Ltd, 201 Felixstowe Road, Ipswich, Suffolk
Tel: Ipswich (0473) 76012

> This is a charity operating an educational film library specializing in documentary and TV films about contemporary problems. It also acts as distributor for films produced by voluntary organizations. It can usually supply copies of the films in the catalogue for outright sale. It produces a useful catalogue (price 40p) which describes each film's content, running time and audience suitability. There are local voluntary projection groups in about ten areas who will arrange to show films for schools, clubs, etc., within a reasonable distance.

MEDICAL RECORDING SERVICE FOUNDATION

Medical Recording Service Foundation
PO Box 99, Chelmsford CM1 5HL
Tel: Chelmsford (0245) 421475

> This is an educational activity of the Royal College of General Practitioners, and provides a very friendly service of short-term loan and hire of audio tapes – with or without slides – and teaching slide sets on most medical subjects. Although the full catalogue is rather intimidating, it would be prepared to send separate details of films of interest to parents of handicapped children, such as its tape–slide documentary on 'An Opportunity Class for Handicapped Children', and the two sets on the work of the Nottingham University Toy Library.

TOWN AND COUNTRY PRODUCTIONS LTD

Town and Country Productions Ltd
21 Cheyne Row, London SW3 5HP
Tel: 01-352 7950

> The company produce and distribute official 16-mm films on games, sports, physical recreation, youth activities, health, welfare and careers. Its catalogue includes the ICAA film 'I Want to Be', a film on the Leukaemia

Research Fund, and on the Riding for the Disabled Association. It was responsible for the production of the Disabled Living Foundation film 'Not Just a Spectator'.

Fostering

The local social services department is responsible for finding foster homes for children in its care, and may also be able to do this when parents need temporary relief. Fostering is subject to strict controls under the Children and Young Persons Act 1969 and other children's Acts, and has to be supervised by the local authority social services department. Some children's societies such as the National Children's Home, Barnardo's and the Church of England Children's Society (see above) make a special effort to find foster homes for children with physical and mental handicaps. A recent report, *Fostering Mentally Handicapped Children: Is it feasible?* (Campaign for the Mentally Handicapped, Inquiry Paper No. 3, price 25p) produces evidence to show that not enough effort is made to find homes for mentally handicapped children. Foster parents cannot claim the attendance allowance for a fostered handicapped child so they should claim an extra fostering allowance in lieu of this.

Campaign for the Mentally Handicapped
96 Portland Place, London W1N 4EX
Tel: 01-636 5020

NATIONAL FOSTER CARE ASSOCIATION

National Foster Care Association
129 Queen's Crescent, London NW5
Tel: 01-485 3929

The aim of the Association is to promote and improve the quality of the foster care service, and to undertake research, discuss problems and find solutions. It has a regular newsletter, *Foster Care*. Membership is open to local groups and individuals.

Genetic counselling

Parents with a handicapped child are usually anxious to know what the chances are of other children being handicapped, or carriers of a hereditary condition. The voluntary societies listed in chapter 2 are often able to give general advice and information. Every GP and hospital should have a copy of the DHSS publication, *Human Genetics*, which includes a list of every genetic advice centre in the country where up-to-date advice can be given about the probability of the risk. Any doctor or consultant should be able to refer you to a centre for counselling. Where there is a risk, a mother can sometimes have a test during the early stages of pregnancy to show whether or not the baby is affected. This procedure is called amniocentesis. The doctor will be able to advise whether this test is appropriate.

A register for the ascertainment and prevention of inherited diseases (*RAPID*) is being developed by the Department of Human Genetics at Edinburgh University in collaboration with the Medical Research Council, but is at present only in its early stages.

Grants

For payments from the Department of Health and Social Security, see **Benefits** above.

FAMILY FUND

The Secretary, Family Fund
PO Box 50, York YO3 6RB
Tel: York (0904) 29241

The Fund was set up by the government to help families with children who are severely handicapped. It is administered independently by the Joseph Rowntree Memorial Trust. It is no longer limited to children who were born handicapped. Families with a severely disabled child who normally lives at home are eligible even if the child has to spend periods in hospital or is at school in term-time. They are *not* eligible if the child lives permanently in a residential home or hospital, although it may sometimes be possible to give help with expenses for visiting. Help may take the form of goods, services or a grant of money for some definite project. It is intended mainly to help in situations which are not covered by other sources or to give emergency help to families who are waiting for a service or payment to be arranged. Your family circumstances generally will be taken into account but there is no actual means test. If the Fund makes a grant, it should not affect the help you are getting from any other source. If you think the Fund could help you, write to the secretary for details of how to apply.

Parents should not hesitate to approach the Fund because they are not sure what to ask for; the Fund is anxious to consider new and unusual ways of helping. Above all it wants to know what families feel they need.

In its first two years, the Fund made payments in 16 000 out of 18 000 applications – mostly help with private transport, clothing and bedding, holidays for the family and washing machines.

Family Fund Research Project
Department of Social Administration and Social Work
University of York, York YO1 5DD
Tel: York (0904) 59861

The Project has been in operation for more than two years. As well as monitoring the day-to-day operation and development of the Family Fund, it has been able to investigate other aspects of the circumstances of families caring for severely handicapped children. It has looked at the responsibilities of local authority social services departments under S2 of the 1970 Chronically Sick and Disabled Persons Act, especially where these overlap with the kind of help the Family Fund can give; at the help which families in receipt of supplementary benefit can get from the DHSS, and has done a very detailed and comprehensive study of the experiences which families with handicapped children have had of the attendance allow-

ance. In addition, it has, of course, built up a large amount
of information on the Family Fund and the social, economic and demographic characteristics of those families
who apply to it.

HANDICAPPED CHILDREN'S AID COMMITTEE

Handicapped Children's Aid Committee
154 Anson Road, London NW2
Tel: 01-452 2627

This is a voluntary charity founded by a group of friends
and neighbours, which in ten years has raised a total of
£250 000 at an administrative cost of less than a farthing
in a pound. It provides specialized equipment for all kinds
of organizations, hospitals and schools for handicapped
children.

INVALIDS-AT-HOME

Mrs J. Pierce (Hon. Secretary)
Invalids-at-Home, 23 Farm Avenue, London NW2 2BJ
Tel: 01-452 2074

Invalids-at-Home aims to help permanent invalids – whatever their illness or disablement – to leave hospital for
home and to remain at home in greater comfort. It makes
grants to meet the heavy additional costs of living at home
and to cope with inevitable emergencies. It may provide
equipment to help ensure safety, comfort and independence, or to help people to earn a living. Interest-free
loans can be made to help buy specialized equipment, to
make adaptations or to meet temporary financial difficulties. An example was the case of a young man who was
speechless and so paralysed that he couldn't even twitch a
finger. Invalids-at-Home helped him to get a head-control
unit to work a tape-recorder and typewriter. With these
aids he was able to get an honours degree and go on to
work for a higher qualification. Invalids-at-Home works
in close cooperation with other organizations and agencies

providing help and all requests to them must be sent through a social worker from the local social services department.

MENTAL HEALTH FOUNDATION

Mental Health Foundation
8 Wimpole Street, London W1M 8HY
Tel: 01-580 0145

The Mental Health Foundation is solely devoted to financing scientific and sociological research into all forms of mental disorder and handicap, and to giving grants to community-based mental health services. Any efficiently organized project of a pioneering or experimental nature which will advance the understanding, treatment or care of mentally ill or mentally handicapped people will be considered sympathetically. The General Projects Committee envisages that pioneering projects will be undertaken with the full support of, and perhaps in cooperation with, the Area Health Authority or local authority. Every project supported by the Foundation fills at least one of the major gaps in existing provision in a new or distinctive way. A number of the organizations in this book have received grants from the Foundation. Four of the six grants made in the first three months of the financial year 1976–7 were for projects involving handicapped children, ranging from £200 for a local holiday scheme for deprived families with a handicapped child to £3000 for an experimental preschool unit for autistic children. In 1974–5 a grant of £10000 was made towards courses for teachers and parents of mentally handicapped children. The Committee will finance projects during an initial experimental period only and some arrangement with a statutory authority for longer-term finance will therefore be necessary in most cases. Helpfully, the Foundation gives a clear order of priority in considering which kind of projects will be eligible for grants.

The Scottish Division has a similar order of priorities. The report, *Pioneering Community Mental Health Services*, which covers all projects for 1974–6 describes four projects from the Scottish Division, including the assessment and education of profoundly handicapped children in Glasgow and a film called 'More Than You Think', made by the Scottish Society for the Mentally Handicapped.

Scottish Division, Mental Health Foundation
13 Bath Street, Glasgow G2
Tel: 041-332 4973

VARIETY CLUB OF GREAT BRITAIN

Variety Club of Great Britain
5th Floor, 1–4 Argyll Street, London W1
Tel: 01-437 9511

The Variety Club is an international charity which helps handicapped and severely deprived children. Since it was formed in Great Britain in 1949, it has given financial assistance to some 4000 national, local and private children's organizations. It can help some individual cases, but prefers its gifts to be of benefit to more than one person.

Guardianship

At the age of eighteen, when people legally reach their majority, very few mentally handicapped young people will be capable of taking the responsibilities of independent adult life. If parents become the official guardians of their mentally handicapped children before they reach this age, they may keep most of the authority over their child that a parent normally has over a younger child. You will need legal advice about this.

See **Law** and **Property**

Help

In every community there are organizations which are prepared to help the handicapped in all kinds of ways, either materially, with gifts of money, or equipment – a special wheelchair, a Possum machine, a tumbler drier, an electric liquidizer – or by providing volunteer help for travelling, babysitting, youth clubs, swimming, holidays. Apart from national organizations like the Water Rats, most towns have a Rotary Club, a Round Table, Trades Council, Chamber of Commerce, Women's Institute, National Council of Women. The list is endless. Their charitable functions vary widely according to the energy and interests of their membership, but if you have a flourishing group in your area, the chances are that they will listen sympathetically to any request for help.

CRIPPLES HELP SOCIETY

Cripples Help Society
26 Blackfriars Street, Manchester M3 5BE
Tel: 061-832 3678

The Society gives a service of personal help to the disabled of all ages throughout the north-west of England. It has been active in welfare work involving children for over seventy years. It provides holidays, parties, outings and Christmas gifts for children in need. Its 'personal services' include arranging recreational activities for handicapped children or grants for something special, such as an electric sewing machine.

WOMEN'S ROYAL VOLUNTARY SERVICE (WRVS)

WRVS, 17 Old Park Lane, London W1Y 4AJ
Tel: 01-499 6040

There are local offices of the WRVS in all towns and in many villages throughout the country. Addresses are in local telephone directories. The organization is involved in trying to help needy members of the community. As far as possible, it tries to include handicapped children in its children's activities. The Young Families Department works through social services departments throughout the country and cooperates with other voluntary organizations. Projects include playgroups, mother and baby clubs, holiday centres, holidays for children alone or for the whole family, riding for gravely disabled children (see chapter 7, **Riding**, page 358). Good-companion schemes operating from more than 150 local W R V S offices provide practical help such as shopping, babysitting with handicapped children or with other children while a handicapped child has to go for treatment. Local W R V S branches may organize their own activities for handicapped children. The Hampshire branch, for example, has taken groups of severely handicapped children for an adventure day in the New Forest including a 'wheelchair ramble'.

Home helps

The local social services department have to provide a home-help service, but the extent of this varies widely from one area to another and demand always seems to outstrip supply. You usually have to get some official support for a request for home help; a recommendation from a doctor, health visitor, social worker, will almost certainly be needed. Home helps provide a few hours help a week (not weekends or holidays) with ordinary household tasks, including shopping.

People have managed to get a home help because a handicapped child seriously disrupts the house.

Although there is normally a charge towards the cost of the help, this is reduced according to the family's circumstances, and may be waived altogether.

Housing

'Many thousands of people, whose only crime is that they are disabled, are being sentenced without trial to imprisonment for life. These are harsh words; but anyone who has lived in a chronic sick ward will know that the analogy with prisons is not simply a figure of speech.' Bitter words from a disabled young man which are quoted by Ann Shearer in *The Handicapped Person in the Com-*

munity (edited by D. M. Boswell and J. M. Wingrove, Open University, 1974). She goes on to describe the nightmare of many parents of handicapped children – that each and every mentally or physically handicapped person whatever his age can become overnight candidates for a long-stay hospital ward, not because his handicap suddenly becomes worse, but because he can no longer rely on the help he needs to keep going.

The Chronically Sick and Disabled Persons Act 1970 required local authorities to 'have regard' to the housing needs of disabled people. The Housing Act 1974 made it possible for disabled people to qualify for 'improvement grants' solely on the grounds of their disability. It extended the Housing Corporation's power to provide capital for housing associations who were building houses for disabled people. But such evidence as exists from official figures suggests that very little is in fact being done. Families with a handicapped child, or young couples one or both of whom are disabled, have very little chance of getting specially designed housing from the local authority. The Housing Officer for the Central Council for the Disabled estimated in October 1974 that current proposals to build would provide one unit for every 595 handicapped people in need of re-housing. *Circular 74/74* from the Department of the Environment, *Housing for People who are Physically Handicapped*, stresses the urgent need for local authorities to improve their provision and recommends 'mobility housing' – i.e. housing units that can suit either an ordinary family or one with a handicapped member.

The suggestion was made at the Annual General Meeting of the Spinal Injuries Association held in 1974 that three types of housing provision are needed to enable people with all degrees of handicap to live in the community: hostels and group homes, sheltered housing and independent housing.

HOSTELS AND GROUP HOMES

These can be less rigid and offer more independence than a

hospital, as long as full support services are guaranteed. Where it is provided by the local authority, this kind of provision would be the responsibility of the social services department rather than the housing department. One very interesting group home is run by Cardiff Universities Social Services. Four students live with five mentally handicapped people who had previously been considered to be too handicapped to be discharged from hospitals.

Hostels and homes are discussed more fully under **Residential care** (below).

SHELTERED HOUSING

Sheltered housing is the type of housing which enables handicapped people to live in the kind of housing they need – for instance, all on one level if they are chairbound – with the help they need to make it possible, situated where they are part of the surrounding community. Some housing associations are doing this – Habinteg, John Grooms, Inskip St Giles, the Scottish Trust for the Physically Disabled among others. Ann Shearer (in *The Handicapped Person in the Community*) describes the philosophy of Fokus, a scheme in Sweden to provide housing for severely disabled people scattered through normal housing blocks throughout the country. Its basic assumption – which is shared by the leading English housing associations – is that the only people who know how the disabled want to live are disabled people themselves. The same may well be true of those who are mentally handicapped. The second assumption, accepted by the government in Sweden, is that the state has an obligation to do all it can to meet these demands. So what sort of disabled people can live in ordinary domestic surroundings? Over three-quarters of Fokus' tenants are in wheelchairs, nearly a quarter need help with eating, a third need help during the night to go to the lavatory. What sort of life can they lead? Over a third of them are married or living together, an increase of about twenty-five per cent since they went to live in Fokus homes. Only a quarter of them are housebound, the rest either work or are studying. How is it done? As well as meticulous attention to practical details, such as the position and adjustability of fixtures and fittings, staff are on call to help at all times. Housewives are paid to come in on a regular basis at 'peak' times – morning, evening and meal times. Ann Shearer claims that many severely disabled people need only around two and a half hours a day of physical help. She concludes that 'it shouldn't be beyond the wit of our social agenc'es to provide this outside a local authority home or hospital ward'.

Some sheltered accommodation is based in communities where disabled people both live and work (see chapter 6, **Sheltered work**, pages 311–13).

INDEPENDENT HOUSING

In her report, *Handicapped School-Leavers*, Mrs Margaret Roberts of the Queen Elizabeth's Foundation for the Disabled asks: 'how many youngsters have been sent straight from school to residential welfare workshops simply because parents live in an upstairs flat with no facility for a wheelchair?' This ought never to happen. This chapter describes some of the many ways in which the local council – the social services in particular – ought to be prepared to help with the daily practical problems of a handicapped person living at home. The BUPA reckoned in 1975 that at the very least it would cost £133 a week for hospital accommodation and basic nursing. Aids, adaptations and home helps are a bargain for the tax-payer in comparison. After all, the tax-payer is paying even if the social services department is picking up the cheque instead of the National Health Service.

COUNCIL HOUSING

If you are on the waiting list for council housing, your application will probably be considered on a points system. A leaflet explaining this should be available in public libraries, family health centres, etc. If you have a handicapped child, the community physician may recommend you for an extra allowance of points. This is unlikely to make much difference to the time you have to wait for a home, but may help if you are already a council tenant and want to get a transfer to more convenient accommodation. You can find out about this from the housing department or speak to a social worker or health visitor at your family health centre.

CENTRAL COUNCIL FOR THE DISABLED

Central Council for the Disabled
34 Eccleston Square, London SW1V 1PE
Tel: 01-821 1871

The bureau of information on housing answers inquiries covering a variety of housing problems, including details of housing associations catering for the disabled and information about conversions and adaptations. The March/April 1975 edition of *Contact*, its official magazine, is devoted to a complete survey of the current housing position, on the occasion of the publication of the *Interim Report of the Working Party on Housing* (price 30p).

They have produced a useful booklet, *Housing Grants and Allowances for Disabled People*, which gives a complete guide to the assistance available to handicapped people with home improvements, housing costs and special adaptations (September 1975; price 25p including postage).

SPINAL INJURIES ASSOCIATION

Spinal Injuries Association
126 Albert Street, London NW1 7NF
Tel: 01-267 6111

The second bulletin of the Association surveys the whole field of housing for paraplegics, and the sources of help, and would be of interest to anyone concerned with housing for people with every kind of handicap.

Income tax

The income tax child allowance or dependent relative allowance may be claimed for a handicapped child or handicapped dependent relative over sixteen who is at home, or is in temporary or permanent care outside the home provided that some money is spent in maintenance including clothes and comforts. A person in *sole* charge of a handicapped child living with him or her who receives an income tax allowance for that child may also be entitled to an additional personal allowance. There are also special allowances for blind people. The Central Council for the Disabled has a pamphlet, *Income Tax Relief for Disabled People,* setting out the position (price 5p, plus postage), and the National Society for Mentally Handicapped Children's *A–Z: Your Questions Answered* (1972) has an entry on income tax. You should always consult your local inspector of taxes, because although the strict legal rules give very little recognition to the needs of handicapped people, it may be possible to negotiate some relief.

Central Council for the Disabled
34 Eccleston Square, London SW1V 1PE
Tel: 01-821 1871

Incontinence

DISABLED LIVING FOUNDATION (DLF)

Disabled Living Foundation
346 Kensington High Street, London W14 8NS
Tel: 01-602 2491

The DLF has lists of useful products and can give advice on every aspect of coping with incontinence.

LAUNDRY SERVICE FOR THE INCONTINENT

Some councils provide a free laundry service for bed-clothes and nightwear where bed-wetting and soiling is a serious problem. There is usually a collection and delivery service once or twice a week. You will probably need a recommendation for the service from your GP, social worker or health visitor. You must normally provide the bed-linen, clothes, etc., yourself, although a few areas provide linen on loan or disposable sheets.

PANTS AND PADS

Area Health Authorities now arrange for the supply of free waterproof pants and disposable pads suitable for adults and children under the National Health Service. Health visitors, the district nursing service or your GP should be able to tell you about it.

Information services

The problem of getting information from people who have it to those who need it has proved very difficult to solve in most areas of public life, but it seems to bear particularly hard on parents of handicapped children. Almost every organization mentioned in this book offers some kind of information service, however modest in size and scope. Under this heading we are simply concerned with organizations which offer a general service, not limited to specific handicap or function, and to which anyone can apply.

Some local councils now run their own information centres – in addition to or instead of support for citizens advice bureaux – and these should be a good source for finding out what local services are available.

CENTRAL COUNCIL FOR THE DISABLED

Central Council for the Disabled
34 Eccleston Square, London SW1V 1PE
Tel: 01-821 1871

As well as all its specialist services, the information service publishes a number of leaflets on statutory provision for the disabled. These include a classified list of Acts of Parliament affecting the disabled, as well as guides and commentaries on various aspects of the Chronically Sick and Disabled Persons Act 1970.

CITIZENS ADVICE BUREAUX (CABX)

National Council of Citizens Advice Bureaux
26 Bedford Square, London WC1B 3HU
Tel: 01-636 4066

Over two million people every year use the services offered by their local CAB, which can give you any information you may need on rights and on problems including family and personal problems, consumer complaints, hire-purchase and credit buying, welfare benefit entitlements, housing, landlord and tenant legislation. Some bureaux hold a weekly legal session where free advice is given by volunteer solicitors. They will also help you to cope with the complexities of making claims, appealing at tribunals, etc. The service is available for everyone, and any problem will be dealt with freely, impartially and confidentially. Many CAB workers are voluntary and unpaid, although some of the larger ones may also use full-time professional staff. You can find out the address and opening hours of your local CAB from the town hall, post office or telephone directory or direct from the National Council of CABx, to which all local CABx are affiliated.

The National Council provides a central information and training service to local bureaux, as well as negotiating with central government. Its monthly news digest gives all local bureaux details of new legislation, as well as developments in social services and general information.

DISABLED LIVING FOUNDATION

Disabled Living Foundation
346 Kensington High Street, London W14 8NS
Tel: 01-602 2491

The aim of the information service is to collect, store and distribute information concerning disability to all those concerned with disabled people, personally or professionally. It undertakes to answer questions on any aspect of disabled living, with the exception of purely medical matters. Its guides and information sheets cover almost every subject, and it also produces reports on its special projects, conferences and inquiries. The general public may use the service free of charge for occasional queries. Organizations and individuals can subscribe to the service, which will entitle them to a full set of indexed information sheets – regularly updated – newsheets and leaflets, and unlimited use of the inquiry service.

DISABLEMENT INCOME GROUP (DIG)

DIG
Attlee House, Toynbee Hall, 28 Commercial Street, London E1 6LR
Tel: 01-247 2128/6877

In addition to its campaign for adequate social security benefits for disabled people of all ages, the charitable trust associated with the group is concerned with the collection and dissemination of information about disabled people. It promotes research and operates an advisory service by post. The advisory service publishes an ABC of services and general information for disabled people, regularly updated.

INSTITUTE FOR RESEARCH INTO MENTAL AND MULTIPLE HANDICAP

Institute for Research into Mental and Multiple Handicap
16 Fitzroy Square, London W1P 5HQ
Tel: 01-387 9571

The Institute aims to encourage collaboration between research workers as well as carrying out research itself; to provide an information centre including a specialist library on every aspect of mental and multiple handicap. Specific inquiries for specialist information are welcomed but inquiries about personal problems are usually referred to more appropriate organizations. Publications include a monthly 'Current Awareness Service', which lists articles, books and meetings on aspects of handicap all over the world. This costs £12 a year. It has also published a comprehensive annotated reading list, *Books for Parents of a Handicapped Child* (June 1976, price 15p). It includes books written by parents and those who are themselves handicapped.

NATIONAL CHILDREN'S BUREAU (NCB)

NCB, 8 Wakley Street, London EC1V 7QE
Tel: 01-278 9441

The Bureau is concerned with children's needs in the family, school and society and aims to improve communication among workers in every profession concerned with family and child care. Its members are mostly organizations professionally concerned with the well-being of children. It has been responsible for the establishment of the Voluntary Council for Handicapped Children (see **General**, above). There is an information service which produces a series of 'Highlights': abstracts and sources on various topics. The Bureau does not give advice to parents, although they may take out individual membership of the Bureau. Its publications include *Spotlight on Services for the Young Handicapped Child* by Jessie Parfit (1972, price £1.50) and a series of booklets, 'Helping the Handi-Child' (price 75p each), which sketch out some ideas on services and help. In 1970, it published one of the first books to look at all round provision for handicapped children, *Living with Handicap*. This was the report of a multi-disciplinary working party, and gives a comprehensive survey of existing services. It makes some fifty recommendations and conclusions which offer a blueprint for future policy and action. It costs £2.50, but should be available from every public library.

NATIONAL COUNCIL OF VOLUNTARY CARE
ORGANIZATIONS

Miss D. E. Cowcher, Clerk to the Council
Turner House, 85 Highbury Park, London N5 1UD
Tel: 01-226 6592

This is a consultative body which acts as a channel of communication for members, particularly the smaller societies, with the government, statutory bodies and other agencies. Membership is open to voluntary organizations helping children and their families. Its members include children's homes, special schools, as well as larger societies such as the NSPCC and Barnardo's.

The Council provides an information service for members and has produced a combined directory of services offered by members which has been circulated to local authority social services departments and other agencies.

SCOTTISH INFORMATION SERVICE FOR THE DISABLED (SISD)

SISD, 18/19 Claremont Crescent, Edinburgh EH7 4QD
Tel: 031-556 3882

This is a voluntary organization set up under the auspices of the Scottish Council of Social Service to record and disseminate information on practical matters of concern to disabled people and those who care for them. Organizations can subscribe to the service, and receive indexed sets of information sheets which are updated regularly, a newsletter and access to the inquiry service. Much of its information is shared with the Disabled Living Foundation. It has produced a useful list of voluntary organizations, directories and handbooks concerned with handicap in Scotland (available free).

Care of Disabled People in Britain

A survey of facilities available for handicapped people in

England, Wales, Scotland and Northern Ireland (published by HMSO, 1975, price £1.20). It describes their historical development and how they work at present. It covers in general terms medical and rehabilitation services, employment, training, social security, personal social services, special education, services for the mentally ill and some of the major voluntary organizations.

Directory for the Disabled: A Handbook of Information and Opportunities for the Handicapped

This handbook by Ann Darnbrough and Derek Kinrade (Woodhead-Faulkner, 1977) is intended to provide, in one compact volume, a wide ranging information service describing the benefits, allowances, facilities and opportunities available to disabled people. Its authors have considerable experience of the problems of disability. The book is available from bookshops or by mail order from Woodhead-Faulkner Ltd, 7 Rose Crescent, Cambridge CB2 3LL.

Sunday Times Self-help Directory

Inquiries to:
Sunday Times, 200 Gray's Inn Road, London WC1X 8EZ
Tel: 01-837 1234 Ext. 534

This book aims to enable people to help themselves by contacting others with similar problems. It was first published in 1975, price £1, and a new edition is planned for 1977.

Insurance

Corporation of Insurance Brokers
15 St Helens Place, London EC3A 6DS
Tel: 01-588 4387

Although in principle it is possible to insure anyone against any risk, people with a disability often find it difficult to arrange and rather expensive. An insurance broker ought to know which firms are most likely to be suitable for a particular type of insurance. Anyone may set himself up in business as a broker so it is always a good idea to go to someone who is a member of a trade association, such as the Corporation of Insurance Brokers. The Corporation can put people in touch with local members; this not only guarantees the standard of security but also means that you can take up a complaint with the Corporation rather than having to go to law to get satisfaction. A good broker ought to be able to find out about any special arrangements offered by particular firms. Voluntary societies concerned with specific handicaps or the Central Council for the Disabled can sometimes give advice about suitable insurance policies.

Jewish services

CENTRAL COUNCIL FOR JEWISH SOCIAL SERVICES

Joint Secretary
Central Council for Jewish Social Services
1 Craven Hill, London W2 3W
Tel: 01-262 3111

In 1976 for the first time the various Jewish welfare organizations are attempting to coordinate and rationalize their efforts under the auspices of a central council. In due course this ought to be able to act as a clearing house, directing parents to the most appropriate source of help.

JEWISH WELFARE BOARD

Jewish Welfare Board
315–17 Ballards Lane, London N12
Tel: 01-446 1499

The Welfare Board is the largest and most general in scope of the Jewish Social Services organizations. There is a professional in-take reception service and a comprehensive information service.

Law

England and Wales: The Law Society
The Law Society's Hall, 113 Chancery Lane, London WC2A 1PL
Tel: 01-242 1222

Scotland: The Administrative Secretary
Legal Aid Central Committee
The Law Society of Scotland, 28 Drumsheugh Gardens
Edinburgh EH3 7YR
Tel: 031-226 7411

Citizens advice bureaux give advice on legal questions. In some areas there are independent community law centres as well, which give free legal advice and assistance on a range of problems to people living in their area who can't ordinarily pay for a solicitor. Any solicitor who does legal aid work may also give advice and assistance under the '£25' or 'Green Form' scheme on any subject usually dealt with by solicitors. To apply for this it is necessary only to tell the solicitor that you want this help and he can grant it immediately subject to a simple means test. Legal aid for court cases and other kinds of legal action have to be formally applied for. Pamphlets about legal aid, produced by the Law Society, ought to be available from any citizens advice bureau or by post direct. Anyone who wants help in paying for legal costs must always complete the arrangements for this before they make the first move in asking advice or taking action – the account cannot be paid retrospectively.

MIND

Mind, 22 Harley Street, London W1N 2ED
Tel: 01-637 0741

Mind have appointed a legal rights officer to review the interpretation and workings of the Mental Health Act. He should be able to advise people about legal rights under this Act, and rights of mentally handicapped people generally. He has, for example, taken up a case with the Department of Education and Science on behalf of a boy

has who received only twenty-four hours, teaching in four
years.

NETWORK — WEST CENTRAL

Centre held at:
Network
23 Hand Court, London WC1V 6JF

For appointments apply to:
Helen Berent
22 Latchett Road, London E18
Tel: 01-504 3001

The law and advisory centre set up by Network at the
end of 1975 is the first one concerned solely with the
problems faced by physically and mentally handicapped
people of all ages and their families. The Network idea
originated with Kith and Kids (see page 28) who hope
to form links with any similar organizations throughout
the country. In his book *Kith and Kids*, Maurice Collins
describes how the working arrangements were arrived at:

At the first working meeting, the lawyers insisted that they were
as much interested in the human problems as the legal ones,
and that parents and disabled people sitting in on cases would
be absolutely essential. Their concept was one of the advice
team. Accordingly, the working evening of Network was
arranged so that clients would fix an appointment by phone
and on arriving at the centre be alloted a legal person and
relevant counsellor.

The centre is open on Thursday evenings. Although it is
best to make an appointment, anyone may call in for a
coffee and a chat. The advice service is free.

Network has produced a series of bulletins: some are
copies of letters to Network and their answers on subjects
such as welfare benefits and taxation; there are reprints
of articles of interest from journals and explanations of
methods and procedures, such as how to get your child
out of care. *Bulletin No. 16* is an index of all bulletins in
print on 1 September 1976. A whole set of bulletins costs

£1; for a single copy just send postage. A bulletin is generally one tightly-packed page and carries the following warning: 'Due to the urgent need to get Bulletins into circulation, certain misprints exist. However, the meaning remains clear in all cases.' So they are useful rather than decorative.

Milk

All children under seven years old are given a third of a pint of milk each day, free of charge, at their school or playgroup. All children aged up to sixteen attending special schools are entitled to a third of a pint a day of free milk and children at special schools for the delicate may get a further third of a pint as well at the local education authority's discretion. Children in special units which are part of an ordinary school do not get these concessions automatically, but any child of any age may be supplied with free milk in school if the school doctor examines him and certifies that it is necessary on health grounds. Handicapped children aged five to sixteen who are not at school are entitled to a pint of milk a day free, regardless of their parents' income. Parents have to apply for this on leaflet FW20 which is available from social security offices.

Mobility

MOBILITY ALLOWANCE

From 1 January 1976, the arrangements for government help with transport to people who are unable to walk have been completely changed. The new regulations provide for an allowance of £5 a week to be paid to everyone over five years old and under pensionable age, who would benefit from facilities to get them about. The money can be spent on public transport, taxis or on helping to run family cars, or sharing petrol costs or anything else.

In April 1977 people between the ages of five and fifty-two were eligible. Other groups will be phased into the scheme in due course.

Eligible people who are living in residential homes and hospitals can pool their allowances, for example, to run a mini-bus. The allowance will be taxable but not taken into account for calculation of entitlement to supplementary benefits, family income supplement, rent and rate rebates and free school meals. DHSS leaflet N1211 gives full details and an application form.

The Family Fund and the Family Fund Research Project have taken a particular interest in the mobility needs and problems of handicapped children and may be able to offer help (see page 136).

JOINT COMMITTEE ON MOBILITY FOR THE DISABLED

Joint Committee on Mobility for the Disabled
Nicholas Elwes (Hon. Secretary)
Wanborough Manor, Wanborough, Guildford, Surrey GY3 2JR
Tel: Guildford (0483) 810484

This is a coordinating committee of organizations concerned with the disabled, set up primarily to lobby Parliament and other statutory bodies to bring about improvement in the facilities available and to exchange information on aids and equipment among the member organizations. It produces some helpful leaflets on various aspects of mobility – details from the secretary (stamped, addressed envelope please).

See also **Travel** and **Transport**

Parliament

MPs may form themselves into all-party parliamentary groups such as the Mental Health Group or the Under-Fives Group to support important campaigns or issues of special concern. Anyone trying to enlist parliamentary support would be wise to start with an all-party group. If you identify your interest with one party, it is likely to make political capital out of it which will alienate all the others. And no party holds office for ever. *Who Does What in Parliament*, by H. Mitchell and P. Birt, will tell you who are doctors, teachers, and so on, and their special interests.

Always in stock at:
Westminster Bookstall, Westminster Underground Station
Bridge Street, London SW1
Inquiries tel: Downland 52044

Possum

The name Possum (the Latin for 'I can') was originally formed from the initials POSM which stood for patient operated selector mechanism. It has now grown with the development of different types of equipment to cover a wide range of electronic aids which enable very severely physically disabled persons to exercise remote on/off control over electrical devices, such as: bell and buzzer alarm system, light, heat, radio, television (with channel change), intercom to the front door to communicate with visitors and an electric door lock, and a specially adapted loudspeaking telephone giving full self-dialling facility and control over volume. (This is the basic unit generally supplied under the National Health Service.) Control systems are also produced to operate individual items of electrical equipment, such as an electric typewriter, calculating machine, tape recorder, dictation machine and any form of keyboard-operated apparatus. So this equipment can give even the most severely disabled people a measure of independence, the possibility of communication, education and employment. Many Possum control systems are mouth-operated by gentle suction and/or pressure down a tube. Some special schools have Possum typewriters. Various departments may supply Possum equipment according to whether the need is, for instance, for education or employment.

POSSUM USERS' ASSOCIATION

Ken Winter (Welfare Officer)
Possum Users' Association
14 Greenvale Drive, Timsbury, Nr Bath, Avon
Tel: Timsbury (0761) 71184

The main aim of the Association is to assist people in buying special equipment. Although one system is available on the National Health Service, the Association has found that even those who qualify have to wait months for it to be installed and they have therefore arranged their own supply so that urgent cases can receive the equipment within a few days. All members of the Association receive a magazine called *Possability*.

Property

Parents may wish to provide for their handicapped child's future by accumulating property and funds in his name or in some kind of trust. It is very important to get legal advice about this. You must remember that any income received by the child is taken into account when entitlement to supplementary benefit and other benefits is being assessed and it must be disclosed to the social security office.

It may be particularly difficult to define exactly when a mentally handicapped person is considered legally to be incapable of handling his own affairs. It depends on a number of factors, including the degree of handicap and nature of the transaction. For example, a mildly handicapped person may be considered capable of making a will, but not capable of selling a house or receiving a legacy. The NSMHC and the Scottish Society for the Mentally Handicapped have a great deal of expertise on these problems and parents would be well advised to refer to them before taking any decisions. The Scottish Society has produced a useful leaflet, *Over Sixteens*, setting out briefly the law in relation to money and property as it affects mentally handicapped people in Scotland.

If someone is incapable of managing his own property,

the Court of Protection in England and Wales and, in Scotland, a curator bonis can be appointed to manage his affairs.

See also **Law**, page 155; **Savings**, page 175; and **Wills**, page 189.

COURT OF PROTECTION

Court of Protection
25 Store Street, London WC1E 7BP
Tel: 01-636 6877

The Court of Protection is responsible under Part VIII of the Mental Health Act 1959 for the protection and management of the property and affairs of anyone over the age of eighteen who is incapable of dealing with his own affairs by reason of 'arrested or incomplete development of mind'. The Court's powers apply irrespective of whether the person is living at home, in hospital or anywhere else. When some action needs to be taken for the protection of a patient's property or to enable it to be used for his benefit, the normal procedure is for the Court to appoint a Receiver to receive the income and administer the property. Where, however, only a small amount is involved, say a couple of hundred pounds, the Personal Applications Branch may help in making an application and in obtaining the necessary order or directions. The Court has a free leaflet explaining its functions.

There are many cases where it will be necessary to instruct a solicitor, such as questions about the sale of property.

CURATOR BONIS

When a major transaction is involved, or more generally, when the handicap is severe and the estate requires protection, a 'curator bonis' may be appointed to undertake transactions and administer funds on behalf of a handicapped person in Scotland. A curator bonis is

A.H.F.P.—F

frequently a solicitor, but may be an accountant or a bank manager, or, in theory at least, any friend or relative of whom the Court approves. To appoint a curator, it is necessary to petition the Court of Session, or in smaller cases, the Sheriff Court, but in either event, certificates will be required from two doctors to the effect that the person concerned is incapable of handling his own affairs. The Court will have to satisfy itself that the proposed curator bonis is capable of carrying out his functions. As an officer of the Court, the curator bonis comes under the statutory supervision of the Accountant of Court to whom he must submit accounts annually. The Accountant sends a note of curatorships in respect of mentally handicapped people to the Mental Welfare Commission for Scotland and the Commission visits all the mentally handicapped people concerned (see page 70).

Curatorship is a relatively complex process and can be fairly expensive although the protection afforded the estate justifies the expense. Approaching the Court of Session requires the services of both an advocate (equivalent to an English barrister) and a solicitor, although the process is largely a legal formality. Expenses in the Sheriff Court, where the services of an advocate are not required, are correspondingly less. The curator may, however, charge for his work only such fees as are fixed by the Accountant of Court. In every case, it is wise to approach a solicitor who can offer advice under the Legal Aid Service at little or no cost.

(This entry was kindly written for us by the Scottish Society for the Mentally Handicapped.)

NATIONAL TRUSTS FOR MENTALLY HANDICAPPED LTD

National Trusts for Mentally Handicapped Ltd
17 Pembridge Square, London W2 4EP
Tel: 01-229 8941/01-727 0536

The National Society for Mentally Handicapped Children – through National Trusts for Mentally Handicapped Ltd – can now become involved in the management of funds which are available for the benefit of a mentally handicapped individual of any age. This can be arranged by bequest or during the lifetime of the settlor (the person making the settlement of property). The settlor would retain the right to decide what purposes the money should be used for while he was still alive. One thousand pounds has to be made available for the costs of administering the trust and arrangements can be made for this to be paid by instalments.

NETWORK

Network, 23 Hand Court, London WC1V 6JF

An information leaflet on how to covenant money and thereby recover any tax paid for the benefit of a handicapped child – through an unfettered trust – is available from Network, who can also advise on this at their law centre.

See **Law**, page 155.

Rates

An extension or room specially built or adapted for a disabled person does not count towards the home's gross rateable value. The position with regard to rates is very confused, but the Central Council for the Disabled can offer help and advice to anyone wishing to appeal to the local valuation officers.

Central Council for the Disabled
34 Eccleston Square, London SW1V 1PE
Tel: 01-821 1871

Registers

Registration is an administrative procedure for recording who needs certain kinds of help and making it possible to see that they get it. There are a number of different registers each with a different function.

OBSERVATION REGISTER

In many areas a register is kept by the Health Service, under the supervision of the district community physician, of all children who have a handicap or might be at risk of developing one (see chapter 1, **Screening**, page 12).

LOCAL AUTHORITY REGISTER

In order to carry out their duties under the Chronically Sick and Disabled Persons Act, local authorities are expected to keep a register of the names of all substantially and permanently handicapped persons (including those who are mentally handicapped) in their area. Registration is voluntary but there is nothing to lose and it helps to ensure that the social services department knows about your problems and can help you to get the care and benefits you need.

In reply to a parliamentary question, Mr Alfred Morris, Minister for the Disabled, said that in 1974–5 the names of 135 000 disabled people were added to the registers of local authorities, nearly 30 per cent more than the previous year.

EMPLOYMENT REGISTER

In addition to the registers of handicapped people of all ages kept by the local authority, there is a quite distinct disabled persons employment register which is kept by the Department of Employment (see chapter 6, Employment, page 305).

BLIND PERSONS REGISTER

There is also a special register of people who are blind or partially sighted (see chapter 2, **Services for blind people**, page 41).

Residential care

The Government command paper, *Better Services for the Mentally Handicapped* (HMSO, 1971), stated that the service in which the greatest expansion was needed was the provision of residential homes for both children and adults. Since 1959 local authorities have had a statutory duty to provide a full range of community services for the mentally handicapped, including residential accommodation. They also have the power to provide residential care for any disabled people who need it. Local authorities may do this by making arrangements with voluntary organizations or paying for places in homes run privately for profit. With the right support many parents want to keep their child at home. However, without adequate support services – physiotherapy, home helps, day care, short-term care, holidays, incontinence aids, transport, babysitting – the stress and strain of coping may be too great for any family. Handicapped children may also need residential care for the same reason that robust and healthy children are taken into care: illness in the family, divorce, poverty or bereavement can all make it quite impossible for parents to continue to look after their own children. The problem is that the local authority's duty to make arrangements for residential accommodation in general terms for all who need it does not seem to mean that any particular individual can claim it as of right. Local authorities with a shortage of places may too readily dismiss appeals for help from mothers who appear to be 'good managers'. Not all families want to admit to the extreme stress they are experiencing or to give in if they can keep going somehow. Yet having hysterics in the social services department or abandoning the child may be the only way of getting proper help – a few days' break or some more permanent arrangement.

There are some crucial questions to which there are not necessarily any clear answers:

1 Who decides whether a handicapped child *needs* residential care? Your GP and/or local authority social worker can make a recommendation. In the

case of a hospital, it will decide whether to make a place available. The hospital social worker's support will help but the consultant in charge will have the final say.

2 Who knows what is available? The Bristol Campaign for the Mentally Handicapped comments: 'Our experience in asking various people who operate and who have used services is that no one seems to have put together what is available in one document so that both parent and social workers can clearly assess the various options.'

3 Who knows the quality of care offered in the various establishments? One parent visited the place recommended by his doctor. When the doctor asked him what he thought of it, he commented: 'I wouldn't send my dog there.' There seems to be no one with responsibility for attempting to apply some consistent measure of standards such as qualifications of staff, facilities, activities for residents as there would be for normal children taken into care. This makes placing a child very difficult for parents and social workers particularly if the residential care is outside the home area as is often the case.

4 Who pays for any place? There is no clear answer. A hospital place is free to both parents and social services departments, although after a time you would lose some social security benefits. But when a child is 'in care', the local authority social services becomes responsible for his keep outside school hours and school terms although parents must make some contribution on a means-tested basis. In some circumstances parents may also have to pay towards the cost of a residential place in a boarding school (see chapter 5, INDEPENDENT SCHOOLS, page 260).

Under the Chronically Sick and Disabled Persons Act, the social services department could give financial help towards the cost of keeping a child in residential care in a voluntary or independent establishment.

HOSPITALS

In 1975 about 8000 handicapped children were living permanently in long-stay hospital wards. A report called *No Childhood* (published by the Council for Children's Welfare, 1975; available from the National Children's Bureau) said: 'It is not an emotional exaggeration to state that the average long-stay hospital is the last bastion of Victorian institutionalization. It needs to be said, for the children live in conditions which are in total opposition to all 20th century knowledge of child care and development.' No child in a children's home run by a local authority would be permitted to endure mass bathing and toiletting, bedtime at four o'clock on a summer afternoon, institutional clothes, the absence of toys and personal possessions or continuity of care. He would not be deprived of education, outings, friends. Yet these situations are endured by many hospital children. The irony is that they may even be deprived of essential medical treatment. For instance, Maureen Oswin (author of *The Empty Hours*, Penguin, 1973) told the *Sunday Times* about a long-stay hospital in the north with 1400 patients which had no physiotherapy service where spastic children of six and seven are growing up with permanent limb deformities which could have been avoided. Two miles away, the Spastics Society has a boarding school for 130 pupils. The staff includes five physiotherapists.

Everyone would agree that no child should live in hospital, that it should never be his only home. But some severely handicapped children may be so destructive, disturbed or hyperactive that no school will keep them, and when parents are left to cope with a child like this all day every day, a place in hospital may be the only way to prevent a complete family breakdown. For children who are fortunate enough to live in an area such as the Wessex Area Health Authority or around Oxford, their hospital place will be locally based in family-sized accommodation where they will be cared for in a homelike way, not in the traditional way based on medical nursing practice.

The problem for hospitals coping with Dickensian buildings, often for historical reasons in isolated and inaccessible positions, is that these conditions, combined with pressure on places, can make it extremely difficult to create any sort of homely atmosphere. The support services which are necessary for families at home are also crucial for the support of nursing staff who are asked to be substitute families. Nevertheless, a change in the atmosphere and morale of children and staff could be created by such simple measures as allowing children to wear their own clothes and a safe place in which to keep their personal possessions and toys. Long-stay hospitals ought to be the concern of Community Health Councils and parents should ask for their support in voicing the needs of the handicapped children who live there.

In February 1975 the Secretary of State for Social Services set up a committee of inquiry into the nursing and care of the mentally handicapped with Mrs Peggy Jay as chairman. The terms of reference focus in particular on residential care. The Jay Committee invited any individuals or groups who wanted their views to be considered to submit evidence to them and in the first year more than 500 pieces of written evidence were sent in. For instance, the Inner London Education Authority said in its evidence that mentally handicapped children in hospital should attend special day schools for the educationally subnormal (severe) wherever possible. It is hoped that the report will be published by the end of 1977.

Younger Chronic Sick Units. A government survey in 1968 found that half the 4200 or so severely disabled people under the age of sixty-five being catered for by the National Health Service were in geriatric wards. As a result £5 million was made available and more than ninety 'younger chronic sick units' were planned. By 1975 only nine of these had been completed. Although the original government memorandum said: 'the aim should be to provide as relaxed and permissive an atmosphere as possible within a hospital setting', many young disabled people would feel that the setting is the wrong one. The tragedy is that a government census of all age groups of physically handicapped people in this type of accommodation found that nearly half of them were only minimally dependent; in other words they were continent, mobile without assistance, able to feed themselves and mentally alert. One of the longest-opened younger chronic sick units estimated that half their patients could live in the community if the right type of accommodation and support services were available (see SHELTERED HOUSING, under **Housing**, page 144).

One-to-One is a volunteer community project aimed at increasing contact between mentally handicapped people in long-stay hospitals and the local community. The focal point of the project is a one-to-one day when volunteers are invited into hospitals where they help the residents to take part in a wide range of activities and entertainments as a way of getting to know one another. The one-to-one days have attracted large numbers of people into hospitals that they hardly noticed before, who discovered that their preconceptions about mental handicap were not just misconceptions but dangerous myths. And sceptical hospital staff have been impressed by the willingness and enthusiasm of volunteers and the capacity for enjoyment and appreciation shown by the residents. When the project was first mooted it was hoped that 10 per cent of those who turned up on a one-to-one day might be persuaded to continue to visit regularly. In the first two years this estimate has been exceeded and regular volunteer contact and participation have been established in most of the hospitals that have taken part.

One-to-One, c/o Spastics Society
76 Cambridge Road, Kingston-upon-Thames, Surrey
Tel: 01-549 5988

In addition to their work providing playgroups and opportunity groups for children in need, the Save the Children Fund recognizes the special need of children in hospital and, wherever possible, answers requests to start playgroups in children's hospitals and children's wards. The Fund also runs two playgroups in Chertsey and Dundee in the wards of long-stay hospitals for severely multiply handicapped children who do not attend a hospital school. Playleaders are specially chosen and trained. They fit in with the daily ward routine, and, for example, join with the nurses in giving the children dinner. They try to establish a warm and caring relationship with the children, to stimulate interest and widen the children's horizons, and help them to become more independent. Outings, visits to nearby shops, choice of fruit for elevenses, a ride in a car, all introduce the children to new experiences.

Save the Children Fund
157 Clapham Road, London SW9 0PT
Tel: 01-582 1414

A study group has been organized by the National Playing Fields Association, the Disabled Living Foundation and the Handicapped Adventure Playground Association to provide play facilities in hospitals for mentally handicapped children. The group aims to bring together people involved in playschemes and the administrators who plan and finance the projects.

Study Group on Play Facilities in Hospitals for Mentally
Handicapped Children
Drummond Abernethby, National Playing Fields Association
25 Ovington Square, London SW3
01-584 6445

See also chapter 4, NATIONAL ASSOCIATION FOR THE WELFARE OF CHILDREN IN HOSPITAL, page 199.

HOMES

Permanent residential homes for children who cannot live with their family may be provided by local authority social services departments, by the long established voluntary children's societies (page 118 above) or by private enterprise for profit.

Everyone now realizes that a residential home should be homely, in small units, with ordinary domestic furnishings as far as possible. The best homes recognize the importance of encouraging parents to maintain contact with their children and always to keep in mind the possibility that the children may eventually be able to go back home.

All private homes must be registered with the local authority in whose area they are situated and be open to inspection. However, in the case of at least one private home in which a child died, the director of social services who licensed the home commented that it was 'kept clean and well-heated'; this authority at least seems to have seen its responsibilities as being limited to the cleanliness and domestic standards and its compliance with fire regulations.

Therefore, however desperate parents are by the time a residential place is offered, and however far away it is, it is important for them to find out for themselves whether certain conditions are fulfilled. These are based on recommendations made by Compassion (see below).

Medical examinations and care should be provided as of right, regularly and automatically. It should not be up to the proprietors of a home to decide whether or not a doctor should visit regularly. Parents should have proper rights concerning visits – full access to their child, be able to see sleeping quarters and so on and be allowed to take the child out.

HOSTELS

The term 'hostel' is often used to describe part-time residential care when the child or adult goes home for the weekend or less frequently and goes to a local school or day centre or employment during the week. In 1975 only about 1800 children were in hostels providing this kind of care. Hostels may be run by local authorities, by voluntary societies or by private enterprise. From its experience in setting up hostels, the Spastics Society argues foi far more local authority provision of this type. In its report, *Everybody's Children* (edited by James Loring, 1975), it quotes its hostels at Manchester and Eastbourne as examples of cooperation between voluntary bodies and local authorities for the good of the community. The local authorities provided the site and £10000 towards the building costs which totalled nearly £200000 each. When the Spastics Society had raised the rest of the money and built the hostels, they were accepted as gifts by the local authority who took on responsibility for the running costs. Both hostels take the form of small housing units linked to communal facilities and playgrounds. The local community is encouraged to use the play facilities and mix with the handicapped children.

These schemes have rescued many children from the 'anonymity' of subnormality hospitals and placed them instead in a family situation in a more normal environment. They need not be beyond the reach of local voluntary groups.

One small local group (albeit a very energetic one), the Enfield Society for Mentally Handicapped Children, managed to raise tens of thousands of pounds to buy, convert and run its own hostel. Another parents' group has thought up an ingenious scheme to create hostels without having to raise the capital needed or to carry the continuing responsibility for the running costs. The proposal is based on the idea that parents should bequeath their family homes to the local authority and the council would then become responsible for the upkeep of the buildings and the support services needed. This scheme is being developed at the moment and Maurice Collins of Kith and Kids should be able to describe the up-to-date position.

Secretary, Enfield Society, 34 Green Dragon Lane, London N21 2LD
Tel: 01-360 6880

Kith and Kids, 58 The Avenue, London N10
Tel: 01-883 8762

COMPASSION

Compassion
120 Salisbury Walk, Magdala Avenue, London N19
Tel: 01-263 1252

Compassion stands for Committee of Parents Against Sub-standard Sub-normality Institutions or Nursing. It is a pressure group set up by London parents of severely subnormal and physically handicapped children after the child of one of them died in a privately run home.

The association promotes the welfare of multi-handicapped children who are cared for in residential institutions. After its campaign about the lack of any adequate official responsibility for children in such institutions, a government study group was set up to inquire into arrangements and communications among parents, local authorities and institutions. The submission from Compassion to the government study group concludes by setting out its recommendations for legislative and administrative changes. The Committee helps individual parents in their dealings with social services departments and arranges mutual visiting of children.

See also MAINTAINED BOARDING SCHOOLS, page 257; **Fostering**, page 135; chapter 8, Holidays, page 371; **Housing**, page 142.

Safety

PLAY SAFE SLIDE SETS

Eric Johnson Film-Strips
430 James Reckitt Avenue, Hull, North Humberside
Tel: Hull (0482) 74044

Eric Johnson has produced three sets of slides to teach safety in home and garden, road and recreation, and farm and country. All three sets feature two boys – easily recognized by the colour of their sweaters – in key situations where one or the other is doing something particularly wrong or something particularly sensible or helpful. One boy is not always the good one; indeed spare slides are supplied which show the roles of good and bad reversed so that the children watching have to be alert to see who is the wrong-doer this time.

Mr Johnson, a retired headteacher, originally produced these slides for primary schools, but they have been used successfully in schools for mentally handicapped children, including schools for children who are severely subnormal. The quality is excellent, both in photographic terms and in the clear way the points are put across. This is the sort of teaching aid which parents can easily use at home. The slides are in plastic wallets neatly packed in small cardboard folders. They all include teaching notes. Each title separately costs £2.50; the set of three, boxed, costs £6.00. Post and packing is 20p.

Salvation Army

ASSOCIATION FOR PARENTS OF THE HANDICAPPED

Brigadier Marsh, Salvation Army
101 Queen Victoria Street, London EC4
Tel: 01-236 5222

The Army has an association for Salvationist parents with a handicapped child and Salvationists who are themselves handicapped. There is a monthly newsletter from headquarters and every corps is encouraged to make provision for handicapped people in some way, either by encouraging them to share in the regular activities or by providing facilities such as day centres for local handicapped people. The Association runs an annual music summer school for handicapped Salvationists on a one-to-one basis.

Samaritans

Samaritans Incorporated, National Office Administration
17 Uxbridge Road, Slough SL1 1SN
Tel: Slough 32713
All local branches are in the telephone directory.

The movement exists to help anyone who is despairing, depressed, isolated or suicidal. A team of carefully selected trained volunteers (more than 18 000 of them) man telephones twenty-four hours a day, 365 days a year from centres in every large town in the country. Smaller branches also give a twenty-four-hour service by transferring calls to volunteers at home or other branches. If you need to talk to a Samaritan you may telephone, write or call in at one of their centres at any time. Home visits are possible if you are tied to the house. There is absolute confidentiality and no one is 'referred' to any other body, nor is information passed on without his expressed consent. Any client who has been helped over a crisis may be introduced to a Samaritan who will visit him at home or on neutral ground and will continue to 'befriend' him until he feels able to cope alone.

Savings

NSMHC, Pembridge Hall, 17 Pembridge Square, London W2 4EP
Tel: 01-229 8941/01-727 0536

Parents who know, or suspect, that their child is mentally handicapped should not put any money or assets in the child's name, whether it is in the form of savings certificates, premium bonds or any other kind of savings account. It may become necessary to go through elaborate legal procedures subsequently to be able to draw on the money for the benefit of the child. Parents should seek legal advice (see **Law**, page 155) as to suitable ways of holding money so that it can be used for the benefit of the child, either during the lifetime of the parents or after. The National Society for Mentally Handicapped Children gives general guidance and warnings about particular forms of savings in their pamphlet, *A–Z: Your Questions Answered* (1972).

See also **Property**, page 160.

Sex

The sexual needs and pioblems of handicapped people had not been recognized or discussed at all until very recently. But now it is beginning to be accepted that handicapped people, whatever their disabilities, have the same needs and should have the same rights as anyone else to form loving and sexual relationships. The Spastics Society, for example, sponsored a film, 'Like Other People', which was shown on TV. It describes the hopes and feelings of a young man and woman who look forward to marriage and a home of their own although they are both severely handicapped. There is now extensive literature and research on the whole issue and society no longer has any excuse for ignoring the social and emotional needs of disabled people.

ALBANY TRUST

Albany Trust
16–20 Strutton Ground, London SW1P 2HP
Tel: 01-222 0701

The Trust was set up to carry out education and research into all aspects of socio-sexual problems. It will see any handicapped youngster or his parents who want individual counselling on particular problems. It believes that young handicapped people should have as normal a sexual life as is possible and that they have the same rights as anyone else in this respect. It is concerned about sex education for handicapped people in residential institutions and opportunities for them to develop loving relationships.

COMMITTEE ON SEXUAL PROBLEMS OF THE DISABLED
(SPOD)

Secretary, SPOD
183 Queensway, London W2 5HL
Tel: 01-727 4426

SPOD is an ad hoc committee of the National Fund for
Research into Crippling Diseases (1 Springfield Road,
Horsham, Sussex), comprising representatives of organizations concerned with the disabled, and individuals with
special experience in this field.

The primary aim of the Committee is to ensure that
disabled people – both physically and mentally handicapped – are enabled to express their sexuality to the full.
It seeks to achieve this aim by research, publicity and the
encouragement of counselling and advice services. It hopes
shortly to set up a referral centre.

Partnership and Marriage for the Subnormal?

Institute of Mental Subnormality
Wolverhampton Road, Kidderminster, Worcs. DY10 3PP
Tel: Kidderminster (0562) 850251

In the September 1975 issue of *Apex*, the journal of the
Institute of Mental Subnormality, Ann and Michael Croft
report on a survey of married couples in Wales of whom
one or both partners have been classified as severely
subnormal, educationally subnormal, or personality
disturbed. They give detailed examples of relationships
and conclude that the chances of happiness in marriage
for the subnormal appear to be greater than for the general
population.

Shoes

ODD SHOES SCHEME

Clarks Ltd, Street, Somerset, BA16 0YA
Tel: Street (045-84) 3131

Clarks Ltd operate an odd shoe scheme to supply pairs of

shoes where one shoe is a different size or fitting from the other. These are supplied in about nine styles each for boys and girls, and are illustrated in their brochure. The range is changed every year. The shoes are specially made so delivery is likely to take up to four working weeks. To help cover the extra cost, there is a 25 per cent surcharge added to the recommended retail price. Clarks cannot supply single shoes. All shoes are sold only through retail shops and they cannot sell direct to the public although they will help if you cannot find a retailer who will make these arrangements for you.

ORTHOPAEDIC ALTERATIONS

Fitting Services Manager
Clarks Ltd, Street, Somerset BA16 0YA
Tel: Street (045-84) 3131

The Craftor Repair Unit at Clarks is registered under the Department of Health and Social Security as a contractor for orthopaedic repairs and alterations. It can also undertake a wide range of work on any type of footwear, such as building up sections of a shoe or reinforcing the toe cap for children who drag their feet. The precise charge will depend on the size of the shoe, the quantity of materials required and the labour cost. The Craftor Repair Unit cannot accept orders direct from the public but any Clarks fitting specialist ought to be able to handle the order. For names of local Clarks fitting specialists, or when problems arise, you should write to Clarks.

SINGLE SHOES

Queen Elizabeth's Foundation
Leatherhead Court, Leatherhead, Surrey KT22 0BN
Tel: Oxshott 2204

Some children may need only one normal shoe, but due to manufacturing procedures it is usually impossible to buy single shoes. Queen Elizabeth's Foundation for the Disabled are now operating an odd shoe scheme. Anyone who wants to buy single shoes should write to Queen Elizabeth's Foundation for the Disabled stating the size, fitting, colour, style (and an alternative colour and style) and whether for men, women or children, for instance: child's left foot, size 6e, brown, sandal. The bill will be sent with the shoe. The maximum charge for a child's shoe in 1975 was £1. People can send any *new* odd shoes they have to the Foundation or take them to any of the Foundation establishments. The proceeds are devoted to the work of the Foundation.

SOLE MATES

Sole Mates Register
Mrs D. Lagden
29 Hillcrest Road, Walthamstow, London E17 4AP
Tel: 01-531 3067

Sole Mates started as a scheme for finding partners for people who needed odd shoes so that they could swop, sell or buy shoes and boots instead of perhaps having to buy two pairs of shoes and throw the odd ones away. It has now developed an information and advice service to help people for whom suitable partners could not be arranged. Mrs Lagden charges a registration fee of 40p to cover postage, etc. Please send a stamped addressed envelope when first writing to her.

Sterilization

The case of the mentally handicapped girl who was made a ward of court in order that the proposal to sterilize her should be considered in a court of law has drawn attention to the serious medical, social and moral problems raised by what *The Times* called 'serious, irreversible operations on minors for non-therapeutic reasons' (*Times Law Report*, 17 September 1975). At present no procedure exists by which such operations can be monitored and sanctioned only after consultation with all the people having responsibility for the child. After the Sheffield case, anyone who knows of a child who is threatened with sterilization can presumably apply for the child to be made a ward of court so that full consideration can be given to the proposal before the operation can be carried out. But this would depend on someone taking a special interest and disagreeing with the doctor concerned. In the Sheffield case this was the girl's shcool teacher and social worker. The National Council for Civil Liberties Report No. 14, *Sterilization of Minors* by Nic Madge (1976), comments on this discussion paper, explains the legal position and discusses the issues involved (price 20p; available from NCCL, 186 Kings Cross Road, London WC1X 9DE; tel: 01-278 4575).

In November 1975 the Department of Health and Social Security issued a discussion paper to health authorities, professional bodies and interested organizations about the whole question of arrangements for sterilization of children under sixteen.

Television

Both the BBC and ITV are devoting more attention to the needs of disabled people nowadays and it is worthwhile keeping an eye on your local programme information to find out what is going on. TV series come and go, but are often repeated, so if you've missed a programme the first time around there is always the possibility of a re-run, particularly if enough people write in to request it.

BBC Publications, PO Box 234, London SE1 3TH
Tel: 01-407 6961

The BBC Further Education Department frequently publishes information sheets and booklets in conjunction with these programmes and these may be on sale long after the series is off the air. One example is *I See What You Mean* (edited by Bill Northwood, 1975), a booklet for deaf people and their families and friends on living with deafness. This was first produced for a series of programmes of the same name. The editor has put together information, ideas and examples from people – deaf and hearing – who know their way around the silent or muted world. He hopes it will help those who want a few answers to questions, but have no idea what to ask and of whom. The booklet is available from bookshops or direct. (Price 85p, plus 26p postage.)

Two examples of programmes put out in 1976 may give some idea of television coverage of the problems of handicapped people. 'Contact' is a BBC TV series of ten twenty-five-minute programmes with the aim of informing disabled people, their families and those professionally concerned with helping them about progress towards integrating disabled and able-bodied members of the community. The programmes cover discussion of misconceptions and the unconsciously hurtful attitudes of able-bodied people towards those who are disabled, how to claim the bewildering variety of allowances or get help from the equally bewildering range of voluntary and statutory organizations offering help, as well as employment, leisure and holidays.

'Link' is a well-established monthly magazine programme for the disabled, first broadcast on the ATV channel in Birmingham. The producer, Richard Creasy, re-examines many of the traditional attitudes towards disability and emphasizes the importance of self-help. The first programme started by telling a fairy tale about a village which is run completely by the wheelchair users with the environment adapted accordingly: for example, doors are built five feet high. A few able-bodied people come to stay in the village and are soon dis-abled by the architecture. They are all marked by the dark bruises they carry on their foreheads from bumping into doors and low ceilings. They become known as the able-bodied disabled. Regular items on the programme will include a guide to aids, to income and welfare rights (produced with the help of the Disability Alliance) and book reviews. Each programme is complemented by an information sheet, giving details of the books and aids discussed, plus full details of the welfare rights items.

Transport

BRITISH RED CROSS SOCIETY

British Red Cross Society
9 Grosvenor Crescent, London SW1X 7EJ
Tel: 01-235 5454

> Some local branches of the Red Cross have volunteers who
> offer transport in their own cars to the disabled or handi-
> capped for a small charge towards the cost of petrol. If a
> driver is available they may arrange to take you for
> appointments, hospital visits and occasionally can even
> take families on holiday. The address of your local branch
> should be available in citizens advice bureaux or from
> the town hall or library.

SOCIAL SERVICES DEPARTMENT

> Some councils have special vehicles for the use of handi-
> capped people and can provide transport where necessary,
> particularly for taking handicapped children to and from
> clubs and on holiday and weekend visits.

TRANS-CARE INTERNATIONAL

Trans-Care International Ltd
Group House, Woodlands Avenue, Acton, London W3
Tel: 01-992 5077

> The service caters on a door-to-door basis anywhere in the
> world for the escort and care in transit of seriously ill,
> injured or disabled people including children of any age. It
> has its own fleet of road ambulances in this country and
> can arrange transport to and from other countries by
> special jet air ambulances or by scheduled flights or by
> special long-distance road ambulances. It claims to be
> able to arrange transport at very short notice to anywhere,
> with escort if necessary (see **Escorts**). Nursing-home
> facilities are avilable for over-night, short-stay or accident
> treatment. This is a commercial service and is certainly
> expensive, but the charges do not seem to be extortionate.

An example of 1975 prices: private ambulance transfer to or from Heathrow Airport and any London hospital, including one hour waiting time and help from the crew with formalities, cost £15.

Travel

AIR TRAVEL

British Airports Authority
2 Buckingham Gate, London SW1
Tel: 01-834 6621

The British Airports Authority with the Joint Committee on Mobility for the Disabled has produced a series of leaflets for disabled passengers describing the facilities of the seven airports which come under the authority (Aberdeen, Edinburgh, Gatwick, Glasgow, Heathrow, Prestwick and Stansted). The leaflets are available from the BAA itself or from the Central Council for the Disabled or the Disabled Living Foundation. They advise you to find out all the details (such as methods of transport to and from the aircraft) and compare the arrangements of the various airlines before choosing an airline and making a booking. Airlines must be given advance notice of the needs of handicapped people, particularly those in wheelchairs. You may be asked to get a doctor's certificate confirming that you are fit to travel. Internal flights on domestic airlines operate some fare concessions for blind travellers with a guide. *Care in the Air*, free from the Civil Aviation Authority, PO Box 41, Cheltenham, Glos., gives full information on air travel.

BUS TRAVEL

Local authorities have the power to operate a concessionary fares scheme for elderly and handicapped people. These usually arrange for people to apply for a permit giving them unlimited free travel (sometimes excluding rush hour). Blind people often get these even where no general scheme for the handicapped applies.

CAR TRAVEL

Disabled Living Foundation
346 Kensington High Street, London W14 8NS
Tel: 01-602 2491

There is a wide range of aids designed to make car travel more comfortable for disabled people, whether they are drivers or passengers. For instance, it is possible to convert car seats so that they can swing round and out beyond the doorway of the car to make it easier to get in and out. The D L F Information Service, List 8, on transport has details of these accessories.

Parking: Orange Badge Scheme. Disabled drivers, or drivers who regularly carry a handicapped person – adult or child – in their car, can get a special orange badge and orange disc which entitles them to parking concessions, such as parking on a yellow line or free parking at meters, as long as this does not cause any obstruction to other road users. The scheme applies throughout Britain, except in some inner London boroughs who have their own arrangements. You apply for the badge to your local social services department and will usually need a doctor's certificate. Blind people were also offered this concession for a trial period, ending July 1976, and this will probably be made permanent.

RAIL TRAVEL

CCD, 34 Eccleston Square, London SW1V 1PE
Tel: 01-821 1871

The Central Council for the Disabled produces a *Guide to London's Underground Stations* (1973) giving details of accessibility. Price 23p. Its *Guide to British Rail* (new edition 1977), a handbook for the disabled person, sets out details of the arrangements British Rail can make for handicapped travellers and access details including parking, refreshment and toilet facilities, telephone number of 300 major stations in Great Britain. Available free for 25p postage from CCD.

British Rail stress their anxiety to help disabled passengers and particularly ask to be notified in advance when a disabled person is travelling so that they can do everything possible to make sure they have a comfortable journey. They ask intending travellers to tell the manager of the departure station their name, date and expected time of arrival at the station, and to explain what assistance would be needed in getting on the train, and off at the other end. The new rolling stock just coming into service allows passengers unable to leave their wheelchair to travel in first-class coaches instead of having to travel in the guard's van as at present. Second-class fares for the wheelchair user and a companion are charged for this. If they have to remain in their chair during the journey and have to travel in the guard's van, the fare charged is now the child's half-fare, for both traveller and escort. Folding 'Mobyle' wheelchairs that can be lifted on to the train are available at forty-four stations and at others if requested in advance. Standard wheelchairs are available at 231 stations. There are special concessions for blind people travelling by British Rail (see chapter 2, **Blindness**, page 42).

Volunteers

More and more people who don't necessarily have any connection with the health or social services are coming forward to offer help to handicapped children. Volunteers of every age can be found helping out with varying degrees of satisfaction both on the part of the helper and the helped. If volunteer help is going to be useful, it is essential for everyone to know what is involved – exactly what kind of help is needed and the extent of the commitment to provide it and to keep on providing it. *The Use of Volunteers* (price 25p), covering all these points and with helpful tips on training, insurance, expenses, etc., is available from the Volunteer Centre (see below). If none of these sources listed here can help, don't overlook the possibility of asking one of the local comprehensive schools; they are often very pleased to have the opportunity of involving their pupils in community work. Local students' unions are also a good source of help.

COMMUNITY SERVICE VOLUNTEERS (CSV)

CSV, 237 Pentonville Road, London N1 9NJ
Tel: 01-278 6601

CSV is concerned with the involvement of young people in every aspect of community service, including work with the mentally handicapped. It offers opportunities for long-term service – between four months and a year – during which the volunteers receive board, lodging and pocket money. CSVs have been attached in this way to hospitals, schools and special units for the handicapped. CSV also runs an information service for schools, producing kits, describing projects done in different areas. It has a special programme to discover ways of involving the disadvantaged, including the educationally subnormal and the mentally handicapped themselves, in service to the community. Handicapped young people aged sixteen and above are welcomed as volunteers.

INTER-ACTION

Inter-Action Trust Ltd
Wilkin Street, London NW5
Tel: 01-267 1422

Inter-Action is a charitable trust set up in 1968 under the energetic and imaginative leadership of Ed Berman, with the aim of involving people in the improvement of their own communities. Amongst a whole range of community activities, they offer an advisory service giving free advice to community and voluntary groups with organizational difficulties, help with film and video-tape productions, group work training, and all kinds of play projects, including a farm which they set up in derelict buildings in a Camden back street.

TOC H

Toc H
1 Forest Close, Wendover, Aylesbury, Bucks HP22 6BT
Tel: Wendover (0296) 623911

> This is a large Christian-based voluntary social service movement, sixty years old in 1975, with members of every race and creed. It has refused to become over-specialized and its 12 000 members are always willing to help where social services leave a gap. Branches will do whatever they can to help their local communities. Activities include summer projects for young people, such as helping to run playschemes or holidays and organizing discos for physically handicapped young people (see chapter 7, **Disco**, page 333). Toc H members started the first hospital broadcasting and one branch runs its own hospital television station.

VOLUNTEER BUREAUX

> Local councils of social service may run volunteer bureaux which act as clearing houses between people wishing to offer help and people in need. Requests for help are mainly channelled through social workers or GPs. A bureau may be able to find volunteers to help with handicapped children. They can often offer help with escort duties and transport.

VOLUNTEER CENTRE

Volunteer Centre
29/33 Lower Kings Road, Berkhamsted, Herts HP4 2AB
Tel: Berkhamsted (044-27) 73311

> The Centre was established with a grant from the Voluntary Services Unit of the Home Office to develop and strengthen relationships between volunteers and the statutory services. It intends to help statutory departments develop initiatives and to coordinate and develop non-statutory efforts.

Wheelchairs

Any child who will always need to use a wheelchair can get it prescribed under the National Health Service by a GP or hospital consultant. Only a limited range of chairs is available on prescription but local organizations, such as the Rotary Clubs or Round Tables, sometimes present more expensive chairs to families who cannot afford to buy them. There is a wide range of chairs available on the market – battery driven chairs of all types, including the Chairmobile (a revoluntary design created by Lord Snowdon), self-propelled chairs and chairs which need someone to push them. Some of these can be seen at the Disabled Living Foundation and other aids centres. The Disabled Living Foundation also has lists of suppliers of wheelchairs, pushchairs and accessories, including the the Quiklock clamp which can clamp chairs to keep them secure in vans, ambulances, etc.

Disabled Living Foundation
346 Kensington High Street, London W14 8NS
Tel: 01-602 2491

The National Fund for Research into Crippling Diseases has funded a two-year research project on children's wheelchair design and in the magazine, *Action*, March 1975 (price 25p plus postage), Dr Stephen Jarvis, the medical research fellow in charge, described some of the limitations he had already discovered which were inhibiting the children's mobility.

Action
1 Springfield Road, Horsham, Sussex RH12 2PN
Tel: Horsham (0403) 64101

If you are going to need a wheelchair for only a few weeks or months, your doctor may be able to recommend you for a chair on loan from the local council or Area Health Authority. Some local Red Cross branches are able to hire out wheelchairs on short-term loan perhaps for a day's shopping or for a visit. The Disabled Living Foundation lists include details of commercial hirers.

The British Red Cross Society has produced a very useful booklet called *People in Wheelchairs, Hints for Helpers* (15p, plus postage).

British Red Cross Society
9 Grosvenor Crescent, London SW1X 7EJ
Tel: 01-235 5454

See also **Aids**

Wills

It is always best to take legal advice before making a will and absolutely essential if parents want a handicapped child to be a beneficiary.

The National Society for Mentally Handicapped Children includes some advice in its *A-Z: Your Questions Answered* (1972) and Network has produced an advice pamphlet and suitable will form, prepared on its behalf by a barrister.

NSMHC, Pembridge Hall, 17 Pembridge Square, London W2 4EP
Tel: 01-229 8941/01-727 0536

Network, 23 Hand Court, London WC1V 6JF

4   Health Services

Structure
People
Therapy and treatment
Support services

Structure

Every parent with a handicapped child is likely to have frequent contact with the National Health Service and the people running it at certain stages of their child's life. For some parents, the NHS will be their main source of help of every kind, not just medical treatment.

The administrative structure of the NHS in England, Wales and Scotland was reorganized by Acts of Parliament from April 1974. Unless you know how an organization is constructed and who is responsbile for taking what decisions, you may experience frustration and a sense of being manipulated when things go wrong in your dealings with it. So we have tried to give you an idea of what all those initials stand for, what the committees and teams are supposed to be doing and what you can do about it if you aren't happy about what is going on. The Court Report, *Fit for the Future* (HMSO), presented to Parliament in December 1976, is a major review of the child health services and contains important sections on handicapped children.

We cannot tell you what to do about medical problems; we have tried to let you know who *can* tell you.

Department of Health and Social Security (DHSS)

DHSS, Alexander Fleming House
Elephant and Castle, London SE1 6BY
Tel: 01-407 5522

The Secretary of State for Social Services is responsible for health services in England; the Secretaries of State for

Wales and Scotland are responsible for their own health services. They are answerable to Parliament for the way in which the services are operated. The Department of Health and Social Security carries out national planning and allocates resources to the regions.

Regional Health Authorities (RHAs)

England is divided into fourteen Regional Health Authorities, each of which contains at least one university medical school. There are no RHAs for Wales, nor is there any tier of authorities corresponding to them in Scotland.

The RHA is accountable to central government for the way in which it plans services throughout the region and how it allocates resources and delegates responsibility to its Area Authorities. Each RHA is made up of Area Authorities – the number varies from three to eleven within a region. The only executive function carried out by the RHA itself is major building work.

All members of the RHA are appointed by the Secretary of State but, with the exception of the Chairman who is paid on a part-time basis, they receive no salary. RHAs are served by professional staff.

Area Health Authorities (AHAs)

There are ninety Area Health Authorities in England whose boundaries generally match those of local government: the county or metropolitan district. In London, AHA boundaries correspond to one or a group of London boroughs. Wales has eight AHAs, corresponding to the county boundaries, which report direct to the Welsh Office from which they receive central guidance and resources. The agencies in Scotland which are equivalent to the AHAs are the Health Boards, of which there are fifteen, directly accountable to the Scottish Office. The Health Board areas correspond to local government areas. The only exception is the Greater Glasgow Region which is split between four Health Boards.

AHAs are the operational authority of the National Health Service. They must assess needs, see that health services in their area are properly run and plan for future developments. They are not, however, the direct employers of family practitioners in any branch of the service (see **Family practitioner committees**, page 204).

AHAs have about fifteen members, appointed by the RHA; at least four of whom are nominated by the local authority and are usually councillors. The chairman of the AHA is appointed by the Secretary of State after consultation with the chairman of the relevant RHA and there is provision in the legislation for him to be paid on a part-time basis. Members are not paid any salary. A fulltime staff of civil servants serves the AHAs.

Health districts

Over half the AHAs are too large for the day-to-day running of health services. So these AHAs delegate this to health districts. The AHA decides on the number of districts in its area and there may, in fact, be anything from two to six districts serving populations between 80 000 and 510 000.

The District Management Team (DMT) consists of a GP, the community physician, a consultant, a nurse, an administrator and a treasurer. DMTs may set up care planning teams concerned with the health care of particular groups of patients, such as children or people with a mental or physical handicap.

These teams are the people who should be on the receiving end of comments on the way the service is running. One parents' group whose concern was handicapped children produced a detailed report for their local child health care planning team about the needs of parents whose babies were handicapped. They covered everything from how parents should be told that their baby was handicapped to suggestions for training in the needs of handicapped children for GPs. They made it clear that their remarks were intended to be constructive; where they were critical they suggested some solution.

Hospitals

The hospital and specialist services of the National Health Service provide all forms of hospital care and treatment in general and special hospitals for in-patients, out-patients and day patients. They also provide specialist opinion and treatment in clinics and, in special cases, can visit patients in their own homes. Every health district has at least one large general hospital and may also have a number of small local hospitals such as maternity and geriatric hospitals or others specializing in one type of treatment. There are thirty-four teaching hospitals (twenty-five in London, nine elsewhere in England) which are actually groups of hospitals with branches and treatment centres of different kinds, totalling 140 establishments.

There are a number of children's hospitals – some of of them world famous – but the trend now is towards children's departments in general hospitals catering for all sick children from the district. Some hospitals have particularly strong specialist departments which accept cases from the whole region. Children's departments include in-patient beds, day beds, out-patient units and comprehensive assessment centres for handicapped children. Increasingly, they are providing overnight accommodation for parents of young children. Even when a child needs treatment which can be carried out only in hospital, more and more investigations and treatment, including certain surgical operations, are being carried out on a day basis.

The Central Office of Information pamphlet, *Health Services in Britain* (HMSO, 1974, price 81p), says that unrestricted visiting helps to give the children – especially long-stay patients – as full and happy a life as possible. It adds: 'Parents of young children are encouraged to stay in the hospital with their children during acute illness, during comprehensive assessment, and from time to time during long-stay care.' A survey published by the National Association for the Welfare of Children in Hospital in 1975 into 800 children's wards showed that 19 per cent permit twenty-four-hour visiting and the majority allow between seven and ten hours a day. But these figures disguised the fact that some hospitals did not want visiting during meal times and before 9.30 a.m. (although the children may have been woken at 6.30 a.m.) or after 6.00 p.m. Parents had found it difficult to visit children on the day of their operation even when this looked possible on paper. NAWCH surveys of visiting hours are published regularly.

Hospital appointments

When we went in to see the specialist I can clearly remember it must be six years ago now, we waited $2\frac{1}{2}$ hours. Now $2\frac{1}{2}$ hours with a broken neck is pretty bad; $2\frac{1}{2}$ hours with two broken legs is pretty bad, $2\frac{1}{2}$ hours with a stomach ache is probably not too bad, but $2\frac{1}{2}$ hours to a mentally handicapped child is murder. . . .

There can be few parents who would disagree with this mother talking to the interviewer in *Something Wrong?* (edited by Liz Cooper and Roberta Henderson, Arrow Books, 1973). Getting to the hospital with a handicapped child for an appointment can be one long obstacle course, but help may be available.

APPOINTMENTS

An appointments system which in general is satisfactory may still be distressing for a handicapped child. As you will see under **Complaints**, page 208 below, you should start by approaching the person in charge – for instance, the consultant responsible for the clinic. On this matter the district management team, and the community physician in particular, would be the next step. Many Community Health Councils have actively taken up this kind of issue.

BABYSITTING

One of the organizations listed in chapter 3 under **Baby-sitting**, **Help** or **Volunteers**, may be able to find a babysitter to look after other children at home and save you dragging them along to hospital appointments. Don't be diffident about approaching them.

TRANSPORT

It is government policy that Area Health Authorities should provide special transport 'when it is medically necessary' so that patients can keep appointments for treatment (section 21, 'Travelling expenses and transport for hospital patients and visits', HM(73)20, HMSO, 1973). The social worker at the hospital should be able to make arrangements for transport directly from the hospital or to put you in touch with voluntary help. If not, try one of the organizations mentioned in **Escorts**, **Help** and **Volunteers** in chapter 3.

Sally Baldwin of the University of York has done a study of the mobility needs of handicapped children for the Family Fund Research Project. She found that three major problems can arise with the AHAs' interpretation of their duty.

1. *The definition of medical necessity.* Some AHAs will not provide transport for children who can walk even if they are blind, deaf, mentally handicapped or hyperactive. Others exclude visits to assessment centres and outpatient clinics. One local spina-bifida association made this comment after reporting that some parents had been told that they no longer qualify for ambulance transport to outpatient appointments: 'I wonder if those responsible for this decision have ever tried getting onto a bus with a handicapped eight-year-old, major buggy, and a bag for spare nappies, etc., in the pouring rain, after waiting half an hour for the bus to appear.'

2. *Distance.* Ambulance transport is arranged in circuits and a child who does not live on a circuit – whether or not he is within the hospital's area – may be refused transport. The greater the distance, the worse the problem is likely to be.

3. *Inconvenience*. Even if you qualify for hospital transport, the service is often inconvenient and unreliable. One mother told Sally Baldwin a typical story of the misery of an hour-long journey that would take ten minutes by car. In any case, the ambulances used are often unsuitable for handicapped children.

Parents who have difficulty over transport to hospital for their child's treatment should first approach the senior administrator of the AHA. If you cannot convince him that transport is 'medically necessary', the support of the consultant in charge of the treatment may carry some weight.

FARES

Patients can claim a refund of travelling expenses to and from hospitals or treatment centres where the cost of these causes hardship. This may include the fares of someone who is accompanying a child. The hospital (probably the medical social worker) can advise on how to claim and provide the necessary form.

People on supplementary benefit or family income supplement should claim automatically.

In practice refunds are not available unless a family's income is very low indeed. There is no other statutory help for parents who may have to travel considerable distances to bring a child for regular treatments. One example quoted by NAWCH was a child living in Kent who had to come to London three times a week for renal dialysis and whose fare bill was well over £1000 a year. Voluntary organizations may be able to help. If the Family Fund has checked that no help is available from any voluntary or official source, it may be prepared to make a grant towards the cost of fares.

WAITING ROOMS

Waiting time in many hospitals is made more tolerable if the waiting room has a supply of toys to help keep the children occupied. This is the kind of thing the League of Hospital Friends or other local group may be glad to provide if they are told that there is a need.

Hospital visiting

Handicapped children may have to spend long periods in hospital, often at a considerable distance from their homes. Although it is generally agreed that it is essential for parents to keep in close contact with their children and to visit them as often as possible, these frequent visits may place a very heavy burden on the family. Quite apart from the stress and difficulty of making suitable arrangements at home, the cost may make it impossible for parents to visit as often as they would like. In the survey conducted by Sally Baldwin of York University she found that 75 per cent of the parents of children who had been admitted to hospital more than five times had experienced difficulties with visiting. However, very little official help towards payment of fares is available.

Parents should discuss any problems with the social worker at the hospital who should know about all sources of help – official and unofficial. The support of the social worker will probably be needed for any application.

Families on supplementary benefit or family income supplement, or those who are not in full-time work and have a very low income may get help from the Supplementary Benefit Commission (see page 113).

Local authority social services have discretion to give financial help to parents who want to visit their child in hospital and may do so in very exceptional cases.

Some hospitals have charitable endowments and funds from which they could draw money to help parents who find it hard to pay for visits to a handicapped child.

Local organizations, particularly branches of societies for handicapped children, may be a useful source of information and practical help.

The Family Fund has been able to give some grants to parents for visits if they have not been able to get help from anywhere else. This has included children in long-stay hospitals who are not, in theory, eligible for help from the Fund. For example, Sally Baldwin, in her work at York University, quotes the case of a child of six with spina bifida whose family lived in Dundee and who spent four months in hospital in Sheffield. The Family Fund made a grant of £200 towards the family's visiting expenses.

The National Council of Social Service has published a concise leaflet giving notes on help with hospital visiting which are intended as a source of reference for workers in the field of child health and for social workers. These are being distributed by NAWCH who have been campaigning since 1972 to get proper statutory recognition of the needs of parents for help with visiting. As a result of their fares inquiry they came to the conclusion that parents should automatically get assistance from the government towards fares whenever the cost of visits is higher than the cost of keeping the child at home (on the basis of the estimate of cost used by the Supplementary Benefit Commission). NAWCH would always like to hear from parents about special problems: they will help with advice whenever they can and all the cases give them more ammunition in their campaign (see page 199).

LEAGUE OF HOSPITAL FRIENDS

League of Hospital Friends
44 Fulham Road, London SW3 6HH
Tel: 01-584 7713

Many hospitals have a local group of well-wishers who work to raise funds, run voluntary trolley sales services in the wards selling magazines, sweets, etc., provide extra comforts and special equipment for the hospital. One of the first groups to be associated with a hospital for mentally handicapped children – at the old Fountains Hospital, Tooting – campaigned for a sea-side branch for the hospital and raised a large part of the funds towards it. Two groups in Southampton have built swimming pools for long-stay hospitals. The League of Hospital Friends has over a thousand affiliated groups and can offer advice together with a model constitution and an insurance policy to cover volunteers in the wards.

NATIONAL ASSOCIATION FOR THE WELFARE OF CHILDREN IN HOSPITAL (NAWCH)

NAWCH, Exton House, 7 Exton Street, London SE1 8UE
Tel: 01-261 1738

NAWCH is well known for its campaign to allow unrestricted visiting of children in hospital and for hospitals and medical staff to recognize that parents have a vital part to play in the care of their sick children. Now that this battle has been won in theory, if not in practice, NAWCH has extended its activities: it campaigns for improvements in children's hospital facilities and child health care in every way and it provides an information and counselling service. Local groups, as well as campaigning, run schemes to help mothers with sick children, such as hospital play schemes, babysitting services, toy libraries, and so on. They may organize visitors for unvisited children. NAWCH produces a useful reading list which includes a leaflet for parents on hospital admissions, describing procedures and including a colouring card for children, called 'Your child in hospital' (price 8p, plus postage). *Simon Goes to Hospital*, a comic for very young children, sets out all the events until Simon is discharged (5p, plus postage). A children's hospital colouring book costs 13p, plus postage. It also publishes reports, survey and reprints of specialist articles, which include a paper on the special needs of long-stay children.

See also chapter 3, **Residential care,** HOSPITALS, page 167.

Family health centres

Most districts have a network of family health centres where clinics are held at which the physical, mental and emotional development of babies and young children is watched and measured. At one end of the scale, this may be a question of weighing the baby every week and making sure that he has his injections at the right time. But at the, other end of the scale, many clinics carry out regular standardized tests on every aspect of a baby's development (see chapter 1, **Screening**, page 12).

Family health centres are staffed by doctors and health visitors who can give advice on all aspects of family health and welfare, including, for instance, questions about feeding and nutrition or dental care.

Centres often hold separate sessions for everything from family planning to sale of welfare foods, so you would always be well advised to check the times or make an appointment before you go along.

No clinic ought to turn away a mother who is worried about her child on the grounds that she has come at the 'wrong time' – but if you do just turn up you may have to be prepared for a long wait.

Dental service

The general dental service is part of the National Health Service and, as in the family doctor service, there is complete freedom of choice by patients of dentists and by dentists of patients. Patients do not register with a dentist. There is no charge for dental services for children.

In addition to the general dental service, children may have dental examinations and treatment arranged through the school health service and treatment may also be carried out at dental hospitals or departments as part of the hospital service.

DO HANDICAPPED CHILDREN HAVE SPECIAL PROBLEMS ABOUT DENTAL TREATMENT?

Handicapped children do not necessarily have special problems of tooth decay although children with some conditions, such as Down's Syndrome, are more likely to have irregular teeth. But, nevertheless, many parents of handicapped children find it very difficult to see that their child has proper dental care. Mrs Eileen Jaffe, Consultant Senior Lecturer of the Dental Department for Children, Guy's Hospital, London SE1 1YR, identifies three main categories of handicap which make it particularly difficult for any dentist to treat a handicapped child:

1 Any physical condition which might interfere with actual technical dental procedure. For instance, a child who suffers from sudden random movements of the head or limbs.

2 Any condition which might cause a risk to the child's health while he is having treatment, such as haemophilia or some heart conditions.

3 A mental or emotional condition which means that there is little chance of making the child understand what is going on and getting him to cooperate actively. Autistic and severely mentally handicapped children are likely to come into this group.

DO HANDICAPPED CHILDREN GET PROPER DENTAL TREATMENT?

The Department of Children's Dentistry at Guy's Hospital carried out a study to discover the need and the demand for dental treatment among physically and mentally or multiply handicapped children. It found that even though the dental needs of handicapped children are similar to those of normal children, they are likely to receive much less treatment. For instance, 72 per cent of the decayed teeth of handicapped children had not been treated in comparison with 32 per cent of decayed teeth in normal children. It was found that mentally or multiply handicapped children were likely to have treatment only in an emergency, such as having a tooth out under a general anaesthetic. This was less true of physically handicapped children who are generally easier to treat – the percentage of those who received *regular* dental care was double that of the other handicapped groups.

For many families with a handicapped child the immediate need may not be dental treatment itself, but becoming used to the idea that regular dental care is as essential for the child as other kinds of therapy. The trouble is that parents with a handicapped child often have so many other problems to worry about that it is only too easy for the child's mouth to be neglected. This may happen even when the child is in pain if he has difficulty in telling anyone about it. One examination of mentally handicapped adults who had showed no sign of being in pain found that, without anyone being aware of it, many of them had conditions such as abscesses and bad decay which normally cause severe toothache.

WHAT CAN BE DONE TO TREAT HANDICAPPED CHILDREN?

The Guy's Hospital Unit has worked out a programme of treatment by which, in their experience, all but about 8 per cent of severely disordered children can accept routine dental treatment, including simple extractions.

The child is not asked even to open his mouth at the first interview. If there is likely to be difficulty over this, they usually give the mother a dental mirror and show her how to practise at home so that by careful, persistent and patient repetition the child can get used to the idea of having his mouth examined.

When the child is first introduced to the drill it is fitted with a rubber cup and used to tickle his fingers. Only when he is reassured that it doesn't present a threat is it gently carried to a front tooth and gradually by stages further into the mouth.

Mrs Jaffe says that a very young child should be examined while he sits on his mother's lap with his head resting in the crook of her arm, 'or, if the child is still unwilling, lying flat on the mother's lap with the shouting end on the lap of the examiner'.

WHERE CAN PARENTS GET THIS SORT OF TREATMENT FOR THEIR CHILD?

It is now generally recognized by the dental service that handicapped children need to have good dental care, not just so that they have a healthy mouth and teeth, but also so that the unsightly appearance of diseased teeth and gums and the accompanying bad breath do not add to their rejection and social isolation.

Every area has an area dental officer with an overall responsibility for dental services and he should certainly be aware of these special needs. He ought to be able to help you find a dentist who is trained and prepared to take on the more taxing job of looking after a handicapped child's teeth. The Guy's Unit has a mobile dental unit for handicapped children which treats about a thousand children from five London boroughs through the AHA. Other areas may well have similar arrangements.

Word gets around parents' groups about dentists and at least one local guide names the dentist in their area who is particularly good at treating handicapped children. So ask other parents.

Every student at the Guy's Hospital dental school – the largest in the country – has some training in the treatment of handicapped children. Mrs Jaffe and her colleagues receive an increasing number of invitations to travel to different areas giving information about their special experience in this field. A reprint of one two-part talk by Mrs Jaffe and her colleague Mrs Pool is available in the *Royal Society of Health Journal* for August 1975.

Although the Guy's Unit cannot treat every handicapped child in Great Britain, any parent who cannot get help from his AHA or find a dentist locally who will take the extra trouble needed to treat his child can contact them. Mrs Jaffe has said that they would do their best to fit them in for treatment.

WHAT CAN PARENTS DO THEMSELVES ABOUT THEIR CHILDREN'S TEETH?

Mrs Jaffe recommends that all handicapped children should take fluoride tablets from birth until they are at least twelve years old.

If it is difficult to keep the child's mouth open while his teeth are cleaned, she suggests propping them open with a metal thimble. Where a child is helpless, it may be easier to clean his teeth if the handle of the toothbrush is softened by heat until it can be bent to a more convenient angle. Sometimes it is easier if you stand behind the child to brush his teeth and lean his head back against you. Parents can massage a child's teeth and gums with a piece of flannel wrapped round their finger.

Mrs Jaffe says that dental disease is almost entirely preventable and that proper diet is the most important means of avoiding decayed teeth. She has found that parents will take part 'eagerly and diligently' in a dental health programme for a handicapped child.

The philosophy of the Unit is that any plan for treating a handicapped child 'should always err on the optimistic side'. Few parents of handicapped children are promised a complete cure for their child's handicap on their endless round of visits to doctors. In contrast, a dentist is almost certainly able to cure whatever is wrong with a child's teeth. So looked at from a positive point of view, a visit to the dentist can be a very cheerful experience for a parent of a handicapped child.

The Unit has produced *A Guide to the Care of Your Child's Mouth,* an attractive illustrated booklet with large print which explains basic dental care to the parents of handicapped children in the simplest possible terms.

Dental Department for Children
Guy's Hospital, London SE1 1YR

Family practitioner committees

GPs, dentists, opticians and pharmacists have always been self-employed. Family practitioner committees contract the services of all family practitioners in England and Wales – GPs, dental and ophthalmic practitioners and pharmacists in retail practice. This is done by the Health Boards in Scotland. The committees are directly responsible to the DHSS for the way these services are arranged in their area. The areas have the same boundaries as the AHAs. Family practitioner committees are responsible for disciplinary proceedings involving the practitioners who are under contract to them.

School health service

Since the reorganization of the health service, local education authorities are no longer responsible for the school health service and AHAs must make arrangements for the medical and dental inspection and treatment of schoolchildren, including handicapped children in special schools. AHAs must provide staff, such as physiotherapists and speech therapists, where they are needed in special schools, as well as nurses and dentists. In some cases therapists will be in school for certain sessions, in others they will be employed by the AHA to work full time in one school.

Parents who are worried about a shortage or complete lack of physiotherapy, speech therapy and so on in their child's special school must therefore approach the AHA, not the local education authority. However, it would be worth trying to get the school governors to take this up as well.

The Community Health Council (see below) ought to be concerned about any lack of facilities in the school health service.

Community Health Councils (CHCs)

Community Health Councils are independent statutory bodies set up and paid for by the RHA. In Scotland Local Health Councils have similar functions. Their purpose is to monitor and evaluate local health services on behalf of the consumer. Although they have not yet had time to test their strength, CHCs have the potential to guarantee a genuinely democratic form of consultation for the community on local health services. They have important rights: the right of access to National Health Services premises, to obtain facts and information and to receive prior notice of any proposed changes which would create 'any substantial development of the health services in the Council's district'. If reasonable access to premises or information is withheld, then the CHC may go to the RHA or to the Secretary of State to obtain their rights. CHC members are local people who are appointed because they already have some special knowledge of the area. These powers can put them in a very strong position in commenting on the priorities and plans of the administrators and pointing out where they fail to meet local needs.

At least once a year the CHC has to publish a report on what it has been doing, with any criticisms of the local health services, to which the AHA must publish a reply.

Each health district has a Community Health Council, but the Council deals direct with the AHA. CHCs have their own premises – ideally on neutral territory and in a position where members of the public can easily call in. Their meetings are open to the public. They appoint their own paid staff; Council members are unpaid. The size of the CHC is decided by the RHA and may vary from eighteen to thirty members. Half of the members of each council are nominated by the local authorities concerned with the district and are usually councillors, appointed on a political basis. At least one third are nominated by voluntary organizations concerned locally with the NHS, such as the Women's Royal Voluntary Service, Mind or the National Association for the Welfare of Children in Hospital. The remainder are appointed by the RHA.

Many CHCs have formed sub-committees which may co-opt members with specialist interests; mental health and handicap are the kind of areas where a number of outside interests may well overlap with health services.

CHCs are intended to be more than a channel for complaints, but they should certainly be prepared to involve themselves in practical details – appointment systems, the state of hospital catering, the absence of toys in waiting rooms – as well as momentous policy proposals. You should be able to find the address of your CHC in the phone book, local library, post office, etc.

We have talked casually to people who have been involved with CHCs in different parts of the country during their early stages. Reactions vary from contemptuous criticism to glowing enthusiasm. The explanation is undoubtedly that CHCs are as energetic or as feeble as their members. Individual parents with a handicapped child ought to be able to look to their CHC for support and understanding in putting things right, clearing up mis-understandings or filling in gaps in the service. Any local groups formed by parents with handicapped children can try to gain a place for one of their members on the council or as a co-opted member of a sub-committee.

In February 1976 *The Times* reported Dr David Owen, Minister of State for Health, as saying: 'I am a tremendous supporter of CHCs. I think they have been one of the most successful aspects of the health service reorganization.'

CHC News
126 Albert Street, London NW1 7NF
Tel: 01-267 6111

A steering committee for a proposed national organization for CHCs began work in March 1975 and at a conference in November 1976 decided that a permanent national body should be set up. This preliminary work was funded by the DHSS, who have also provided the finance for *CHC News*, a monthly newsletter for members of CHCs, professional and voluntary organizations and anyone else interested. It contains information about the Health Service, parlia-mentary and legal reports and provides a forum for the exchange of ideas, views and practice generally, including advice about how to get things done. It costs £2.50 a year. Associated with *CHC News* is an information service which can give advice on practical problems of CHC work and sources of reference. It publishes a *Directory of Community Health Councils*, regularly updated, which gives details of addresses and membership of all councils (price 60p, including postage). Both the steering committee and *CHC News* have offices at the King's Fund Centre pending the permanent establishment of a national organization.

Complaints about the Health Service

If you want to complain about something that happened at a hospital, clinic, health centre or surgery write direct to them in the first place. If their answer is unsatisfactory you can take it further.

For complaints about a hospital or clinic, write to the district or area administrator. The family practitioner committee deals with complaints about GPs, dentists, opticians or pharmacists. Always send a copy of a letter of complaint to the CHC.

To go one step higher: from the AHA you can appeal to the Health Service Commissioner or from the family practitioner committee to the Secretary of State.

HEALTH SERVICE COMMISSIONERS

Health Service Commissioner for England
Church House, Great Smith Street, London SW1P 3BW
Tel: 01-212 7676

Health Service Commissioner for Wales
3rd Floor, Queen's Court, Plymouth Street, Cardiff CF1 4DA
(Also has an office at Church House)
Tel: Cardiff (0222) 394621

Health Service Commissioner for Scotland
71 George Street, Edinburgh EH2 3EE
(Also has an office at Church House)
Tel: 031-225 7465

England, Scotland and Wales each have their own Health Service Commissioner who can investigate complaints from members of the public who feel that they have suffered injustice or hardship as a result of:

(a) a failure in a service provided by a health authority
(b) a failure by one of these authorities to provide a service which it has a duty to provide
(c) maladministration affecting any other action taken by or on behalf of one of these authorities.

Complaints should reach the Commissioner within one year of the events to which they relate and they must first have been brought to the attention of the authority responsible for the service involved, who have to be given an adequate opportunity to investigate the matter and reply.

The Commissioner can act only within certain defined areas; he cannot, for instance, investigate purely clinical matters nor the services provided by practitioners who are under contract to the family practitioner committees or, in Scotland, the Health Boards.

So before you take a complaint to the Commissioner, look carefully at his terms of reference. A leaflet should be available in citizens advice bureaux, local libraries, and so on, or you can get one direct from the Commissioner's office.

PATIENTS' ASSOCIATION

Patients' Association
Suffolk House, Banbury Road, Oxford
Tel: Oxford (0865) 50306

This is the only association that represents the views of patients in the National Health Service. It is independent of government, the health profession and the drugs industry, and is financed by members' subscriptions and donations. It takes up causes such as the implementation of the DHSS circular on teaching and the right of patients to be consulted where students are carrying out or observing treatment. It keeps a watching brief on patients' interests, particularly on complaints procedures. It helps individual patients with difficulties in their medical treatment and has published a series of leaflets on patients' rights and medical procedure. One of these, *Can I Insist?* (price 20p, plus postage), sets out the thirty commonest queries the Association receives from worried patients and gives practical answers.

'Which' survey

In 1975 *Which,* the consumer magazine, published two excellent reports on the National Health Service. The first in April 1975 explains how the NHS works and has useful advice on how to make your views about local health services known. The second, in August 1975, examines how well the service works and its regional variations. It concluded: 'There are big variations among the health regions in the amount of money spent and the facilities provided. So the standard of care the NHS provides for you may depend very much on where you live.'

Which is obtainable only by subscription to the Consumers' Association, but it is usually available in the reference section of the public library.

Consumers' Association
14 Buckingham Street, London WC2N 6DS
Tel: 01-839 1222

People

Community physician

The administrative staff of the AHA must include a doctor who is a specialist in community medicine to have overall charge of all child health services, including the school health service.

At district level, a district community physician (DCP) of consultant status is employed by the AHA as part of the district management team. He is involved in planning and coordinating services and particularly in the health care planning teams. As a specialist in community medicine, he can advise his clinical colleagues in the district – GPs and consultants – on community health care. He is in charge of preventive services in the district, including vaccination, immunization and screening. He may also be in charge of the local school health service. School health service functions which are still the responsibility of the local education authority will be under his supervision and may, in fact, be carried out by him.

To sum up then, the DCP has probably the greatest influence on the planning and priorities of the local health services and the philosophy underlying them, particularly as they affect children.

Consultants and specialists

These are the top medical posts in the hospital service and consultants are often in charge of a department or unit. They may have part-time appointments and are seldom in one hospital all the time. It is worth remembering that though you may be given an appointment to Mr X's or Dr Y's clinic, you may in fact see one of his registrars (full-time experienced doctors working their way up to a consultant's post). Mr X's clinic may be hospital shorthand for a clinic under his general oversight but in which he sees only a few special cases.

In many hospitals, the doctors now wear identity labels but, if not, and you are in any doubt, check on whom you are talking to before you start. It is an all too common discourtesy for the person conducting the consultation not to introduce himself or to explain if he is standing in for someone. This is very disconcerting for anyone who assumes that he is talking to the person in whose name the appointment was made.

Family doctors

You can choose a family doctor (general practitioner or GP) from the list compiled by the local family practitioner committee and displayed at the post office. You are entitled to visit him first, before making up your mind, and the doctor, too, is entitled to refuse you, without having to give a reason. If you have any trouble finding a doctor, the family practitioner committee will be able to help you. It is still the case that some areas of the country are very badly supplied with doctors. *Which* found that in 1975 over a quarter of GPs in the West Midlands had more than 3000 patients on their lists, whereas in the South West, only one doctor in twelve had as many.

Your GPs recommendation is needed for many medical and social services – for most hospital treatment, for some national insurance benefits, for home nursing and often for home help, laundry and other services offered by the local authority social services department.

More GPs nowadays work in group practices or health centres; you must still register as a patient. A group practice is a sort of halfway house between the conventional GP partnership and a health centre set up by the AHA. The work is shared among four or more doctors and they may employ a nurse or social worker. Health centres, built and maintained by the AHA, are staffed by GPs, dentists, midwives, pharmacists, social workers and nurses, all under the one roof.

You can change your doctor if you want to. If you or the doctor moves or if the doctor agrees, you can register with a new doctor straight away. If you have some other reason for changing doctors, you can still do so by informing the family practitioner committee but the transfer will then take at least a fortnight.

Health visitors

Health visitors are state registered nurses (SRNs) who have taken special extra training. They are employed by the AHA. A good one can provide an invaluable service, not only to mothers and young children, but also to the whole family, including older people. They can offer advice about health, management of young children, child development, home safety and so on. They can also help you to get help from other sources, particularly social services departments. They are usually based on family health centres, but some are attached to group practices and health centres.

The criticisms expressed by one parents' group are not untypical of the experience of parents of handicapped children:

Many parents, both with and without handicapped children, we believe, are concerned about the level of service given by health visitors. We would like to see at least one, possibly two health visitors assigned specifically to the care of handicapped children, with training in the problems of handicapped children and their parents. We believe this service, like so many others, is grossly understaffed for the population it is meant to serve.

Home nurse

It is the duty of the AHAs to organize a home nursing service for sick people who need skilled nursing care at home. They may arrange for voluntary organizations like the Queen's Institute of District Nursing to do this work for them.

Home (or district) nurses work under a doctor's direction and arrangements for them to call are usually made through your GP. In many areas they are in short supply.

Medical social worker (MSW)

Most people are familiar with the 'lady almoner's' function in a hospital; nowadays this title has generally been dropped, and its place taken by 'medical social worker'. MSWs ought to be able to help parents who have difficulty in coping with hospital visits by arranging transport or help with fares and so on. They can help with practical problems over work and money and with emotional worries. MSWs are employed by the social services department of the local authority although they work in the health service.

Psychiatric social worker (PSW)

Psychiatric social workers are medical social workers who have had special training to help with the personal and social problems of patients who are mentally ill or emotionally disturbed. They may also be used by psychiatrists to take case histories from patients and their families.

Psychiatrists

Psychiatrists are doctors who have qualified in medicine and then taken further special training in the diagnosis and treatment of mental illness. Some psychiatrists use similar treatments to those used for other illnesses – pills and physical treatments. Others believe that psychiatric disorders are a result of personal or personality conflicts and use counselling and psychotherapy either alone or combined with some treatment with drugs.

Psychologists

A psychologist has an academic training in psychology, the study of behaviour. There are various specialisms within the field of psychology: clinical psychologists, for example, have studied the use of psychology in the assessment and treatment of mental illness; educational psychologists must also have training and experience in teaching.

Psychologists may make use of a variety of tests – the best known of which is the intelligence test – in order to help in assessing the precise nature of the child's difficulties.

Professor Peter Mittler of the Hester Adrian Research Centre has made this comment on the intelligence test. He says that it 'reliably and validly classifies and categorizes the individual, and is reasonably successful – within fairly generous limits of error – in predicting future educational or occupational achievement. But it tells us very little about the person as an individual.'

Therapy and treatment

Art therapy

BRITISH ASSOCIATION OF ART THERAPISTS

British Association of Art Therapists
13c Northwood Road, London N6 5TL

This is an association of professional teachers, affiliated to the National Union of Teachers. The terms 'art therapists' and 'remedial art teacher' are used to describe someone with the same qualifications, depending on the setting in which he is working: in a psychiatric ward the therapy would be emphasized; in a school for handicapped children the remedial teaching would be more important. Art therapy differs from art teaching in that it is more concerned with the emotions expressed and the personal development of the individual than with the end product. The secretary has said that the Association should be able to provide expert information on the various ways in which remedial art education/art therapy may be adapted to all the major handicaps.

Child guidance

Child guidance services should be available to all children, including children under the age of five, whose behaviour is causing serious problems or who have emotional or learning difficulties or difficulty in adjusting to a disability. There should be a network of services provided by the local education authority and the AHA through the school health service or the local hospital service. Hospital clinics are particularly common in London and are often called child psychiatric clinics.

Parents who want their child referred to a child guidance clinic can ask for it to be arranged through their GP, the social services department or the child's school.

It is generally recognized that treatment of a child cannot be carried out in isolation from the family. So 'family psychiatry' rather than 'child psychiatry' is carried out in many clinics, and parents are often expected to attend the clinic for sessions themselves.

Music therapy

BRITISH SOCIETY FOR MUSIC THERAPY

British Society for Music Therapy
48 Lanchester Road, London N6 4TA
Tel: 01-883 1331

The object of the Society is to promote the use and development of music therapy in the treatment, education, rehabilitation and training of children and adults suffering from emotional, physical or mental handicap. The Society can organize a free assessment session and put parents in touch with the right kind of therapist. It has an annual conference and produces publications which, like membership of the Society, are available to interested parents as well as professionals.

COUNCIL FOR MUSIC IN HOSPITALS

Sylvia Lindsay (Organizing Secretary)
Council for Music in Hospitals
340 Lower Road, Little Bookham, Surrey
Tel: Bookham 58264

For the last twenty-five years the Council has been organizing concerts of classical music in hospitals, including children's wards and those for the mentally ill and mentally handicapped. The performers are chosen not only for their technical ability but also for their skill in communicating with the captive audience; they introduce their own programmes and encourage the audience to join in whenever possible. The concerts have been particularly successful in psychiatric wards where some withdrawn and non-communicating patients have begun speaking again. The Council also encourages patients to make their own music after the concerts and can help with organizing lectures, clubs, choirs and other musical activities.

NORDOFF MUSIC THERAPY CENTRE

Nordoff Music Therapy Centre, Goldie Leigh Hospital
Lodge Hill, Abbey Wood, London SE2 0AY
Tel: 01-311 0712

Paul Nordoff, a composer and pianist, and Clive Robbins, a teacher of handicapped children, have developed a method of music therapy which stimulates a response from even the most brain-damaged or autistic children. Therapists can now take a full-time course, leading to a diploma, in the Nordoff–Robbins technique of music therapy. The department also holds weekend courses for teachers, playgroup leaders and all those interested in work with handi-

capped children. This work is sponsored by the Music
Therapy Charity Ltd.

Occupational therapy

BRITISH ASSOCIATION OF OCCUPATIONAL THERAPISTS

British Association of Occupational Therapists
20 Rede Place, London W2 4TU
Tel: 01-229 9738

Occupational therapists, still trying to live down their
old-fashioned image of basket-making, have special
expertise in helping handicapped children to become more
independent and to overcome mental and physical limitations. Their primary aim is to maintain clients in their
normal place in the community. They are trained to assess
individual needs, to advise colleagues and clients on
practical ways of meeting them, to instruct and supervise
clients in the use of aids and adaptations, to initiate and
advise on activities at training and day centres and at
home, and to act as one of the links between the local
authority social services and the National Health Service.

An occupational therapist may be asked to call at your
home – by your doctor, consultant or social worker – to
assess what structural adaptations or aids could minimize
the restrictions on a handicapped child's freedom.

Physiotherapy

Physiotherapy is the treatment of a disability by external
means such as exercise, heat, massage or hydrotherapy. A
Sunday Times report described what may happen to some
spastic or brain-damaged children without physiotherapy:
'. . . . their limbs are twisted and rigid. Some have spines so
bent that they cannot be turned over or legs so tightly
crossed they can never now be straight'. And the consultant in charge of the hospital criticized in that report
said: 'At least half these adults need never have been so
crippled. They should have been treated when they were
young. . . .'

Physiotherapists are concerned with the assessment and treatment of any physical handicap. As well as preventing irreversible deformity, they can help handicapped children to develop their physical skills to a maximum and to achieve more personal independence. Like occupational therapists, physiotherapists teach the handling, use and care of aids and equipment.

It is important for parents to have regular meetings with their child's physiotherapist, even if the treatment is given in school time, so that they can help with the exercises and make sure that the child doesn't do things the wrong way at home and un-do some of the good the treatment is doing him. One of the many revealing remarks made by parents talking to Dr Mervyn Fox (*They Get This Training but They Don't Really Know How You Feel*) came from a mother of a spastic boy. She said: '. . . one day when he was sitting down and had his legs in a funny way, he got up and said "I mustn't sit that way, I must sit this way" and I said "Why?" and he said "Because the physiotherapist says so". I thought, if somebody had told me to keep an eye on him indoors, I could have done that. . . .'

Physiotherapists work in special schools and hospitals and are all in the employment of the AHA if they work within the NHS. You will be able to get physiotherapy provided by the NHS only if your doctor recommends it, and if there are enough physiotherapists working in local hospitals or in your child's school to fulfil the demand.

If you want to try to get private treatment for your child, the State Registration Board publishes a geographical list of private practitioners in its *Annual Register* (price £2).

Council for Professions Supplementary to Medicine
York House, Westminster Bridge Road, London SE1 7UH
Tel: 01-928 2612

CHARTERED SOCIETY OF PHYSIOTHERAPISTS

Chartered Society of Physiotherapists
14 Bedford Row, London WC1R 4ED
Tel: 01–242 1941

The Society produces a directory of its members in private practice, available to medical practitioners. It has helped to produce an invaluable guide to the lifting and moving of disabled people – *Handling the Handicapped* (1975). This is the first book to illustrate for lay people the professional skills involved in lifting and moving handicapped people in everyday situations and in activities like swimming and riding. As one hospital physiotherapist pointed out: 'Heavy children are as big a problem to move as many adults.' The book costs £1.95, plus 25p postage, and can be ordered direct from the publishers if you can't get it locally.

Available from:
Woodhead Faulkner Ltd
7 Rose Crescent, Cambridge CB2 3LL

ASSOCIATION OF PAEDIATRIC CHARTERED PHYSIOTHERAPISTS

Miss D. B. Woods (Hon. Secretary)
Association of Paediatric Chartered Physiotherapists
Katherine Elliot School, Monkmoor, Shrewsbury, Salop

The Association is a new special-interest group formed from members of the Chartered Society who work with children. There are branches in most regions which hold courses and meetings on many aspects of physiotherapy for handicapped children. It is hoping to produce publications and has a regular newsletter.

COMMUNITY PHYSIOTHERAPY PROJECT

Superintendant Community Physiotherapist
Southampton General Hospital, Southampton
Tel: Southampton (0703) 777222

The Southampton and South West Hampshire Health District has a well-established community physiotherapy project. Under the supervision of Mrs Ann Compton, who initiated the scheme (she is possibly the only Superintendant Community Physiotherapist in the country), young handicapped children have physiotherapy in their own homes through the NHS. Mrs Compton explained the advantages when she talked to Action for the Crippled Child in September 1974. She said:

I used to have to rely on parents to do exercises they had been taught for the children at the hospital; but the following week they would say, 'We can't do them at home', because they seemed unable to adapt from the hospital to the home environment. By going into the homes, I can see exactly what facilities a family has. I can show parents how to do exercises with their handicapped child, using their own furniture. Most parents don't have much time but in the home I can demonstrate practical ways of helping a handicapped child - exercises which fit into a parent's normal everyday life.

Mrs Compton found that in the hospital the physiotherapist rarely sees anyone except the mother, but by visiting at home she is able to involve the whole family – father, brothers and sisters and grandparents – in the treatment.

The Health District has thought out its own scheme for standardizing its physiotherapy assessments so that as the children move on from groups for babies at the hospital clinic, to opportunity groups and later on to school, each successive physiotherapist knows the precise criteria used by her predecessors. The Health District pays for a physiotherapist for two hours a month at each of the five or six local opportunity groups as part of the assessment process and the playgroups supplement this treatment out

of their own funds, usually by employing the same physiotherapists.

HOME PHYSIOTHERAPY GROUP

Inquiries to: Mrs G. Sawyers
98 Cannons Close, Bishop's Stortford, Herts
Tel: Bishop's Stortford (0279) 51784

One physiotherapist has been treating handicapped
children in her home on a voluntary basis for the past
eight years. She takes individual children, referred by
local paediatricians, three afternoons a week. She helps the
parents in many ways with advice about equipment, toys
and ways of handling the children. She makes frequent
home visits and the parents all know she can be contacted
by phone at any time. The parents have held various
events to raise money for equipment as she receives no
financial aid or help at all. One of her mothers writes:
'We are a happy group of Mums and helpers and children.'

LAMPS NATIONAL PHYSIOTHERAPY SERVICE

Head Office, Lamps
19 Hammersmith Broadway, London W6 8AF
Tel: 01-748 4058/9

Lamps runs a group scheme through which members can
contribute 5p a week at their place of work (usually by
deduction from wages) to cover the member and his
dependents for up to twenty physiotherapy treatments a
year. Physiotherapy is given by qualified people on the
instructions of a doctor. If a parent is a member of the
scheme at work, his child can obtain benefit treatment and
advice. Lamps can also give information to parents
about qualified physiotherapists in their locality from
whom they could get private treatment and advice for a
child. The Scottish Advisory Council looks after the
scheme in Scotland.

Mobile Physiotherapy Service Association
94 Old Broad Street, London EC2M 1JB

This is a voluntary service which provides physiotherapy in the homes of people who are unable to attend a hospital department where treatment is free under the NHS and who cannot afford the full cost of private treatment. All treatment is provided by chartered and state registered physiotherapists. Local groups in fifteen areas of Great Britain raise all the money for a specially equipped van, its maintenance and the salary of the physiotherapist/driver. Visits are arranged on a doctor's recommendation. A small charge is made for visits, but is kept as low as possible.

Remedial gymnastics

Remedial gymnasts form part of the team working under medical officers in medical rehabilitation centres, special schools and in private practice. They treat disease and injury by means of all forms of physical exercises, games and recreational activities.

SOCIETY OF REMEDIAL GYMNASTS

Society of Remedial Gymnasts
County Ground, Northampton
Tel: Northampton (0604) 21794

The Society will be able to tell you whether a member is in private practice in your area.

Skin camouflage

DOREEN TRUST FOUNDATION

Peter and Doreen Trust
Wester Pitmenzie, Auchtermuchty, Fife

Doreen Trust has fought for many years to establish skin camouflage as a new health care service within the ethical control of the NHS and freely and safely available to all who are in need of care. The society exists to investigate the needs and social and psychological problems as well as cover treatments of men, women and children whose skin is disfigured. Doreen Trust is herself disfigured by a birthmark and has devoted her life to the study of faulty skin structures and cosmetic concealment of severe skin damage. She has always refused to operate commercially but has struggled to persuade hospitals to arrange for her to treat their patients in their clinics. Appointments are still arranged only through hospitals and the society cannot arrange a clinic unless invited to do so. Because she and her husband have received no official support, they have run into serious financial problems and can answer inquiries and give advice only to subscribers to *Talkabout Camouflage*, the society's newsletter (£3 a year, including postage). There are local groups of the society in nine areas of the country and there are plans for a national council. It may be difficult to contact them but as they are based in Scotland the Scottish Information Service for the Disabled can give information about them (see page 152).

Social skills

Inter-Action Advisory Service
Wilkin Street, London NW5
Tel: 01-267 1422/01-485 1672

Every summer holidays since 1972 the parents' action group, Kith and Kids (see page 28), has been running a programme to teach social skills. The whole programme is described in *Two-to-One*, an Inter-Action Advisory Service handbook. This gives comprehensive information about how the programme was set up; how it operates; work programmes and work sheets; training sessions. This would be invaluable to anyone wanting to set up a similar scheme. In his foreword Dr Albert Kushlick, writes: 'Because of the modesty and joyousness of the style, the reader may fail to notice that it is, in fact, a very detailed description and evaluation of a complex cycle of joint activities between parents and handicapped children, volunteers and professionals.' The pamphlet, published in 1976, costs 60p post paid.

Speech therapy

Speech therapy is the treatment of every kind of speech and language disorder and can also help to coordinate the throat muscles and alleviate eating problems. Speech therapists give diagnosis, advice and treatment in hospitals, schools and other units. They welcome the opportunity to cooperate with parents during treatment. Children are usually referred for speech therapy by the doctor at school or by the family health centre and/or their own GP. Children ought always to have their hearing tested before speech therapy is prescribed.

COLLEGE OF SPEECH THERAPISTS

College of Speech Therapists
47 St John's Wood High Street, London NW8 7NJ
Tel: 01-586 1958/4189

The College publishes a series of pamphlets for parents on how to help their children with speech problems and can put anyone in touch with qualified speech therapists in their area. In 1977 they will be moving to: 6 Lechmere Road, London NW2.

AFASIC MOBILE SPEECH THERAPY CLINIC

There is never enough speech therapy to go round so voluntary societies may try to make some sort of provision for their own members. But the Afasic Society went one better than this. In November 1974 it presented a specially adapted and fully equipped van to the Gloucestershire AHA. The van provides a pleasant environment in which to carry out assessments, consultations, discussions and treatment. It has led to an invaluable saving in time, money and energy both for the therapist, who no longer has to work in impossible conditions, and for the patients and their parents who no longer need to take days off school and work in order to make long journeys for speech therapy sessions. The appearance of the Mobile excites interest and comment wherever it goes and in itself is producing interesting results in the field of public relations. The parents and children feel that it is a personal service for them, it comes to *their* village for *them* and this has greatly improved attendance figures, especially during the holiday periods.

Let Me Speak

This book, by Dorothy M. Jeffree and Roy McConkey (Souvenir Press Ltd, 1976), is written primarily for parents whose children are slow in acquiring language but it should prove useful to anyone, parent or professional, who is interested in furthering any child's language development. Throughout the emphasis is on practical suggestions for games and activities. All aspects of language development are covered, from the early stages, even before the child begins to talk, right up to the use of language in thinking. The book is in four main sections and the introduction explains how to find out which section is right for your child's stage. Section 2 is called Language Skills and it has, in turn, five 'booklets' covering games to help the child learn to name things; games to help the understanding and use of verbs; the meaning of prepositions; putting two words together and helping the child to structure sentences. Many of the games in the book were developed in the context of the Parent Involvement Project at the Hester Adrian Research Centre which was directed by the authors. The paperback edition of the book costs £1.75.

Treatment

Various techniques have been developed in an attempt to help severely mentally or physically handicapped children. In some cases centres have been established where these techniques are put into practice. A fee may be charged for

A.H.F.P.—H

these services, but none of the organizations we have listed is profit-making.

BEHAVIOUR MODIFICATION

Behaviour modification is a technique for teaching a variety of skills to a child. These can range from self-help activities, such as feeding or dressing, to complex areas such as language or social relations. The technique is based on a careful step-by-step analysis of what the child must learn in order to acquire a particular skill. Teaching proceeds through careful structuring of the task and consistent reward for success. Behaviour which is harmful or causes serious problems to the family can also be reduced or eliminated by consistently ignoring it, by teaching alternative, acceptable behaviour, or in extreme cases, such as self-induced vomiting, by use of punishment. Although it is possible to teach parents the principles of behaviour modification, parents should not be expected to cope by themselves. There will be many cases in which parents, through family circumstances, could not be expected to take on a time-consuming programme for their child. One psychologist told a conference that there could be a risk of changing confident parents who felt they were coping well with their mentally handicapped child into guilty non-coping parents. Continuing support from professionals and other parents through workshop courses and so on help to keep a check on the progress of the whole family. Reputable organizations such as the Hester Adrian Research Centre and the Institute of Mental Subnormality (see chapter 2, **Mental handicap**, pages 67–8) are involved in projects in this field and are constantly discussing and developing their understanding in courses, reports and publications on the whole area of behaviour-modification techniques. It is a controversial field and they are well aware of the ethical problems involved. In January 1976 the Institute held a conference specifically to discuss the ethical implications of behaviour modification, particularly in cases of mental subnormality. Apart from the general ethical issues, some people are worried about the scope it offers for exploiting mentally handicapped people unless there are adequate safeguards.

BOBATH CENTRE FOR PHYSICALLY HANDICAPPED CHILDREN

Bobath Centre, 5 Netherhall Gardens, London NW3
Tel: 01-794 6084/5884

A registered charity offering a widely recognized form of physiotherapy for children whose posture and movements are abnormal. Normal patterns of movement are encouraged through repeating exercises based on instinctive reactions. A great deal of the work is with spastic children and for more than twenty years the Centre was known as the Western Cerebral Palsy Centre. Team-work is essential among physical, occupational and speech therapists, the child's teachers and parents so that treatment can be reinforced in his everyday life. The Centre does not charge fees for treatment. Therapists in many different professions are trained at the Centre in its special techniques.

CENTRE FOR EDUCATING YOUNG HANDICAPPED CHILDREN AT HOME

Dr Geoffrey Waldon
Strathmore, 636 Wilmslow Road, Didsbury, Manchester M20 0AH
Tel: 061-445 2411

Dr Waldon's Centre aims to help parents of young handicapped children by planning and organizing an individual programme for parents to teach their child at home. Parents attend the Centre with the child at regular fortnightly or monthly intervals. Between visits parents spend about an hour every day giving the child a special 'lesson'. All kinds of developmental disorders are catered for, except where hearing impairment is the main problem. Dr Waldon likes to accept children as young as possible, but the work of the Centre now extends to older schoolchildren. Children are accepted only on referral from medical or educational authorities and parents who write direct are asked to get this kind of support. A full assessment is given, with the parents' help, before a child is accepted. About sixty children attend the Centre at present, mostly from about twenty miles radius of Manchester, although some attend from further afield. Dr Waldon would like to see his Centre as a prototype for a nation-wide system of centres working in association with local schools. Fees: £15 for original consultation, £10 for each subsequent visit.

DOWN'S CHILDREN'S ASSOCIATION

Down's Children's Association
Quinborne Community Centre,
Ridgacre Road, Birmingham B32 2TW
Tel: 021-427 1274

The Association is a voluntary body of part-time and unpaid workers giving guidance and assessment for young Down's Syndrome children to give them the maximum chance of developing their full potential. The Director, Mr R. Brinkworth, has received widespread recognition from professionals throughout the field of mental handicap for his special methods of training and education for Down's Syndrome children. To avoid the secondary retardation which often occurs in this condition, the training should start from birth. Children are seen only with their doctor's consent or referred direct from hospital. The book, *Improving Babies with Down's Syndrome* (by Rex Brinkworth and Joseph Collins, 1969), explains to parents what they can do to benefit their baby. One parents' action group recommends this as the most readable and helpful book for parents. Detailed training schedules are available free to members of the Association (with their GP's approval). The Association now has several branches to provide local bases for parents and spread the work of the Association.

DOMAN–DELACATO METHOD

The theory underlying this method of treatment is that even when an area of the brain is seriously injured – destroying millions of cells – there must be some cells which survive uninjured. The aim of the Doman–Delacato method is to activate the surviving cells and 'pattern' them to take over the functions of the dead cells. Messages, which rapidly reach healthy brain cells as a normal child spontaneously learns a process such as crawling, take far longer to reach inactive cells and the messages cannot be sent spontaneously. The method therefore involves an intense programme of 'patterning' exercises which artificially reproduce the movements needed to crawl until the brain 'learns' how to do it. Although each session lasts for only a few minutes, the exercises must be repeated at frequent intervals throughout the day. Some of the exercises use five helpers at a time to position the child's head and limbs and it has been said that the programme for an individual child may involve more than 100 voluntary helpers. In many cases, this treatment has to be maintained over the course of several years.

This treatment is highly controversial. Before they make the decision to embark on it, parents should look not only at the dramatic successes which have been reported; they should also take the failures into account and then the decision must be carefully weighed against the cost of a commitment to the training programme, not just of money, but also in time and disruption of family life.

The Voluntary Council for Handicapped Children are producing an information sheet on the Doman–Delacato method. This will consist of a list of sources of information and reports on and references to the method in practice.

Voluntary Council for Handicapped Children
8 Wakley Street, London EC1V 7QE
Tel: 01-278 9441

The following organizations are those offering treatment by the Doman–Delacato and similar methods in Great Britain:

British Institute for the Achievement of Human Potential
Knowle Hall, Knowle, Bridgwater, Somerset
Tel: Bridgwater (0278) 684060

> The British Institute is one of the Institutes for the Achievement of Human Potential whose focal point is the Philadelphia Institute where Glenn Doman is the Director. Patients attached to the British Institute must first attend the Philadelphia Institute at their own expense for assessment and planning of the child's individual programme. The home training programme is then supervised by the British Institute whose staff were trained at Philadelphia and who carry out re-assessments three times a year. If the British Institute decides that a child needs a further visit to Philadelphia, it meets the cost.

National Society for Brain-Damaged Children
35 Larchmere Drive, Hall Green, Birmingham B28 8JB
Tel: 021-777 4284

> The Society gives evaluation and assessment based on the Doman–Delacato method, although its staff have worked independently since they trained in Philadelphia. Assessment and treatment must be paid for privately – the Society is a registered non-profit-making charity. Children come from all over the British Isles to the centre at 85 Homer Road, Solihull, Warwickshire. The initial assessment takes three days and the Society can recommend friendly local guest houses used by children who attend the centre.

Temple Fay Centre
119 The Promenade, Cheltenham, Gloucestershire
Tel: Cheltenham (0242) 56265

> Temple Fay MD was the American neurologist and neurosurgeon whose work formed the theoretical basis on which Doman founded his method of treatment. The purpose of

the Temple Fay Centre is to bring to children in this country Temple Fay's therapy. The centre describes this as 'developmental sensory/motor stimulation', beginning with stimulation of developmental reflexes and progressing through the well-defined stages of normal neurological development. A full assessment is undertaken at the Centre and a programme for therapy then taught to the parents to be carried out at home. The Centre claims that its programmes are considerably less rigorous for both parents and children than the Doman–Delacato system. It hopes that the methods will eventually become available at day centres and this is already happening in Durham with NHS staff who have trained at the Centre.

Friends of the Karen-Robert Centre
39 Rutland Road, Hazel Grove, Stockport, Cheshire

This group is trying to establish a new centre where home programmes will be devised and treatment undertaken using specialized equipment.

Support services

Ambulance

Ambulance and hospital car services are free, but can be ordered only by the family doctor or hospital except in special circumstances. These are maternity cases; any accident, at home, outside or at work; sudden illness *outside* the home – at work, in public places or in the street. To call the ambulance you dial 999 and ask the operator for 'Ambulance' when she asks you which service you require. For cases of illness at home you must first send for your GP unless it is a real emergency.

Bathing

The home nurse (district nurse) may be able to help with bathing a handicapped child. You will need a recommendation from your GP who will arrange the application.

See also chapter 3, **Aids**, page 104, for sources of help with bathing equipment.

Bedwetting

If a school-age child has a persistent bedwetting problem which has nothing to do with a physical handicap, the school doctor or your GP may be able to arrange for him to attend a special clinic for expert help and advice. See also chapter 3, **Incontinence**, page 147.

Behaviour problems

Family health centres ought to be able to give help and advice with behaviour problems of preschool children. School-age children who have minor behaviour problems such as food fads, not sleeping or constant attention-seeking, may be able to go to a school health service clinic. Serious problems should be referred to the child guidance service (see page 215 above).

Diets

If a child has to be on a special diet, the hospital dietitian will be able to give you diet sheets and lists of 'dos and don'ts'. Special diets are necessary for people with certain disabilities and the voluntary societies often produce more elaborate and detailed lists of approved brands and menus to make the diet more interesting. For gluten-free diets, see **Coeliac disease**; for diets which are low in sugar, see **Diabetes**; for diets which are low in protein phenylalanine, see **PKU** – all in chapter 2.

Drugs

A Teacher's Guide to Drugs

NCSE, 1 Wood Street, Stratford-upon-Avon, Warks.
Tel: Stratford (0789) 5332

Published by the National Council for Special Education, 1974, this pamphlet is written by a consultant psychiatrist. It describes the use and effect of some of the commoner drugs used in the treatment of handicapped children. It costs 20p, plus postage.

Glossary

Medical jargon can be very alarming to patients and their families. The Central Council for the Disabled has a publication called *What Is It*? which is a glossary of medical terms in everyday use (price 15p).

Central Council for the Disabled
34 Eccleston Square, London SW1V 1PE
Tel: 01-821 1871

Hearing tests

All preschool children should have a hearing test as part of their routine check-ups. Schoolchildren have their hearing tested by the school health service in the first place; if there is any sign of abnormality or if parents have worries about their child's hearing, they can be referred to the audiology clinic of a hospital by their own GP, the school doctor or the doctor at the family health centre. Hearing aids are available on free loan from the NHS. The audiology clinic will arrange for them to be fitted and supplied at a hearing aid centre run by the NHS.

See chapter 3, **Aids**, page 104.

Identity bracelets and necklets

MEDIC-ALERT FOUNDATION

Medic-Alert Foundation
9 Hanover Street, London W1R 9HF
Tel: 01-499 2261

Medic-Alert identity bracelets and necklets have a red Medic-Alert emblem on one side and the immediate medical problem of the wearer engraved on the other. This may be a warning about an allergy, details of drugs being taken or contact lenses worn; of mental handicap or of a medical condition such as epilepsy or diabetes. Additional medical information and other personal information is filed at Emergency Headquarters. Reversed-charge phone calls can be made to Emergency Headquarters twenty-four hours a day by authorized persons (doctors, hospital casualty departments, police, etc.) to ask for additional information from the file about the wearer. Each emblem is registered and the serial number is engraved on the reverse side, together with the telephone number of the Emergency Headquarters.

Injections

A home (district) nurse may be able to call at your home to give injections which are necessary as part of a short course of treatment or on a long-term basis. A doctor's recommendation will be needed.

Medical treatment away from home

TEMPORARY AND EMERGENCY TREATMENT

If you are away from home and need a doctor you can become a 'temporary' patient of any NHS doctor who will treat you. If it's an emergency and you can't get hold of a doctor, ask the police or the telephone operator for help. If you are there for only twenty-four hours or less you are technically an 'emergency' patient. For any longer period, up to three months, you are a 'temporary' patient. You will have to sign a form and, if possible, give your NHS number. Children at boarding school are usually registered with a doctor near the school, and use the 'temporary' arrangement for holidays. Students can decide whether they prefer to be registered at home or near their college, according to where they are likely to spend most time.

MEDICAL TREATMENT ABROAD

Reciprocal emergency health cover for employed persons and their dependents (but not for those who are self-employed) is available throughout the European Economic Community. It is necessary to apply for a certificate of entitlement (Form E111) and this may be done through any DHSS office. It is worth applying at least four weeks before travelling. Further information is in leaflet SA28 from any DHSS office. In addition, the UK has bilateral health service arrangements with a number of other countries which generally cover urgent medical care. These facilities are not necessarily as comprehensive as those provided under the NHS and they are not always entirely free. Information on the services available is given in leaflet SA30. The advice of CHIVE and DIVE (see chapter 8, **Visits and exchanges**, page 385) is to carry enough medicine for the duration of the visit, but also to be sure to keep a list of the prescriptions and dosage in case of emergency.

Obesity

In many areas the school health service runs special clubs and clinics to help overweight schoolchildren. Where a weight problem has no direct medical link with a handicap and the doctor has not prescribed a special diet, the school clinic may be able to help.

Prescriptions

Medicines and various appliances which are available on prescription are automatically free to all children under sixteen years of age. People over sixteen do not have to pay prescription charges if they have an exemption certificate which is available to people who suffer from certain chronic conditions or who have a physical disability which prevents them from leaving the house except with someone else's help. DHSS leaflet EC91 gives general information on exemptions and refunds.

The family practitioner committee is supposed to see that at least one chemist in the area is open at all reasonable times. Local chemists usually agree on a rota for opening late and on early closing days and Sundays. If there is a rota, details should be displayed on a notice in every chemist where it is visible when the shop is closed. This information is often given in the local papers. Your GP should be able to tell you where to get a prescription filled if you have any difficulty.

Vision tests

Parents who are worried about their child's eyes should get advice immediately. For instance, a baby with a squint should be examined even if he is only a few weeks old. Family health centres will probably be able to help and there may be a vision clinic in the area.

Almost every local education authority tests pupils when they start school for variations in eyesight, but not all of them have a programme for re-testing them at regular intervals. These routine tests are mostly carried out by nursing staff and any children who appear to have defective sight are referred to an ophthalmologist for a full test. Eye tests usually include a test for colour blindness. The vision test carried out in schools is a primitive one and parents should not rely on it if they suspect that their child is having difficulty in seeing properly.

GPs have to fill in a form recommending an eye test the first time anyone has this done under the NHS.

Eye tests may be conducted by ophthalmic opticians (who also sell glasses) or by ophthalmic general practitioners (who prescribe glasses but do not sell them). Alternatively, your doctor may refer you to the hospital eye service.

All children under sixteen, and older children who are still at school full-time, may be supplied free of charge with glasses using standard NHS lenses in NHS frames from a special children's range. In addition, no charge is made for standard NHS lenses for children over ten using any other NHS frame, but the appropriate charge is made for the frame.

The Vernon Committee of Inquiry into the education of visually handicapped children, which reported in 1972, recommended that schools for visually handicapped pupils should be visited regularly by ophthalmologists and opticians and that this standard of care should also be available to visually handicapped pupils who attend normal schools or special schools for other handicaps. However, in 1972 – before the reorganization of local authorities and of the NHS – there was the equivalent of only sixty-seven full-time ophthalmic specialists working in the school health service. (See chapter 2, NATIONAL FEDERATION OF THE BLIND, page 38.)

Wigs

Wigs may be supplied under the NHS if the doctor in charge of the case considers that it is necessary. Children under sixteen, or those in full-time attendance at school, are exempt from payment of any charge.

5 Special Education

The structure of the education system
Ascertainment
Special schooling
Miscellany

'Special educational treatment' is defined by Section 8 (2) c of the Education Act 1944 as education by special methods appropriate for persons suffering from any disability of mind or body. The Education (Scotland) Acts 1962 use a similar definition. Special education may be given 'either in special schools or otherwise'.

In November 1973 Mrs Margaret Thatcher, who was then Secretary of State for Education, announced to the House of Commons that a Committee of Inquiry was to be set up under the chairmanship of Mrs Mary Warnock, an Oxford philosophy don. Its terms of reference are:

to review educational provision in England, Scotland and Wales for children and young people handicapped by disabilities of body and mind, taking account of the medical aspects of their needs, together with arrangements to prepare them for entry into employment; to consider the most effective use of resources for these purposes; and to make recommendations.

The Committee has twenty-six members of whom one was appointed to represent parents of handicapped children because she is the mother of two hearing-impaired daughters. There are no disabled members on the Committee. The Committee has research funds of £160000 and is undertaking its own research projects and surveys.

It is not expected to publish its report before 1978 but in the meantime the whole field of education for handicapped children is in its shadow. Every organization and individual concerned with this aspect of handicap have had to concentrate their thoughts to prepare their evidence for

Warnock. And as the evidence is published, the lines of consensus and conflict emerge. We have come a long way in the five years since Parliament first decided that no child – not even the most severely handicapped – was ineducable.

Membership list and terms of reference available from:
Press Office, Department of Education and Science
Elizabeth House, York Road, London SE1
Tel: 01-928 9222

The structure of the education system

Central government

ENGLAND

DES, Elizabeth House, York Road, London SE1
Tel: 01-928 9222

The Department of Education and Science (DES) has responsibility for all aspects of education in England, some responsibility in Wales and control over universities throughout Great Britain. The political head of the DES is the Secretary of State who is a senior member of the government with a seat in the cabinet. Other MPs are assigned to the DES as Ministers of State and Parliamentary Under-Secretaries.

WALES

Welsh Education Office
31 Cathedral Road, Cardiff CF1 9UJ
Tel: Cardiff (0222) 42661

The Secretary of State for Wales is responsible for all schools, including primary, nursery, special, direct grant and independent schools. These are administered by the Welsh Education Office which is part of the Welsh Office in Cardiff. The DES is responsible for other aspects of education in Wales.

SCOTLAND

Scottish Education Department
New St Andrew's House, Edinburgh EH1 3SY
Tel: 031-556 8400

The Scottish system is quite separate from the rest of Great Britain. Education is one of the services administered by the Scottish Office, under the Secretary of State for Scotland, who is directly responsible to Parliament for all the departments making up the Scottish Office. The Scottish Education Department supervises all aspects of education and youth and community services in Scotland (except universities).

DEPARTMENTAL ORGANIZATION

The Departments are staffed by civil servants who are, of course, permanent and non-political. The Departments control and direct the education service by issuing regulations, administrative memoranda and circulars. Those which apply to both England and Wales are published jointly by the DES and the Welsh Office. Regulations have the force of law and are properly called statutory instruments. They normally fill in the details of how a general clause in an Act of Parliament is to be put into practice. The regulations which deal with the practical details of special education are the *Handicapped Pupils and Special Schools Regulations 1959* (SI 1959 No. 365 amended by SI 1962 No. 2073 and SI 1966 No. 1565).

Scottish education is controlled by its own Acts of Parliament and its own regulations and circulars. These generally coincide with DES policy.

In what follows about the education system we have not given all the references to Scottish law, but where Scottish practice differs in any important way from the English system we have tried to make this clear.

INFORMATION ON THE EDUCATION SYSTEM

The Law of Education by G. Taylor and J. B. Saunders (Butterworths, 8th edn, 1976) gives a complete run-down of all the English and Welsh Education Acts, current regulations and circulars, with an explanatory commentary and notes. Be sure to use the latest edition. It should be in your local reference library.

List 10, published by HMSO, is an index of all current circulars and administrative memoranda issued by the DES and the Welsh Office. *Circular 939*, issued by the Scottish Education Department, lists all current circulars and memoranda issued by the Department. The Department also issues a table of statutory instruments and orders in council.

The Education Act: How it Provides for Handicapped Children (1976)

This is a transcript of a lecture by John C. Morris given at a conference of the North London Dyslexia Association in March 1976 (see also page 55). This give basic legal information which applies to the education of *all* handicapped pupils and to those who are dyslexic in particular. The rights of parent and child are fully and clearly explained. Highly contentious points are identified which are soon likely to be the subject of alterations in the law. (Price 70p including postage).

North London Dyslexia Association
78 Whitehall Park, London N19 3TN
Tel: 01-272 1331

Local education authorities (LEAs)

The central government is responsible for the education system but it does not actually provide the education – that is done by the local education authorities.

There are 104 LEAs in England and Wales and nine regional and three island authorities in Scotland. Lists of all officers and education committee members for each LEA are published in the *Education Committees Yearbook* which is available in reference libraries. This shows whether an authority has any committees specifically concerned with special schools and whether they employ any inspectors, advisers, organizers or officers with a responsibility for special education.

The duties of LEAs as regards the education of handicapped children are established by Parliament in Education Acts. The 1944 Education Act (Section 34) states that it is: 'the duty of every local education authority to ascertain what children in their area require special educational treatment'. Having found out who needs special education, it is the duty of the LEA (Section 8 (2) c) to make provision for them to be given it 'either in special schools or otherwise'.

The Act (Section 33 (2)) said that the more severely handicapped children should be educated in special schools. Where education in a special school is impracticable or undesirable, or where the disability is not serious, a child may be given a place in any other suitable school.

The Acts (Section 56 of the 1944 Act, Section 14 of the Education (Scotland) Act 1962) allow LEAs to provide education 'otherwise than at school' in extraordinary circumstances. This provision has often been used to provide home tuition for handicapped children.

So the law was designed to leave no loopholes for LEAs to get out of their duty of providing a suitable education for every single handicapped child living in their area, although it was only in 1970 (1974 in Scotland) that the education authorities' responsibility was extended to include children classified as severely subnormal.

Any parent who is worried about his child's education and cannot get satisfaction from the school or the LEA officers ought to take it up with his local councillor. A councillor can contact senior officers on behalf of constituents and can get pertinent questions asked in education committee meetings.

Ascertainment

The term 'ascertainment' covers the whole process of finding out which children need special education. So every step in discovering that a baby is not developing normally, in diagnosing what's wrong and in assessing the effects, is part of ascertainment. Family health centres, GPs, hospital assessment centres, audiology or other special units, or – particularly in the case of educationally subnormal and maladjusted children – the schools may all have something to contribute to this process.

England and Wales

In 1975 the DES and the Welsh Office issued identical circulars on *The Discovery of Children Requiring Special Education and the Assessment of Their Needs* which aimed to 'clear up uncertainties and confusion which surround the subject of ascertainment, and to provide a fresh statement of what is involved in discovering which children require special education and in recommending the form it should take.' DES *Circular 2/75* (Welsh Office *21/75*) says how important it is for teachers to be on the alert throughout a child's school career to see if he needs special help. Teachers should be able to consult educational psychologists and school doctors. The circular warns of the difficulty of assessing children whose native language is not standard English. (The immigrant community have produced evidence to show that a high proportion of West Indian children are allocated to special schools simply because of the idiosyncracies of West Indian English and differences in West Indian culture.)

The most significant change recommended in *Circular 2/75*, and one which many parents and teachers will feel is overdue, is the suggestion that the first steps in a full-scale investigation of a child's difficulties should always be to 'obtain a report from a teacher who knows him well, describing the child's progress and behaviour in school and indicating the problems as the teacher sees them, and to consult the parents.'

The next steps are to obtain the opinion of a school doctor and an educational psychologist. A new series of forms has been produced for teachers, school doctors and educational psychologists. A head teacher concerned about a child will fill in form SE 1. The school doctor will see this form when completing SE 2, and the educational psychologist will see both forms when completing his own report on SE 3. The forms will be summarized on form SE 4, a summary and action sheet, which includes a descriptive list based on educational needs rather than diagnostic labels. This is intended to ensure that educational judgements are made by people with educational qualifications instead of by doctors as they were previously.

Assessment shouldn't end when a child is sent to a special school. His progress should be periodically reviewed and the possibility of him going to an ordinary school reconsidered.

Although circulars do not have the force of law, this one could eventually have a profound effect on the whole process of ascertaining handicapped children. At the present time, many children are found a special school place without any formal legal procedure. Parents may be involved in discussions from an early stage, their opinions about the child and his capabilities asked for and taken into account. They may be encouraged to visit the special school, unit or class suggested for their child. But there are still occasions when a decision that a child should have special education may be the focus of bitter conflict between the parents and the LEA.

FORMAL PROCEDURE FOR ASCERTAINMENT

Circular 2/75 describes when formal procedures are, and are not, needed. They should not be used unless there is a good reason to believe that parents will refuse to send a child to a special school. They may also be used when parents who have agreed to send their child to a special school fail to send him to school regularly. In these cases the authority must notify the parents in writing that the child is to have a medical examination. This applies to any child who has reached the age of two. Parents can be fined for refusing. The LEA must give parents details of the time and place of the medical examination so that they can be present. *Circular 2/75* adds that 'although not required by the Education Acts, it is desirable that the parents should similarly be given an opportunity to attend an examination by an educational psychologist'.

According to the ascertainment procedure set out in the 1944 Education Act (Section 34(5)) the advice given by the medical officer as a result of the formal examination 'shall be communicated to the parent of the child and to the local education authority'. The parents or the LEA can also require the medical officer to issue to both of them a standard certificate showing whether the child is suffering from any disability and, if so, the nature and extent of it. However, the LEA cannot require a certificate unless it needs it in order to take proceedings against parents for not sending their child to school.

PARENTS' RIGHTS

It is quite clear that a fundamental principle of Section 34 was that parents should have the right to see any report on which the decision about their child's future is to be based. The new summary and action sheet (form SE 4) introduced by *Circular 2/75* recommends what kind of special education a child needs and what kind of school it should go to. The form is headed with these instructions: 'The information on this form must be restricted to those professionally concerned with the child.' When you look at the information called for under the heading 'Home background and parental attitude' (see page 246) it's not surprising that they don't want parents to see what they have said.

The North London Dyslexia Association would like to see the instructions on the form altered to read: 'The information on this form must be restricted to those professionally concerned with the child and to his/her actual

31. Parental attitude to child: supportive

    neutral

    over-protective

    rejecting

32. Siblings and place in family
    (tick for subject and ring as appropriate for others).

    1   2   3   4   5   6   7
    M F   M F   M F   M F   M F   M F   M F

33. Parental attitude to special education: in favour

    indifferent

    unknown

    opposed

home
background
and
parental
attitude

34. Other factors.
    Specify:

35. Special need for school to enlist home support if
    placement is to be effective.

36. Need for counselling of parents before special education
    may be initiated.
    Specify appropriate agency:

parents. The parents should be provided with a copy of this form if they so wish. If there is any part of the material they do not regard as being grounded in fact, they must be permitted to have their opinions on such matters accorded equal status on the form.'

At the moment it seems likely that a persistent parent could insist that the provisions of Section 34, even though the prescribed report form had been changed, gave him a right to see the report: this right is statutory and a circular cannot remove it. However, *Circular 2/75* says that when an opportunity for amending legislation occurs, the statutory provisions for the issue of a certificate in a prescribed form to the authority and the parent when either require it will be reviewed. Parents ought to have a right to know what is being said about them and their child and these moves can make nonsense of the excellent sentiments expressed in the circular that parents should be brought into consultation in all stages of the assessment process.

Scotland

New procedures for ascertaining which children need special education in Scotland were introduced after the passing of the Education (Scotland) Act 1969. Parents can ask for a medical examination for the child from the age of two, and the LEA can call for medical and psychological examinations for any child of that age onwards. The parents must allow their child to attend these examinations, and can be present at the medical. The LEA receives reports on special forms from the child's headteacher as well as from the school doctor and the educational psychologist who examine the child. The form for headteachers includes specific questions on what sort of help the child has already received, what other circumstances – such as frequent changes of address, oversize classes, poor attendance – may have affected the child's development and about his behaviour in and out of the classroom. The headteacher is supposed to interview the parents and discuss the child's problems before completing the form.

The medical and psychological forms have a tear-off summary sheet which is sent to the child's school. The Director of Education writes to the parents to tell them about the LEA's decision. This letter should explain that parents have a right to ask for a statement of reasons for the decision and to appeal against it to the Secretary of State. Scottish parents have a legal right to an annual review of their child's case, and can appeal against any decisions taken at that review.

Circular 733 explaining the effect of the changes laid great stress on the 'importance of gathering together all available information about a child before reaching a decision on his case, to involve parents at all stages, and (where the parent is not convinced that the decision taken was right) to give him considerable opportunities to press for a review.' Children must be ascertained before they attend a special school or other special educational provision.

The Scottish Education Department has published a series of working-party reports on ascertainment of children with different handicaps, which would be of interest to parents. The report on the ascertainment of deaf children is particularly impressive in its scope and imaginative proposals (*Ascertainment of Children with Hearing Defects*, HMSO, 1967).

However, the resources needed to carry out assessment and ascertainment procedures envisaged in the reports and circulars are not always available, and so procedures may fall short of what is recommended.

PARENTS' RIGHTS

The Scottish regulations made in 1969 ensure that parents have a right to ask for a statement of reasons if their child is ascertained as needing special education. *Circular 733* states that this should be 'as informal as possible, consistent with the need to give the parent clear information on which to judge whether to agree with the education authority's decision.'

De-ascertainment

A formal certificate of ascertainment may be cancelled by the LEA or, on appeal by the parents, by the Secretary of State. The LEA must notify the parents of this and must not continue to provide special educational treatment for the child.

Once a child is registered at a special school, whether or not the statutory ascertainment procedure has been carried out, he may not be withdrawn from the school without the LEA's consent. Parents can appeal to the Secretary of of State if the LEA refuses to let the child leave. The Secretary of State cannot direct a child to attend a special school unless a certificate of ascertainment has been issued.

Categories of handicap

The *Handicapped Pupils and Special Schools Regulations 1959* (and later amendments) described ten different categories of handicap, each of which was defined in terms of educational needs. For instance, there was no such category as spastic, autistic or dyslexic so those children had to be slotted into the category of school which the doctor thought most suitable, such as physically handicapped, mentally handicapped or maladjusted. In 1974 the *Statistics of Education* published by the DES distinguished between nineteen different categories of school, each catering for a different description of handicap (with hospital schools as a separate category). For instance, these included 'Deaf and partially sighted' and 'Delicate and maladjusted'.

Nine categories of handicap are recognized in Scotland: blind, partially sighted, deaf, partially deaf, mentally handicapped, epileptic, maladjusted, physically handicapped, and children suffering from speech defect.

However detailed the specification, it is almost impossible to define categories which will cover the whole range of complex disabilities. Professor Gunner Dybwab of

Brandeis University, USA, talks about '*labels* which in the technical sense become *libels*'.

The DES considered the changing population of special schools in *Circular 4/73*. It points out that, since increasing efforts are being made to cater for less severely handicapped children in primary and secondary schools, the population of special schools contains an increasing proportion of the most severely handicapped. The circular also says:

Modern methods of diagnosis and assessment have shown that handicapped children rarely have a single uncomplicated disability; educational backwardness and psychological disorder are the most common additions to a specific handicap. A survey (carried out in the Isle of Wight in 1964/65) indicates that the proportion of handicapped children suffering from two or more disabilities is probably not less than 25 per cent. The proportion of such children in special schools will be much higher, since the handicapped children in ordinary schools will not include many with two or more disabilities.

The new procedure for assessment set out in *Circular 2/75* is intended to provide helpful experience to put before the Warnock Committee when it 'seeks to reach conclusions about the statutory categories and, if they are to be abolished, about the descriptive system required in their place.'

Integration

One of the controversies on which the Warnock Committee will have to reach some conclusion is that of integration versus segregation. Those who take a hard line in favour of separate special schools insist that handicapped children need special skills and a protected environment, that handicapped children in normal schools may feel (in the words of the National Association of Head Teachers to Warnock) 'isolated and stigmatized'. Supporters of integration on the other hand lay great stress on the importance of allowing handicapped children to play a full and equal part in society which to a large extent depends on educating society to accept the handicapped on equal terms. The DES has produced a booklet in the 'Education Today' series, called *Integrating Handicapped Children*, which surveys the whole question of integration and special schooling.

Most voluntary societies have produced some discussion of this problem. The Spastics Society has set up an extensive research project (in cooperation with the London University Institute of Education) into the progress of handicapped children who are being educated at ordinary schools. The National Foundation for Educational Research have undertaken a comparative study of blind and partially sighted children in ordinary and special schools, due to be completed in 1976. Elizabeth Anderson, whose research into integration of physically handicapped children in primary schools was published as *The Disabled Schoolchild* (Methuen, 1973, price £6 hardback, £2.90 paperback), concluded that the children were generally happy in school, that teasing was a confinable problem, and that, not surprisingly, academic progress depended on the preparation and specialized help given.

It is clear that integration, as an end in itself, is not going to help handicapped children get the education they need and deserve unless there is planning, proper provision of resources and specialized training of teachers. Whether the children in all *special* schools have the benefit of careful planning, adequate resources and trained teachers is another question.

Some people are just getting on with making it work without waiting for the results of large research studies. For example, when autistic children from a hospital school for fifty severely disturbed children were exposed to standards of normal behaviour in a south Midlands primary school, their own behaviour improved markedly; a thalidomide armless boy at a Stevenage comprehensive learned to write with his feet and won second prize in the school diving contest; a six-year-old with spinal atrophy at an Oxfordshire primary school progressed well beyond her estimated potential in one year alone.

A parent who wants his handicapped child to be educated at an ordinary school may have trouble convincing the authority and it will be difficult to succeed without the enthusiastic and properly qualified help of the school itself. But integration is already mandatory in the state of Massachusetts, USA, so it can be done.

Special schooling

Preschool

There is one subject on which everyone agrees – the vital importance for handicapped children even more than for others of beginning the education process as early as possible and the almost total inadequacy of existing arrangements for preschool education. LEAs have the power to compel a parent to submit any child who has reached the age of two for medical examination to decide whether the child needs special educational treatment, and parents have a similar right to ask for an examination. If the child is found to need special help the LEA is supposed to provide it. Yet, in fact, very few handicapped children get any special help before they reach the age of five. The official *Statistics of Education* records that in England and Wales in January 1974 over 130000 pupils were attending special schools full time; of these 3457 were under the age of five. Some may be found places in nursery classes at special schools, some may attend special playgroups attached to hospital clinics, others may get a place at a playgroup or nursery school run by social services departments or voluntary organizations either for handicapped children alone or for handicapped and other children together. Local authority social services departments have to register all playgroups in their area so they should be able to tell you what is available locally. Having said that, it seems carping to point out that mere attendance at a playgroup may not in itself achieve anything unless the handicapped child's individual needs and progress are properly understood. According to Professor Peter Mittler: 'The company of talking children does not magically produce a flow of language from a silent child unless there is a systematic attempt to meet all the learning needs of the individual.'

PERIPATETIC TEACHERS

Some LEAs are now employing peripatetic teachers to visit young handicapped children in their homes and give support and encouragement to their parents. Dr Elizabeth Newsom, at a conference on opportunity groups organized by the Preschool Playgroups Association, said: 'Parents want home visitors who will enable them to learn to work with children themselves. They don't want a social worker's shoulder to cry on but someone who will put tools, techniques and ideas into their hands.' A good peripatetic teacher can provide this. You can find out about any local arrangements for peripatetic teachers from the local education office.

PRESCHOOL PLAYGROUPS ASSOCIATION (PPA)

PPA, Alford House, Aveline Street, London SE11 5DH
Tel: 01-582 8871

Scottish PPA, Playgroup House, 7 Royal Terrace, Glasgow G3 7NT
Tel: 041-331 1340

The Association encourages member groups to make provision for handicapped children. Handicapped children are encouraged to join playgroups and opportunity groups, where the handicapped/normal ratio is higher. Some member playgroups are for handicapped children only. The Association produces publications on handicapped children and playgroups – list available from head office. It has a special needs committee to collect together expertise on specialized areas of work with preschool children, including children in hospital.

Since the opportunity groups started by Dr R. E. Faulkner of Stevenage merged with PPA it also runs a sub-committee for handicapped children. The sub-committee maintains a register of opportunity groups which now number more than sixty. An opportunity group, as founded by Dr Faulkner, is a playgroup where children with any form of handicap and normal children can play together and where mothers of handicapped children can meet one another. Opportunity groups, unlike usual playgroups, are available from birth, so that handicapped children can benefit from the learning situations and planned play activities as young as possible. A well established group would have twenty children, a maximum of thirteen of these being handicapped. Dr Faulkner's *Notes for Opportunity Groups* is available from PPA, price 20p, plus postage.

The PPA has appointed a national adviser with responsibility for children with special needs who will be able to give help and advice on any aspect of handicapped children and playgroups.

Mrs Delphine Knight
67 Cranleigh Road, Feltham, Middlesex
Tel: 01-890 9393

THREE-FOUR-FIVE LTD

Kiddicraft, Three-Four-Five Ltd
Godstone Road, Kenley, Surrey CR2 5YS
Tel: 01-668 4181

A twelve-month course of nursery education designed to be used at home. The parts arrive by post each month and include brightly coloured graded activity cards, suggestions and notes for parents and a 45 rpm record of songs. The activities are based on pre-reading preparation, and development of speech and number sense. The course has been used by handicapped children. It costs £15 for the twelve-month course.

Special schools

The Secretary of State for Education has the power to make regulations about the conditions which any special school must comply with and may decide whether a school is suitable for providing special educational treatment.

These conditions are set out in the *Handicapped Pupils and Special Schools Regulations 1959*. The legal requirement for primary and secondary education to be provided in separate schools does not necessarily apply to special schools, which may take pupils from two years to sixteen or over.

In *Living with Handicap* the National Children's Bureau listed thirteen different kinds of arrangements for providing special education. At one end of the spectrum children were educated full time in residential special schools or hospitals, at the other end they were fully integrated in ordinary schools. But in between there were children living in residential homes and special schools who went out for some of the time to join ordinary local day schools, children in special units on the site of ordinary schools or actually part of an ordinary day school with the extra support of a special resource centre. There were children being educated at home and peripatetic teachers offering extra specialist support in schools, units or at home. In 1975 not one education authority could offer this full range of choices to the handicapped children in its area.

The DES publishes *List 42* which contains all special day and boarding schools for handicapped pupils in England and Wales, arranged by handicap. This publication includes non-maintained and independent schools. The list has not previously given any details about the schools, but in 1975 the Secretary of State told a conference on special education that future editions would give detailed descriptions of the schools so that educational psychologists or special education advisers could match individual children more accurately to the appropriate school place.

Available in reference libraries or from local offices of HMSO or: Mail Order Department, HMSO, PO Box 569, London SE1 Tel: 01-928 6977

The Scottish Education Department's *List G* gives brief details of all educational provision for handicapped pupils in Scotland – residential and day special schools, special classes, regional councils providing child guidance services, hospital schools and H M Inspectors for Special Education.

Available from:
New St Andrew's House, St James's Centre, Edinburgh EH1 3SY
Tel: 031-556 8400

CHOICE OF SCHOOL

Parents have only a limited right as far as choosing any state school is concerned, and any choice which would cause unreasonable public expense can be overruled by the LEA (Education Act 1944 Section 76 and Education (Scotland) Acts). *Circular 2/75* recommends that parents should be encouraged to visit any special school, unit or class suggested for their child. But it is unrealistic for parents to expect much choice for a severely handicapped child; only a small number of schools are suitable for a particular child and there are often long waiting lists. The choice of a special school may be restricted still further if the LEA's schools have catchment areas linked to transport arrangements (see **Transport**, page 274). Nevertheless, parents may always appeal direct to the Secretary of State under Section 68 of the 1944 Education Act or to the Secretary of State for Scotland – simply by writing a letter to him – if they think that the LEA is acting unreasonably in refusing to take account of their wishes. If parents have good grounds for arguing that the school suggested would be unsuitable for their child they could also report the case to the local ombudsman on the grounds of maladministration.

MAINTAINED DAY SCHOOLS

Some handicaps are now so rare that an LEA may have only a handful of children suffering from a particular one and may not have a day special school for those children anywhere in the whole authority. In 1974, according to the *Statistics of Education*, there were no maintained day schools at all for blind children in England and Wales (there was one in Glasgow) and only fifty-two blind children were being educated as day pupils (in boarding schools) compared with about 1000 blind children who were boarding pupils. In contrast, more than 75000 educationally subnormal pupils were at day schools in England and Wales and nearly 800 schools were catering for them. So, with some handicaps parents who want their child to go to a day school may have a long, hard struggle to get a satisfactory education for their child unless they have the good fortune to live within easy reach of a suitable school. Even when a place at a day school is found, it is likely to cover a wide catchment area, especially in view of the DES's official encouragement to LEAs to combine and plan special schools on a regional basis serving more than one area. As the National Confederation of Parent–Teacher Associations pointed out in their evidence to Warnock: 'The result is that children have to spend up to three hours a day in school buses in extreme physical discomfort.'

MAINTAINED BOARDING SCHOOLS

A child with a handicap has the same right to a free state education as any other and it is the duty of his LEA to provide it. So if a pupil cannot get to a suitable school every day the LEA must pay either for lodgings near a school or for a place at a boarding school.

The question of whether or not the parents could afford to pay doesn't enter into it. In 1974 about 20 per cent of all maintained special schools in England and Wales were boarding schools. (The percentage is very much lower in Scotland.) But within that average the percentage varied from 100 per cent in the case of schools for blind children to 38 per cent in the case of schools for physically handicapped children down to 15 per cent of schools for educationally subnormal children.

Reports on Education No. 77, 1973, *Special Education: a Fresh Look*, says that in planning provision of special schools LEAs should 'work towards a situation in which children who cannot attend a school as day pupils would have a suitable boarding school sufficiently near for them to be able to go home at weekends. Some existing boarding schools in country areas suffer from an isolation that is educational and social as well as geographical. . . .'

The National Deaf Children's Society published a report in 1974 called *Weekly Boarding: Why and How*. It found that practice varied widely. At one school a mere handful of children stayed at school over the weekend, at another the majority stayed. It found, not surprisingly, that 'the further children live away from school, the less likely they are to return home at weekends, and beyond 70 miles the likelihood decreases very sharply.' Nevertheless, 24 per cent of LEAs in their survey sent deaf children to boarding schools between sixty and 151 miles from the centre of the authority (see **Transport**, page 274).

NON-MAINTAINED SCHOOLS

In 1974 there were 113 non-maintained special schools in England and Wales. These schools are administered either by their governing boards or by voluntary societies such as the Royal National Institute for the Blind, but catering only for pupils whose fees are paid by local education authorities. For some handicaps they are a major source of educational provision: fifteen of the seventeen schools for the blind, three of the four schools for children with speech defects are in the non-maintained sector. Pupils are placed in these schools through LEAs who pay all the fees. Section 6 of the Education (Miscellaneous Provisions) Act 1953 lays down that all tuition and all board and lodging should be free to parents, whatever the parent's personal means may be if 'the authority are satisfied that the pupil requires special educational treatment and that it is expedient in his interests that such treatment should be provided for him at a special school not maintained by them or another local education authority.' Non-maintained schools are subject to the *Handicapped Pupils and Special Schools Regulations*, Part IV. These state that the school shall not be conducted for profit. It also brings them into line with maintained schools as far as arrangements for medical examinations, provision of milk and meals and general record-keeping are concerned. Apart from these administrative requirements, non-maintained schools are virtually independent. They may be isolated from the educational mainstream because, as the DES has pointed out, they have no links with other schools in the area and no access to educational advisory services. Non-maintained schools are not accountable to the local authorities which pay their pupils' fees. When the National Association of Governors and Managers surveyed the composition of the governing bodies of thirty-three non-maintained special schools used by one local authority, only thirteen had representatives of the LEA on their governing boards. Yet the activities of a non-maintained special school will affect not only the school itself, but the pattern of educational provision in a particular area for a particular category of pupil and LEA provision (or lack of it) is often closely linked with the provision in the non-maintained special school sector.

In Scotland the nearest equivalent to this type of school is the fourteen residential special schools which are grant aided under the *Residential Special Schools and Orphanages (Scotland) Grant Regulations 1948*.

SPECIAL UNITS AND CLASSES IN ORDINARY SCHOOLS

Government policy has long been that no handicapped child should attend a special school if his needs can be met by an ordinary school. But provision is very uneven. The Campaign for the Mentally Handicapped was told by the DES in 1974 that in two and a half years only two out of 103 replacement building projects included provision for special classes in ordinary schools and probably well under 2 per cent of retarded children are being educated in ordinary schools. In January 1974 over 2000 partially-hearing pupils in England and Wales were attending full-time special classes at maintained primary and secondary schools, but only 112 partially sighted children were in this type of class. The Scottish *List G* gives details of seventy-seven special classes, of which seventy-three were for mentally handicapped children, one for maladjusted, one for partially sighted and one for partially deaf children. It may be thought that these special classes or units solve the problem of reconciling the need of a handicapped child for specialist facilities and teaching skills with the need to mix socially and work together with children without handicaps in the normal community. In 1973 the DES gave a warning about what could happen if special classes were not carefully planned and organized: 'It can be the worst of all worlds for a handicapped child, if without the range of facilities provided in a special school, he has little contact with the other staff of an ordinary school and is not accepted as an equal by the other children. . . .'

INDEPENDENT SCHOOLS

England and Wales. All independent schools in England and Wales must be registered with the DES. Only those which meet the standards of facilities and educational provision which satisfy Her Majesty's Inspectorate are recognized as efficient. Independent schools are not regarded as providing suitable special educational treatment unless they are recognized as efficient by the DES, although exceptions can be made in particular cases. If parents choose an independent school in preference to the school offered, the LEA may help towards the fees at its own discretion. The LEA has to make a grant if there is no other suitable place available for your child.

Scotland. All independent schools in Scotland have to be registered with the Registrar for Independent Schools and conform to certain standards of facilities and staffing. There is no provision for 'recognition as efficient' in Scotland. English readers should note that the Scots are more logical about what they call their schools – in Scotland 'public schools' are the state schools.

The Scottish Education Department has issued a circular (No. 821) on the use of independent special schools, which draws the attention of LEAs to their responsibility to see that the independent school concerned can fully meet the child's educational and other needs.

HOSPITAL SCHOOLS

The school, the education welfare officer, and the hospital are all supposed to notify the LEA when a child is admitted to hospital for a long stay. It is not the responsibility of the hospital or the health authority to provide education, however long a child is likely to stay there. They are expected to cooperate in making arrangements so that teaching can take place, but the duty to provide the education belongs to the LEA. If there are likely to be at least twenty-five children who should receive education, the LEA has a duty to be sure that there is a proper school with a headteacher in charge and its own board of governors (*Circular 5/74: The Education of Mentally Handicapped Children and Young People in Hospital*). Where there are fewer than twenty-five children it may be necessary to make arrangements to educate the children 'otherwise than at school' under Section 56 of the Education Act 1944. The official statistics of education showed in January 1974 that there were 155 hospital schools in England and Wales catering for nearly 10000 children. In Scotland *List G* gives details of nineteen hospitals which provide special education and training for mentally and severely mentally handicapped pupils. The Scottish Education Department also states that some provision is made for physically handicapped patients in hospital for long periods. There were, according to the official statistics, less than eight pupils for each teacher. These statistics conceal another story. A report was published by the Council for Children's Welfare in 1975 called *No Childhood – the Handicapped at Home and in Hospital in the 1970s* (available from the National Children's Bureau). Its research shows that in 1972 there were approximately 8500 physically and mentally handicapped children permanently living and being educated in long-stay hospitals in England and Wales. It found that 'the provision of education within the hospital is often inconsistent, e.g. priority is sometimes given in the form of extra staff and expensive equipment to a department dealing with a "popular handicap", while in an adjoining department dealing with a less interesting handicap, the children are retained in severely deprived conditions.' Although the DES has recommended (*Circular 312 1956*) that every child should have the opportunity to join in classes, even if it's for only a week or so, it is difficult to ensure that school-age children, who might be scattered through several wards in a hospital, are in fact receiving any education at all. Adolescents are particularly difficult to help as they may be placed in an adult ward where a teacher is not welcome because of ward routines geared to nursing sick adults. *Circular 5/74* says that children should not be educated in their own ward, or only 'very exceptionally' and wherever practicable should go out to a special school in the community. But *No Childhood* describes how a severely physically disabled spastic boy had to stay on his ward in a long-stay hospital because the purpose-built school in the hospital grounds was not purpose-built enough to take a child in a wheelchair. A hospital school should, ideally, have the same relationship with parents as any other school. *Circular 5/74* says that parents should be encouraged to make regular visits to the hospital school, and although advance notice of visits is a help to staff, visiting should not be restricted to particular hours.

Although there may not be the same clear distinction between school terms and holidays as in other schools, there will be breaks in the teaching routine. Visits by children to their homes should if possible be arranged so as not to interfere with their education. Parents who are concerned about the education provided for their child in hospital may find that the Community Health Council is the best source of help. Although the responsibility for the education belongs to the LEA, the Community Health Council ought to be actively concerned with every aspect of the quality of life of children in hospital.

Home teaching

In 'extraordinary circumstances' an LEA has the power to provide a free education for a child 'otherwise than at school' for up to five half days a week. This may mean providing teaching at home. Most LEAs have some system for arranging this. The LEA decides whether a child's circumstances are extraordinary enough. Living a long way from a suitable school is not in itself the kind of extraordinary circumstances covered by this section, since the authority should provide board and lodging in those cases. However, parents who don't want their child to live away from home could ask for home teaching under Section 56. Parents whose children are waiting for a special school place ought to have home-teaching provided. In January 1974, 5554 handicapped children were officially recorded by the DES as receiving education 'otherwise than at school' and this figure included those who were receiving home tuition.

The Scottish Education Department recorded seventy-three children as having home teaching in September 1975; this figure included children who were not handicapped.

Staffing

ENGLAND AND WALES

The *Handicapped Pupils and Special Schools Regulations 1959* used to have clauses which prescribe the maximum class sizes for each type of special school and for special classes in ordinary schools. These clauses were revoked in April 1973 (*Circular 4/73*) and the formal safeguard of staffing standards in special schools is now the general clause in the Regulations which says that 'there shall be in every school a headteacher, who shall take part in the teaching, and a staff of assistant teachers able to provide full-time education suitable to the ages, abilities and aptitudes of the pupils.' An equivalent clause covers the staffing of special classes. The circular sets out some general considerations which should be kept in mind by an LEA (or by the governors in non-maintained schools) in deciding on the number of teachers needed in a particular school. The first principle is that the more severe the learning handicap, the smaller should be the teaching group (as distinct from class size). The younger the children the more favourable the staffing ratio needed. The circular goes on to comment on the considerations relevant to specific handicaps with precise details of the staff needed in schools of a particular size according to the age of the children and the nature of the handicap.

Teachers of the blind and of the deaf and partially deaf are supposed to have additional specialist qualifications (*Handicapped Pupils and Special Schools Regulations 1959*, 15 ii). These are not a requirement for other handicaps, although a considerable number of specialist diploma courses are available. However, a survey in England and Wales conducted by the National College of Teachers of the Deaf in 1975 showed that even in schools for the deaf one in three teachers does not have the proper special qualifications. So parents cannot assume that staff in special schools will be specially qualified.

Ancillary staff – non-professional helpers – are recognized as an indispensible part of the staff of special schools. With younger children, *Circular 4/73* suggests that it may be desirable to have as many ancillary helpers as teachers.

SCOTLAND

All teachers in Scottish schools have to have a full professional training, recognized by the General Teaching Council. No exemptions from this requirement are permitted. This means, for instance, that schools for severely subnormal children – the former junior occupation centres – must be staffed by teachers who have taken a full primary school training.

It is up to local education authorities to decide on staffing policy. Although a consultative document was issued in 1973 by the Scottish Education Department about desirable staffing levels, this is still being discussed with local authorities.

School governors

ENGLAND AND WALES

The 1944 Education Act said that every school should have a board of governors and it published a Model Instrument, suggesting who might be suitable to serve as governors, and Model Articles, suggesting what their powers might be. In 1975 the National Association of Governors and Managers (NAGM) conducted a survey to discover how many authorities appointed parents, teachers and pupils to the governing boards of their schools (*School Governors and Managers: Some Facts and Figures*, NAGM, 1975). They discovered that of the ninety-one LEAs replying to the survey, sixty appointed parents to serve as governors in special schools, compared with sixty-five in primary and seventy in secondary schools. For teachers the figures were fifty-one in special schools, fifty-six in primary and sixty in secondary schools. Twenty-six LEAs involved pupils in governors' meetings in some capacity – as observers if not full governors with a right to vote. Of these only one (Ealing) appeared to include pupils at schools for the physically handicapped. Another NAGM publication (*Proposals for More Effective Functioning of Governors and Managers of Non-Maintained Special Schools*, 1974) found that three out of thirty-three non-maintained schools used by one local authority had parents on their governing boards. The large catchment areas of most special schools make it difficult to define the community they serve and therefore harder for the governors to 'form a link between the school and the community' as their function is frequently described. Yet this public-relations role may have a special importance for schools whose pupils are 'different'. Parents who are concerned about school facilities ought to to be able to get influential support from the school governors, but they will not be able to rely on their point of view being heard until every special school, both maintained and non-maintained, has parent governors.

NAGM
Holbrook Centre, Holbrook Road, London E15

SCOTLAND

Until May 1975, when local government was reorganized in Scotland, there were no Scottish equivalents of the managing and governing bodies of English and Welsh schools. However, from that date LEAs had to set up school and college councils to manage and supervise individual schools or groups of schools and further education colleges. The councils include representatives of parents, teachers, churches, industry, commerce and other local interests.

Waiting lists

The HMSO *Statistics of Education* in England and Wales for 1974 show that over 7000 children were awaiting admission to special day schools and approximately another 4000 were waiting for a boarding place. Of these, 5292 had been waiting for more than a year. It was a slight improvement over the figures of the previous three years. Different handicaps have different prospects, the physically handicapped generally being better off. According to DES official sources, the vast majority of these children were being educated in ordinary schools or at home while they waited for a place at the right special school, but 583 of them were not receiving any education at all. Of these children 394 were described as severely subnormal. The LEA has a duty to provide education for every child and the Secretary of State has powers (under Section 99 of the 1944 Education Act) to give directions to any LEA which fails to discharge its duties. Some attempts are being made, at the time of writing, to persuade the Secretary of State to take action against LEAs which are failing to provide a child with any education. However, there is no record of any Secretary of State ever having used his powers under this section.

The Scottish Education Department was unable to supply figures about children waiting for a suitable special school place. This is in line with the finding of the Scottish Society for Mentally Handicapped (SSMH) in *Regional*

Patterns in Education and Training of Severely Mentally Handicapped School Age Children in Scotland (by J. N. Richardson, 1975, price 25p) that local authorities simply do not know how many handicapped children there are in their areas. For example, the Lothian region had records of 373 severely mentally handicapped children, whereas at least 480 children were living there.

SSMH, 69 East Regent Street, Glasgow G2 2AN
Tel: 041-331 1551/2

Miscellany

General

DISABLED LIVING FOUNDATION

Disabled Living Foundation
346 Kensington High Street, London W14 8NS
Tel: 01-602 2491

The information service has a fund of information about helping handicapped children which could be very useful to special schools, ranging from suggestions about school furniture to incontinence aids. It is concerned that this doesn't seem to be reaching schools and education authorities who may not even know that it exists. In its annual report for 1974, the DLF describes how a volunteer worker is carrying out an inquiry into the use of this information in special education. It hopes that as a result it will be able to get a better idea of the kind of information services schools think would be most helpful to them.

WHEELOCK SPECIAL EDUCATION CENTRE

Wheelock Special Education Centre
Crewe Road, Wheelock, Sandbach, Cheshire
Tel: Sandbach (093-67) 7398

Wheelock Special Education Centre has been set up by the LEA as a focal point for all concerned with the total development of handicapped children in Cheshire. It provides a resource centre for books, equipment, toys and aids suitable for handicapped children. It is a base for in-service training, induction courses and conferences for all those working with handicapped children within the education service. Parents, voluntary societies, professional associations, a toy library and opportunity groups all use the centre as a meeting place. It is the base for home tutors and for peripatetic teachers of the handicapped and their equipment. Its management committee consists of representatives from parents' groups, voluntary organizations and the health, social services and education departments.

Audio-visual aids

LEARNING DEVELOPMENT AIDS (LDA)

Learning Development Aids
Park Works, Norwich Road, Wisbech, Cambs PE13 2AX
Tel: Wisbech (0945) 2011

The LDA catalogue, *Materials for Children with Learning Difficulties*, contains a range of aids designed to help children's development in specific areas – auditory skills, visual perception, motor skills, conceptual skills and language. A new venture, undertaken in cooperation with the Hester Adrian Research Centre, is the production of several series of Barnaby books, concerned with language, memory, imagination and problem-solving in daily life. The first book in the 'Help Yourself' series tells how a young boy gets his shoes dirty and then cleans them. Opposite each of the twenty-eight pictures is a list of ideas, games and concepts carefully graded in difficulty. *Learn to Look: Ball, Cup, Bottle and Bus* shows these four objects in different, more and more complex, contexts with games to play that give practice in looking at colour, shape and spatial relationships.

VIDEOTAPES

Jill Lumb, Woolley Wood School, Oaks Fold Road, Sheffield 5

Jill Lumb, a teacher at an ESN school, is working on a programme of experimental TV films for mentally handicapped children with the help of Sheffield University's TV service and a gift of equipment from Rank Xerox. The programmes are designed to reinforce or emphasize something already being taught by a teacher by presenting it in much more simple terms than the ordinary Playschool-type programme. Her first programme, which lasts seven minutes, is on body images; parts of the body appear as if by magic in the context of a story about an invisible man. The programmes are made on videotape so that they can be repeated over and over again on closed-circuit TV systems. Although the films are designed for use in schools, anyone with access to a videotape recorder could contact Miss Lumb for details of how to borrow copies.

'Whatever Next'

ETV, Tennyson Street, London SW8
Tel: 01-622 9956

Tony Wise of the Inner London Education Authority's educational television service has produced a series of twelve television programmes for deaf children of junior school age. The aim has been to give the teacher pictorial material which can be used to extend vocabulary and develop language.

Videotapes of the programmes are available on hire.

Details from:
Guild Sound and Vision
Woodstone House, Oundle Road, Peterborough
Tel: Peterborough (0733) 63122

See the Index for other audio-visual aids.

Compulsory school age

ENGLAND AND WALES

At present, compulsory school age is calculated as starting from the beginning of the term after the child's fifth birthday. It ends when the child is sixteen. Children who are sixteen between 1 September and 31 January may leave school at the end of the spring term; children whose birthdays are on or between 1 February and 31 August can leave at half-term in the summer term (normally the spring bank holiday week-end).

When the normal school leaving age was fifteen, special-school children had an extra year at school because they had to stay on till they were sixteen. Many people concerned with the education of handicapped children have criticized that fact that these children, who normally develop more slowly than their unhandicapped contemporaries, have to leave school just as they are beginning to show some progress. Although LEAs have the duty to provide education in school for pupils up to nineteen years of age if they or their parents require it, very few children in special schools can stay on after sixteen because of shortage of places. The official DES *Statistics of Education* for 1974 shows that there were only 1487 pupils over the age of sixteen in special schools. Over 800 of these were seventeen years old, about 300 were eighteen and the same number were nineteen. For example, only sixty-three educationally subnormal children over the age of sixteen, out of a total of all ages of 53353, were in full-time special schools.

This is another example of how educational resources are unfairly distributed. Just a little of the money spent on sixth-form education, which is often uneconomically organized, could revolutionize the educational chances of many handicapped children, especially the mentally handicapped.

SCOTLAND

Although compulsory school age is effectively the same in Scotland as in England and Wales, the administrative arrangements for deciding the exact date on which a child must start or may leave school are different. Proposals for revising these are contained in a Bill to be presented in Parliament some time in 1976.

Educational psychology

Most LEAs employ educational psychologists as part of their child guidance service and also to help them in carrying out their duty of identifying children who need special education. Educational psychologists, who are normally qualified teachers in addition to their psychology qualification, are specialists in the assessment and treatment of learning problems. Because the problems dealt with are primarily educational, children are mostly referred through their schools, rather than through the usual medical sources for other assessments. *Circular 2/75* especially recommends that schools should normally consult parents before referring a child to an educational psychologist although they have no legal obligation to do so. It also suggests that parents should be given the opportunity of being present at examinations by an educational psychologist. Where there are long delays in being referred for an assessment some parents may be tempted to speed up the process by making a private appointment. The North London Dyslexia Association, which has considerable experience in this field, had this to say in their annual report for 1973: 'it is uncertain how much influence the report of an educational psychologist, working in a private capacity, will have with a local education authority. Furthermore, if the child has already been referred to the schools' psychological service, a medical assessment by a neurologist or a paediatrician may be more helpful.'

Educational therapy

Mr and Mrs V. Arkwright, 36 Essex Park, London N3
Tel: 01-349 9633

This is an American qualification. Educational therapists diagnose the exact nature of a child's difficulties in learning; they plan an individual programme to meet his special intellectual needs and strengths. Parents are fully involved in the programme and the therapy.

Education welfare service

Most LEAs in England and Wales have some kind of education welfare service. The first detailed report on the working of the education welfare service published in 1974 showed that the structure and organization of the service differed widely between LEAs. One of the main duties of the education welfare service has always been the enforcement of school attendance, but the title of school attendance officer, with its punitive associations, has generally been dropped. Nowadays they see themselves as providing a link between the school and the family, and consequently between the family and the education service as a whole, so as to help children in some kind of difficulty or hardship at school. Where the service is well organized, the education welfare service will be concerned with seeing to a child's direct needs, such as free dinners and clothing grants, and with less easily identifiable problems relating to suspected family difficulties, moral welfare and the possible need for special education. Parents can find out if they have a a local education welfare service and how to contact it from the school or from the education office. They can often take the initiative and approach the education welfare service themselves if they want help.

SCOTLAND

In Scotland there is no service directly comparable to the education welfare service. The nearest equivalent is the school attendance service. Welfare problems in schools are the responsibility of the guidance staff. Headteachers are responsible for specific administrative duties such as applications for free meals and, according to the Scottish Education Department, 'distribute forms as appropriate'.

Examinations

A variety of arrangements are possible for candidates who are blind or have some physical handicap or are in hospital. Extra time is usually allowed and candidates may be allowed to use typewriters or to dictate their paper to someone who writes it down. Surprisingly, the simpler expedient of dictating into a tape recorder does not yet seem to have been accepted.

Holidays

The longer the special school holidays, the more ground may be lost in terms of education and specialist forms of treatment such as physiotherapy. Moreover, for the more severely handicapped children, boarding school is a form of residential care and the strain on the family during long school holidays may be considerable. Similarly, day schools are a form of day care, essential for the welfare of the family. So the pattern of terms and holidays which suits ordinary schools may be quite unsuitable for special schools. Some attempts have been made to solve this, such as the four-term year with shorter holidays. According to *Circular 4/73*, some LEAs keep one or more boarding schools open during the school holidays. The circular suggests that day schools could copy the idea. Some voluntary societies make a particular point of offering regular holiday care where the child can feel that he is returning somewhere he really belongs for the school holidays. The report, *No Childhood* (published by the Council for Children's Welfare, 1975, available from the National Children's Bureau), deplores the fact that many children are sent to long-stay hospitals for school holidays because they have no homes or because their parents can't have them at home for some reason. The report says: 'Hospital is the last place for a child to spend his school holidays.' It describes one child: 'When she goes back to her school, her classmates will talk about where they have been, they will write about it in their school news books, she will hear about their family outings, etc. But all she will be able to think about is a dull ward where she spent four weeks without going anywhere at all.'

Circular 5/74 on the education of children in hospital also stresses the problem of holidays. It recommends that holidays for mentally handicapped children should last at most three to four weeks and that the hospital staff should arrange suitable activities and experiences during the holidays to divert and stimulate the children. It suggests using voluntary help if there are not enough staff to do this.

See chapter 8, Holidays, page 371

School meals

Although the charge to be made for school meals for children at ordinary schools is fixed by the Secretary of State, the price to be charged for school dinners for pupils at special schools is at the discretion of the LEA. The *Provision of Milk and Meals Regulations* allow LEAs to provide, in addition to school dinner, 'such other refreshments as the authority consider appropriate'. Some authorities have made use of this clause to provide breakfast for children in special schools.

Transport

All children are entitled to free transport provided by the LEA to and from schools if they live more than a regulation distance from the school – measured by the shortest possible route, whether this is a cart track or busy lorry route. This distance is two miles for children under eight, three miles for children over eight. LEAs may either lay on a school bus (which they may hire from a subcontractor) or pay for fares on public transport. Section 55 of the 1944 Education Act allows LEAs to be more flexible and generous than this if they want to and can afford to. They can provide transport for handicapped children under this section. The catchment areas of special schools may well be worked out in conjunction with transport arrangements and parents who want to choose a school on a different 'bus run' from the one which passes their home will not necessarily be able to have both the school of their choice and LEA transport. Unreliable school bus services are a constant cause of complaint. In some cases, parents are told to contact the bus contractors direct. By all means do this if the LEA suggests it, but they cannot 'pass the buck' to the contractor altogether since it is the LEA's responsibility to be sure that the arrangements are satisfactory. The school parent–teacher association and the governors ought to be prepared to lend their support to long-standing complaints.

The LEA is legally responsible for the safety of all children travelling on buses hired by them and should employ people to supervise them.

BOARDING SCHOOL

LEAs must pay for children's transport to and from school at the beginning and end of term. The problems arise with visits during the term, and particularly if weekly boarding is the norm at the school or parents prefer it. LEAs vary widely in their generosity in paying fares or arranging transport for visits home during the term. Coming home every weekend, or frequently, can involve parents in considerable expense. In fact the fares may cost more than they will save by having the child away at school.

LEAs have discretionary powers to pay fares for parents to visit the child at school 'if they are satisfied that without a visit, the child's special educational treatment would be impaired, and that the parents cannot afford the cost' (*Administrative Memorandum 6/66*).

Voluntary educational groups

CONFEDERATION FOR THE ADVANCEMENT OF STATE
EDUCATION (CASE)

CASE, 1 Windermere Avenue, Wembley HA9 8JH
Tel: 01-904 1722

> A pressure group of parents and teachers which interests
> itself in every aspect of the quantity and quality of state
> education. There are local associations throughout the
> country which are often active fighters for improvements
> in their area. Local associations may take up questions
> to do with special education. An outstanding example of
> what a CASE group can do is the series of well-produced
> publications from the Enfield Association for Education
> which includes *Education for Children with Mental Handi-*
> *caps, Education for our Children with Visual Handicaps* and
> *Education for our Children who are Deaf and Partially*
> *Hearing.*

Copies available from:
Mrs M. Jepson, 25 Forestdale, London N14 7DY
Tel: 01-886 4725

NATIONAL ASSOCIATION OF GOVERNORS AND MANAGERS
(NAGM)

NAGM, Holbrook Centre, Holbrook Road, London E15

> NAGM was established in 1970 to form a link between
> governors and managers all over the country, to help
> improve their effectiveness, and to press for reforms which
> would strengthen their role of reflecting the interests of the
> local community in its schools. It has branches in all parts
> of England and Wales, as well as a strong individual
> membership. NAGM issues policy and discussion papers,
> and runs courses and conferences on the work and function
> of governors and managers. It has a regular newsletter.
> In its evidence to Warnock, NAGM stressed the im-
> portance of every special school having its own governing

body including parents, teachers and, where possible, pupils. Membership is open to anyone interested in its views, whether or not they are governors or managers.

NATIONAL CONFEDERATION OF PARENT—TEACHER ASSOCIATIONS (NCPTA)

NCPTA, 1 White Avenue, Gravesend, Kent
Tel: Gravesend (0474) 60618

Many special schools have active school groups affiliated to the National Confederation whether or not they are formally set up as a PTA. They are concerned about how difficult it is for parents to make contact with one another since special schools draw their pupils from such large catchment areas. The National Confederation can advise on the setting up of an association and on how to plan and organize a suitable programme for a PTA as well as providing a range of other services and publications.

6 Leaving School

Careers guidance and assessment
Education and training
Employment

Careers guidance and assessment

Parents of *young* handicapped children can now be sure
that they will get some kind of assessment. The picture is
quite different at the end of their school career. What they
need is a realistic assessment of their potential, and practical
advice about opportunities for further education and work.
Sadly, their chances of getting it are minimal. These are
the main sources of help; you may have to try them all.

1 The school
2 The LEA careers service
3 The Manpower Services Commission
4 Voluntary organizations.

Some further education colleges also offer assessment
courses.

See Education and Training, page 285.

In school

Careers education has been defined as 'preparation for
adult life'. This is a continuous process in which guidance
and help in choosing a career are part of a concern for the
development of each individual pupil, not something
which can be done by a total stranger who sees them only
once at the end of their school career to fix them up with a
job.

The majority of ordinary secondary schools – 94 per cent
in a recent DES survey – have at least one staff member
with responsibility for careers advice and education. The

same survey looked at the provision for careers education in 281 special schools in England and Wales which had pupils of secondary school age. (These schools tend to be small and to cover the whole range of compulsory school age.) Half of them had no designated careers teacher and, where there was a careers teacher, over half had received no form of training (*Careers Education in Secondary Schools*, HMSO, 1973).

The HMIs who conducted the DES survey found that philosophy of careers education in special schools tends to be based more on a concern with social development and acceptance than with a preparation for work. Careers education is therefore a matter of 'infusion' rather than of timetabled periods, although two-thirds of the schools in the survey did devote a few periods specifically to it.

However, Margaret Morgan, Head of Social Work and Employment of the Spastics Society, has said:

So often discussions about post-school plans are left until the last year, or even the last term at school. The young people and their parents will, however, often have been speculating and worrying about the future for some years, though they may have been apprehensive about raising the topic themselves, for fear of disappointment and disillusionment.

It isn't a question of special schools not caring about the prospects for their pupils once they have left school. The DES report comments: 'If patience, sympathy, forbearance, encouragement and common sense are attributes of careers education, then special schools do not lag behind in this respect.' So it would seem that although parents can be sure of a sympathetic hearing if they discuss with the teachers their worries about the future, they cannot rely on getting the information they need from the school about all the possibilities for further education, training and employment.

Some schools have undertaken major projects such as the one run by the Cliffdale Secondary School for educationally subnormal pupils in Portsmouth. They set up an industrial training workshop for pupils who were ill-equipped to make the sharp transition from school to open employment. The workshop unit is supervised by a works board, which includes five managers of local companies, and five representatives of the LEA and the school governors. Children from other local special schools are also accepted on to the course. A panel consisting of the headmaster, careers teachers, LEA careers officer, an educational psychologist and a school doctor was set up to help educationally subnormal school-leavers. The whole programme includes activities like a school-leavers' club for pupils in their last term, ex-pupils and their friends, backed by a parents/supporters association. The London Borough of Hillingdon has set up a similar scheme, run by the careers service.

LEA careers service

LEAs have a duty to provide and maintain their own careers service to help anyone receiving education to decide what training they need and to help them find a suitable job. The careers service is not necessarily limited to those in education and anyone may go to them for help in choosing a suitable career. LEA careers officers are expected to work in close collaboration with the schools and visit them regularly. Some LEAs have careers officers who specialize in helping handicapped school-leavers.

Manpower Services Commission

EMPLOYMENT SERVICE AGENCY

In 1973 the Employment and Training Act set up the Manpower Services Commission to make sure that people would get help in 'selecting, training for, obtaining and retaining employment suitable to their ages and capabilities'. The Employment Service Agency and the Training Services Agency carry out the policies of the Commission. The Employment Service Agency is responsible for modernizing the employment service; the Training Services Agency is responsible for the provision of training and the Training Opportunities Schemes.

The Employment Service Agency is therefore responsible for local employment offices (not, however, for unemployment benefit) and for all services for rehabilitation and employment of disabled people. The place to contact the service is the local employment office or job centre whose address will be in the post office.

DISABLEMENT RESETTLEMENT OFFICERS (DROs)

The Employment Service Agency employ special officers known as disablement resettlement officers. They are based mainly in the larger employment offices though some of them work in hospitals and rehabilitation centres. Their job is to know about all the facilities available for disabled people in further education, training and employment. They should work closely with hospitals and doctors, social workers and local employers, and, where young people are concerned, with the careers service in arranging suitable employment and training. Any job centre or employment office can put you in touch with a DRO.

In 1975 there were 530 DROs and thirty specialist officers helping blind people (blind persons resettlement officers).

After a major review of the DRO service in 1974 the Employment Service Agency has made plans to improve the training of DROs. Various experimental projects in assessment for handicapped people are being undertaken with a view to improving and expanding the Agency's service for disabled people.

JOB CENTRES

Job centres are the new version of the employment exchange. They are modelled on the more attractive style of the best commercial employment agencies, and, like them, sited in main shopping centres. Anyone over compulsory school age may go to a job centre. One part of the service is simply a job supermarket where clients make their own selection from the lists of jobs on display. Staff should be able to advise on training and qualifications.

Anyone needing more detailed advice and guidance can make an appointment with a trained vocational guidance counsellor, or a disablement resettlement officer.

EMPLOYMENT REHABILITATION CENTRES

These centres (the old industrial rehabilitation centres) are run by the Employment Service Agency. Although they were originally intended mainly for people recently sick or injured who need extra help in getting back to work, handicapped school-leavers may also be recommended to them by the careers service or the DRO. They provide work experience, occupational guidance and aim at improving the physical condition and mental outlook of disabled people. In 1975 there were twenty-six centres in different parts of the country, including a residential centre. There is residential accommodation at two others and lodgings can be found near all the centres where necessary. Courses last from seven to nine weeks, or longer if required. A realistic working environment is provided, including modern workshops and a commercial and clerical section, but the centres do not attempt to train people for a trade. They do assess the capacity of those taking courses over a range of basic industrial and commercial operations and can recommend and arrange further training elsewhere if they think this is desirable. The emphasis has generally switched from the rehabilitation of recently disabled people towards help in solving personal problems which may be the main barrier to employment. Over the last five years, work preparation courses for mentally retarded and other handicapped school-leavers have been provided at a few rehabilitation centres in collaboration with local authorities. Applications for courses are submitted through the DRO.

OTHER REHABILITATION SERVICES

The Employment Service Agency also makes grants of various kinds, usually allowances to trainees, to voluntary bodies providing workshop facilities designed to prepare people for open employment. They include industrial therapy associations in Birmingham, Ealing and Epsom, centres for the blind run by the RNIB, residential rehabilitation centres run by the Spastics Society at Welwyn Garden City and Lancaster.

Voluntary organizations

BANSTEAD PLACE

Banstead Place, Park Road, Banstead, Surrey SM7 3EE
Tel: Burgh Heath 56222

As the outcome of its experience and of the research by Mrs Margaret Roberts (published as *Handicapped School-Leavers*, 1972), the Queen Elizabeth Foundation for the Disabled established Banstead Place as a purpose-built residential centre for the assessment and further education of thirty-two physically handicapped (including multiply handicapped) young people of both sexes of school-leaving age. It provides total assessment – educational, personal, medical, vocational, social. The main criterion of entry is the student's ability to learn through his individual programme how to accept increasing responsibility for himself and to understand the demands of normal, everyday life. An initial assessment is arranged, preferably during the last year at school, so that the student, his parents, the school and the local authority's careers officer and social worker can coordinate plans.

It is important to stress the role which Banstead Place hopes to play in achieving the correct placement of the students after they leave. The organizers believe that there is no point in theoretical assessment unless its findings are translated into practical action. The staff of Banstead Place continue to offer support to all concerned after the student has left. Application forms may be obtained from the Principal and fees are normally paid by the appropriate local education authority. When he has received a formal application the Principal arranges a preliminary visit.

SPASTICS SOCIETY

Social Work and Employment Department
Spastics Society, 16 Fitzroy Square, London W1P 5HO
Tel: 01-387 9571

The Spastics Society arranges short residential assessment courses for physically handicapped school-leavers at their centres in different parts of the country. Many people come to them for the first time at this stage for advice on further education, vocational and occupational opportunities and residential care. Although the reason for this is that many of the other services which have provided support up to school-leaving age peter out when it is time to leave school, Miss Morgan, the head of the Social Work and Employment Department, sees a positive side to it. She says: 'Although, clearly, the reports and views of those most closely connected with the young people are very valuable in building up the whole picture, the fresh appraisal at adolescence may be best undertaken by people who have not been closely involved with the child during the growing-up process.' The Spastics Society has its own further education and work and training centres.

Handicapped School-Leavers

National Foundation for Educational Research, Book Division
2 Jennings Buildings, Thames Avenue, Windsor
Berks SL4 1QS

A report published in 1973 by the National Children's Bureau on the education, training and employment of a sample of handicapped school-leavers attempts to assess how far such needs are being met at the present time. The individual cases described in the report show very clearly how far the services available can fall short of meeting these needs. It makes recommendations for an efficient and coordinated service for handicapped school-leavers. The report costs 85p.

Education and training

It is not very easy to find out what is available in the field of further education for people who are mentally or physically handicapped. The National Bureau for Handicapped Students (see page 301) intends to keep a current register in due course.

It is particularly disappointing that a purpose-built short-term residential college for the physically handicapped had to close within a year of its opening because of insufficient endowments and the toll of inflation. This was Prospect Hall at Selly Oak, Birmingham, which shared a campus site with eight other colleges.

There are a number of further education and training establishments which cater specifically for people with a particular handicap. The organizations involved with that handicap ought to know what is available in their own field and may very well have their own establishments. For instance, both the Spastics Society and the National Society for Mentally Handicapped Children run further education colleges offering a variety of types and levels of courses. The larger establishments which offer courses on a regional or national basis to students with a particular handicap are listed as Appendix A in *Handicapped School-Leavers* (National Children's Bureau, 1973, see above).

Manpower Services Commission

TRAINING SERVICES AGENCY

The Training Services Agency of the Manpower Services Commission organizes government-sponsored training under the Training Opportunities Scheme. This may be in skill centres (formerly called government training centres). Handicapped school-leavers may be referred to these, perhaps after a course at an employment rehabilitation centre (see page 282 above). They may attend from sixteen years of age and take longer courses than the normal one year maximum. The centres provide training on modern machine and hand tools, given by skilled craftsmen.

Special supervision and help are provided for disabled trainees.

The Scheme may also sponsor students at further education colleges, particularly in clerical and commercial courses at residential further education colleges. The Professional Training Scheme may be able to sponsor students for higher education and professional qualifications. The careers service or DRO will be able to give advice on what help is available from the Training Services Agency. Finding a job after a course is the responsibility of the placement officer at the centre or the employment office in the trainee's own area.

A leaflet, *Training Opportunities for Disabled People*, (TSA L15) was published by the Training Services Agency and the Central Office of Information in 1976.

Special further education

We have given details here of any colleges we could find out about which are not linked to one specific handicap. We do not claim that this list is exhaustive.

DELROW HOUSE

Delrow House, Hilfield Lane, Aldenham, Watford WD2 8DJ
Tel: Radlett 6006

Delrow House is one of five Camphill Village Trust Centres in this country associated with the Anthroposophical Movement founded on the work and teaching of Rudolph Steiner. It has been going for twelve years, first as an assessment centre, now as a residential college for rehabilitation and further education. Fifty mentally handicapped or disturbed students study courses designed to help them to achieve independence in the community. There are lectures, discussion groups, courses in speech therapy, movement, music and drama. Practical work includes crafts, gardening, cooking and housework. The age range is sixteen to sixty and the courses may last anything from a weekend to several years. The Trust says ιhat no matter how slow the progress, no student is treated as a failure. Delrow College is supported by fees – mostly paid by social services departments, allowances from the DHSS, donations, covenants and local fund-raising.

HEREWARD COLLEGE OF FURTHER EDUCATION

The Principal, Hereward College, Bramston Crescent,
Tile Hill Lane, Coventry CV4 9SW
Tel: Coventry (0203) 461231/4

A residential college for the further education of one hundred physically handicapped young people over sixteen. It opened to students from all parts of the country in September 1971 and was the first college to be established with national support from the DES and LEAs to fill a gap in provision for physically handicapped school-leavers. The college provides courses similar to those provided in colleges generally and acts as a bridge to employment, to 'ordinary' further education or to advanced courses in polytechnics or universities. Admission will not necessarily depend on academic qualifications and applicants with a wide range of physical handicaps – paraplegic, spina bifida, cerebral palsy, chest conditions, etc. – will be considered. Most students entering the college take a foundation course designed to bring them up to the standard for further courses or work experience.

MICHAELMAS TRUST

Secretary, Michaelmas Trust
Sherbrook, Towers Road, Poynton, Cheshire SK12 1DA
Tel: Poynton (099-67) 4233

This is a charitable trust which is seeking funds in order to set up a rural training unit, probably in Cheshire. The unit would provide a two-year residential further education course based on agriculture and horticulture and with continuing basic education where necessary. It will cater for forty to fifty mentally subnormal trainees of both sexes

up to a maximum age of about twenty-six yea.
will be selected from the whole of England and
according to suitability, aptitude and because they sh
enthusiasm for working on the land and with livestock.
Preliminary arrangements for selection procedures have
been made in cooperation with the Hester Adrian Research
Centre. It is expected that LEAs will meet the fees of
about £1200 a year for each trainee. They expect to move
into their own premises in 1977.

NATIONAL STAR CENTRE FOR DISABLED YOUTH

National Star Centre
Ullenwood Manor, Cheltenham, Glos GL53 5QU
Tel: Cheltenham (0242) 27631

An independent specialized residential college of further
education for physically handicapped students offering a
range of courses from general remedial work to university
courses. Great attention is paid to building up a rich
community life and encouraging students to develop a
greater degree of independence. All kinds of social,
cultural and sporting activities are arranged by the
students' executive committee. There is an experimental
POSM room where severely handicapped students can
learn new skills. Applications are usually submitted by
LEAs.

PORTLAND TRAINING COLLEGE FOR THE DISABLED

Portland Training College, Mansfield, Notts. NG18 4TJ
Tel: Blidworth (062-34) 2141/2

A voluntary residential college with 200 places available to
all categories of handicapped students (except totally
blind people) from school-leaving age. Its aim is to equip
students for open competition in employment. There are
three main departments. The department of further
education offers one-year education courses for which
students are sponsored by LEAs, and twelve-week literacy/
numeracy courses sponsored by the Training Services

Agency. Careful assessment is made before students are
offered a place on these courses. Assessment course groups
are arranged in each month of the year and applications
should be made well in advance. The vocational training
department offers a variety of courses, sponsored by the
Training Services Agency, in business studies and technical
studies. These prepare students for RSA, City and Guilds
and Pitmans examinations. There is also a sheltered
employment department, with some accommodation
facilities, offering workshop employment. Although candidates are normally sponsored by LEAs, local authority
social services departments or the Training Services
Agency, individuals can apply direct to the college.

REHAB – BRITISH COUNCIL FOR REHABILITATION OF THE DISABLED

REHAB, Tavistock House (South), Tavistock Square
London WC1H 9LB
Tel: 01-387 4037/8

A voluntary organization for handicapped people of
school-leaving age and over offering full assessment, information and advice. Further education courses are
planned in over 120 different subjects and arrangements
are made with local education authorities over payment of
fees. Some recognized correspondence courses are proposed
or personal tuition organized. All handicaps are catered
for except the blind.

The Council also operates a diagnostic and treatment
centre for people with specific learning difficulties.

ST LOYE'S COLLEGE

St Loye's College, Fairfield House
Topsham Road, Exeter EX2 6EP
Tel: Exeter (0392) 55428

The primary function of the College is to train physically
disabled people in skilled trades so that they can obtain
employment. The College has accommodation for a total

A.H.F.P. – K

of 200 people from all parts of the country with almost any disability except those who are blind or mentally ill. The College has a further education department catering for up to fifty physically handicapped young people between sixteen and eighteen years of age who are of average or below average academic ability. Students are sponsored by their local education authorities. A purpose-built teaching centre, opened in September 1975, provides facilities for assessment and pre-training in all the commercial and technical skills taught at the College, together with intensive remedial tuition in basic subjects and a broad-based programme of general studies and social studies courses. All applicants are required to attend a one-day assessment at the College, for which the date can usually be offered within six weeks. There may occasionally be a waiting list for boys.

Outside working hours the young people are cared for by house-parents and are encouraged to take part in sporting and social activities both in and out of College. Applications for entry into this department of the College are normally made through careers officers of local authorities direct to the College. There are no fees at all to the young people and they receive pocket money direct from the DHSS. The College is a voluntary organization registered as a charity, with government grants to cover running costs.

The majority of students spend an average of eighteen months in the further education department before transferring to one of the College's vocational training courses for adult men and women under Training Services Agency sponsorship.

HOSPITAL PATIENTS

Patients in long-stay hospitals who are over school-leaving age ought to be put in touch with the education services so that they can take advantage of further education courses (*Circular 5/74*). It is the responsibility of the LEA under the 1944 Education Act to make adequate provision for education for everyone over school age, including disabled people, and for the health services to make it possible for hospital patients to take advantage of this. One example of how further education for mentally handicapped adults can be organized within the hospital service is the scheme run jointly by Wiltshire LEA and the Wiltshire AHA. There are two full-time tutors based on two major hospitals and an educational adviser/tutor who oversees education and training teams headed by a nursing officer and including teachers seconded from the LEA in other hospitals in the group. Funds are provided both by the LEA and the AHA. In a report on the scheme, included in the King's Fund Centre publication, *Adult Education for Mentally Handicapped People* (1975), the educational adviser claims that the success of the scheme is dependent on the close working knowledge and involvement with the hospital world as well as the commitment to education.

RADIO CLUB SPECIAL – AN EDUCATIONAL BROADCASTING VENTURE FOR THE MENTALLY HANDICAPPED

Stanley Vince, Radio Club Special
40 Lodge Hill Road, Birmingham B29 6NG
Tel: 021-472 0881

On Tuesday 18 May 1974 the first broadcast was transmitted from BBC Radio Birmingham of 'Radio Club Special', written by Stanley Vince, an education officer for the mentally handicapped. These are broadcasts which contain elements of educational techniques basic to work for the handicapped. Their main aim is to help the retarded toward an understanding of the everyday world and contain features such as buying a railway ticket, travelling on a bus, shopping, visiting friends, etc., and also cultural items. Listeners are encouraged to become involved with the programme. Mr Vince hopes that these broadcasts might also help to show how much an extension of education beyond the statutory obligations of the Education Act is needed. All work on the broadcasts is voluntary, no finance being available from any source. Family, friends and a mentally handicapped adult helped to read scripts of the first transmissions.

Latter-day stringent economies upon local radio expenditure make future broadcasting dates uncertain, but BBC TV has shown interest in a screen version of 'Radio Club Special'. Taped copies of 'Radio Club Special' and programme notes with suggestions for follow up activities are available for anyone else interested. Please send a stamped, addressed envelope when contacting Mr Vince.

Further education colleges

Further education colleges are becoming increasingly conscious of the needs of the handicapped members of the community, and some of them are trying to find the best way of helping. Any further education college is able to set up a course for handicapped school-leavers, given the resources and, most important of all, the will. Teachers, governors and parents should approach their nearest college to see what can be done. We have given a few examples here which might give you some useful ideas.

AIREDALE AND WHARFEDALE COLLEGE OF FURTHER EDUCATION

Airedale and Wharfedale College
Calverley Lane, Horsforth LS18 4RQ
Tel: Horsforth (097-34) 87234

Following a detailed investigation in the Leeds and Bradford area by members of the College staff, a full-time one-year further education course for physically handicapped young people was established in September 1974.

Approximately half the week is devoted to general education and the remainder to practical work. For this part of the course handicapped students are integrated into ordinary classes of adults, vocational students or older school pupils following linked courses. The practical work may be regarded as vocational or non-vocational depending upon individual interests and inclinations. A great deal of attention is given to continuous assessment and as a picture emerges of the type of work a student will be able to perform, the careers officers search for possible employers. The course is based at Pudsey Centre where there are specially developed workshops and craftrooms, situated almost entirely on the ground floor. There is easy access to all parts of the building for people in wheelchairs. There are no fees for this course.

BRIXTON COLLEGE FOR FURTHER EDUCATION

Brixton College for Further Education
65 Brixton Hill, London SW2
Tel: 01-737 1166

This College runs full-time courses for hearing-impaired students – from profoundly deaf to partially hearing. Some students undertake one of the ordinary courses offered by the College, with the support of tutorial help and other assistance from specialist staff. Alternatively, there is a general education course especially designed for hearing-impaired students. They would normally study either commercial or technical subjects as well. Students are integrated with hearing students for PE, optional subjects and commercial subjects. A speech therapist is assigned to the 'Deaf Unit' and all students have speech therapy sessions twice a week. The College also organizes day-release courses for hearing-impaired students.

The College runs a series of linked courses with local special schools, most of which have some vocational content. A number of the students from these linked courses have been able to make the transition into a more normal educational and social situation and have become successful full time students of the College.

PARK LANE COLLEGE OF FURTHER EDUCATION

The Principal, Park Lane College
Park Lane, Leeds LS3 1AA
Tel: Leeds (0532) 443011

Since 1971 the College has run a special full-time further education course for school-leavers from local special schools, including a hospital school for the ESN. The course, which takes seventy students, lasts three years and attempts to create educational programmes in keeping with the chronological age of the students and yet realistic enough to meet their actual needs. Work is therefore highly individual and each task is geared to the student's attainment and capability and varies from simple dressing and hygiene practice to going out unaccompanied and travelling by public transport. The academic programme includes speech development, number and reading, telephone practice, conceptual building tasks. In the afternoon each group has periods of art and craft, music and sporting activities. Students are encouraged to mix with other students at the College and share its facilities. Transport is provided to and from College, and meals are provided by the school meals service.

WEST BRIDGFORD COLLEGE OF FURTHER EDUCATION

The Principal, West Bridgford College
Greythorn Drive, West Bridgford, Nottingham NG2 7GA
Tel: Nottingham (0602) 812125

The department of science and general studies of this College now operates a full-time course for handicapped young people over the age of sixteen. Students have a variety of handicaps and a wide range of abilities and interests. Some find difficulty with the basic language skills of reading and writing while others are ready to cope with GCE work. Each student's programme is tailored to meet his or her individual needs. Most students are given the opportunity to work in other departments of the College or may be seconded to them full time. At present all students are ambulant but ramps are being constructed around the College by West Bridgford Comprehensive School to cater for any future students who may be confined to wheelchairs. The College works in close cooperation with the county careers office and it is hoped, in spite of some difficult cases, that suitable employment will be found for students as they become ready for work.

Universities and polytechnics

In common with other public institutions, universities and polytechnics are beginning to make positive efforts to cope with the difficulties faced by handicapped young people who hope to work for a degree. The University of Leeds is one of those universities and colleges who have appointed a committee to make sure that physically handicapped staff and students are given as fair a chance as possible in university life. Their Senate has issued a formal declaration of intent, one of the main points of which is that no application will be turned down just because of handicap. All handicapped applicants will be given a chance to discuss their needs with the admissions officer. At least one polytechnic, the North East London Polytechnic, has a coordinator for handicapped students. Lancaster University has a media services unit where handicapped students can listen to films and recorded repeats of lectures and demonstrations.

The University Grants Committee has produced a free leaflet, *Provision for the Disabled at Universities – Notes on Implementation of the Chronically Sick and Disabled Persons Act 1970*. This is also of interest to polytechnics and further education colleges.

UGC, 14 Park Crescent, London W1N 4DH
Tel: 01-636 7799

ACCESS

Physically handicapped young people hoping to go to a university or polytechnic can consult *Access to University and Polytechnic Buildings* (price 20p) which gives detailed information about access to sites, faculty buildings, social facilities and living accommodation.

Central Council for the Disabled
34 Eccleston Square, London SW1V 1PE
Tel: 01-821 1871

UNIVERSITY OF SUSSEX

One example of the way in which handicapped students can be helped to enjoy university life is Kulukundis House at the University of Sussex, a residential building designed especially for them. This is a unit consisting of four study bedrooms, a common room with kitchen area, bath, shower and toilet facilities, and a small self-contained flat for the nurse in attendance. There is also a terrace and patio garden. The site of the building was deliberately chosen to encourage social contact with other students. The building is specially equipped and furnished and has an alarm and warden intercom system in each room. The cost of £40000 was met by private donations, largely by one from the President of Burmah Oil, Mr Elias Kulukundis.

During vacations some of the rooms may be available for Open University summer-school students or holidays.

The University of Sussex has also published a *Guide for Wheelchair Users* with a plan and details of access to all buildings and grounds.

CHESHIRE HOSTEL FOR HANDICAPPED STUDENTS AND
UNDERGRADUATES

The Warden,
Taylor House, 16 Osler Road, Headington, Oxford
Tel: Oxford (0865) 66322

> Under the auspices of the Cheshire Foundation, a group of
> people in Oxford has bought and converted a house in
> Headington as a hostel to enable five students to study for
> degrees and diplomas at any college in Oxford. It is run
> by a warden and assistant warden trained by the Cheshire
> Homes, who also provided the capital for the enterprise.
> The costs of running the hostel, including staffing and
> repayment of the Cheshire loan, are subsidized by volun-
> tary contributions.

OPEN UNIVERSITY

Open University, Walton Hall, Milton Keynes MK7 6AA
Tel: Milton Keynes (0908) 74066

> It was clear from its inauguration in 1969 that the Open
> University would be an ideal source of higher education
> for handicapped students: no formal academic qualifica-
> tions are needed to enrol for courses and the medium of
> instruction is correspondence course type material, backed
> up by radio and TV broadcasts and summer schools.
> There are regional offices and study centres where students
> can meet tutors, counsellors and fellow students.
>
> The University's evidence to Warnock – a fat pamphlet
> of over 100 pages – gives a full account of everything it is
> doing for handicapped students, and how it plans to help
> them in the future. It has a coordinating committee for
> disabled students, which keeps an eye on all the different
> aspects of catering for disabled people; also a full-time
> senior counsellor for disabled students who can be con-
> tacted on any problem relating to handicap.
>
> In April 1975 the University issued a policy statement on
> disabled students. Its nine declarations included a promise
> to give special consideration in its admission policy to

handicapped students, a pledge to take all possible practical steps to enable them to participate in all aspects of university life, and an intention to treat all disabled students as equal members of the University.

In 1975 the University knew of at least 1100 disabled students studying with them. This seems to be about twice as many as at all the other higher education institutions put together. A survey of success rates showed that their overall pass rate was slightly higher than average, and that those with multiple handicaps were the most successful. Because so much of the material is written, people can work at their own pace. Tapes are available for blind students and also for people with dyslexia. Broadcasts can be taped and repeated.

A project for deaf students has been in operation since 1972 through which a group of deaf students has received intensive support, with extra tutorial courses, supplementary visual aids, experimental communications systems, etc., and a special summer school for deaf and hearing students. A report on the project so far is available from the University. All deaf students who need it are offered special help at the summer schools including a personal helper whose expenses are paid by the University or a local authority.

The University is offering a new post-experience course 'The Handicapped Person in the Community'. Although it is really intended for people professionally concerned with the care of handicapped people, much of the course content would be of interest to parents of handicapped children. Books, films and tapes can be bought from the Marketing Division whether or not you are a registered student. Details are available in a leaflet describing the course. One of the textbooks which has already been published, *The Handicapped Person in the Community* (edited by D. M. Boswell and J. M. Wingrove, Open University, 1974), was described in the *Times Educational Supplement* as a 'beautifully produced masterpiece, unlikely to be superseded'.

The Open University Students Association works to help handicapped students participate fully in its activities, and offers several voluntary services to them. For example, OUSA organizes study tours abroad in connection with some of the courses. It thought that disabled people should have a chance to join in, so as an experiment a study tour of Rome was organized for students with impaired mobility. Ten disabled students, five totally wheelchair bound, with fellow students as assistants, spent two weeks in Rome with a tutor and group leader. One tour member summed it up like this: 'Living in close proximity taught us all a lot. Not only about the wonders of Rome but about ourselves – how the fit and disabled can help each other – in a situation which was new to us.'

A book on their experiences, *Have Wheels: Will Travel*, is published by Educational Explorers Ltd (price £1.65). It should be obtainable from bookshops or direct from the publishers – cash with order. It has photos as well as a fund of advice for intending travellers, and a frank and informal account of disasters as well as successes. All the proceeds from the book are going into a disadvantaged students' travel fund sponsored by OUSA.

Educational Explorers Ltd
40 Silver Street, Reading RG1 2SU
Tel: Reading (0734) 83103

Grants for education and training

ENGLAND AND WALES

The LEA may pay an educational maintenance allowance for people who stay on at school after school-leaving age. In addition to the standard student grants statutorily available to all students following an approved course of higher education, the LEA grants now include an extra allowance for disabled students. Any handicapped student who can show that he incurs additional expenditure related to study because of his handicap – for instance, having to buy an essential typewriter or tape-recorder or paying a fee to a reader – can claim to this extra allowance (not exceeding £140 a year in 1977).

Under the Education Act 1962, Section 2, LEAs can also make discretionary awards to students in further education – the generosity of these varying from area to area – and the extra disability allowance is available of right to any such award holder. All these awards are adjusted according to a means test.

SCOTLAND

LEA. Higher school bursaries may be granted to pupils who remain at school after compulsory school age as a contribution towards the child's expenses in the fifth and sixth years at secondary school. The amount depends on the parents' income and is prescribed in regulations issued by the Secretary of State for Scotland. Bursaries may be granted to students at full-time or part-time courses of further education or the Open University dependent on the generosity of the LEA and the financial circumstances of the student.

Scottish Education Department. The Department pays grants under the student allowance scheme to all students on first degree and comparable courses depending on parent's income. An extra allowance of up to £120 a year is payable to disabled students who have extra expenses because of their disability.

DHSS – SUPPLEMENTARY BENEFIT

Students on a grant are not eligible for supplementary benefit during term time, but may be able to claim special allowances for certain needs and conditions. Students who are not on a grant, maintained only by their parents, are eligible for supplementary benefit on income grounds. In the words of the DHSS, it is always worth applying to your local social security office for support during any educational or training course.

Most of the colleges and courses for handicapped students described in this section mention that the students receive supplementary benefit, even if it is described only as 'pocket money'. The college will be able to help anyone make an application.

EMPLOYMENT GRANTS

Any trainee on a course sponsored by the government (for instance in an employment rehabilitation centre, a skill centre, or a course recommended by a government agency) is eligible for allowances towards the cost of any fees and maintenance. These vary according to the type of course and the individual circumstances of the trainee. Details from any DRO or job centre.

SOCIAL SERVICES DEPARTMENTS

It is the responsibility of the local education department to give grants for conventional academic courses. However, many of the courses described in this chapter offer social and leisure activities as well as education and training. So social services departments, which have very wide powers to help handicapped people, may also be prepared to give grants for this type of course.

CHARITABLE TRUSTS

Many voluntary organizations and charities are able to make grants for aids to study or to supply equipment and aids at reduced prices or on loan.

See chapter 3, **Grants**, page 136.

Students' organizations

NATIONAL BUREAU FOR HANDICAPPED STUDENTS

National Bureau for Handicapped Students
City of London Polytechnic
Calcutta House Precinct, Old Castle Street, London E1 7NT
Tel: 01-283 1030

The National Bureau was established in 1975 to meet the

growing needs of handicapped students who want to follow some form of higher education course and find employment afterwards. It is intended to act as a clearing house of information and advice; to help coordinate the work of voluntary and statutory agencies where necessary, both in providing courses and in careers guidance and placement; to initiate research projects in the field of handicap, with special reference to education and employment.

A governing council representing the whole field of handicap will decide policy. It is intended that both the council and the staff will include a number of handicapped people. Membership of the Bureau will be open to institutions, organizations and individuals.

Once the Bureau's operations are under way, it should be possible for anyone with a handicap who wants to take up a college course to get all the information about special facilities, welfare services and help of all kinds from the Bureau.

NATIONAL UNION OF STUDENTS (NUS)

NUS
3 Endsleigh Street, London WC1H 0DU
Tel: 01-387 1277

The education and welfare department welcomes inquiries from disabled students and their parents about admissions, grants, access or any other individual problems.

With the help of a grant from Action Research for the Crippled Child, the NUS set up a research project on educational opportunities for disabled students. A report on the project, *The Disabled Student*, was published in 1976 and is available from NUS publications (price 40p, plus 15p postage). The report is divided into three main sections: admissions procedures in the tertiary sector; the role of the special school; local authority policy and provision. A major survey was undertaken into admission procedures in universities, polytechnics, colleges of education, further education colleges and other miscellaneous institutions such as agricultural colleges and colleges of art, music and drama. One result of the survey showed that almost a fifth of those replying to the survey took *no* handicapped students at all during 1972–5 and about one half took between one and four disabled students during the same period. The survey also covered such topics as reasons for not admitting handicapped students, criteria of entry handicapped students had to meet, whether any special committee or working party to discuss the needs of handicapped students had been set up. The results were equally disappointing.

The special school section looked briefly at the 'take up' rate of disabled school leavers into higher education and the difficulties encountered by schools in trying to place suitable students. The local education authority section discussed the thirty replies from LEAs in England, Wales and Scotland, 50 per cent of which 'were lacking in any significant information regarding services or provisions for handicapped people. . . . The response from the Scottish LEAs was entirely unhelpful and displayed the same lack of concern that was noticed in our examination of special schools in this area.'

The report concludes with a series of recommendations, the first of which typifies the NUS approach to the question of disabled students: 'The applications of all handicapped persons wishing to enter further or higher education must be treated solely on the basis of their academic merit so that they have opportunities equal to those of able-bodied candidates.'

Employment

We had to draw the line somewhere and this is it. But we try to give you some glimpses of what lies on the other side of it so that you know what to expect.

Research

EMPLOYMENT EXPERIENCES OF HANDICAPPED
SCHOOL-LEAVERS

National Children's Bureau
8 Wakley Street, Islington, London EC1V 7QE
Tel: 01-278 9441/7

This two-year study was set up in 1975 to look at the
employment experiences of some 400 handicapped young
people, aged between sixteen and eighteen. The group is
drawn from the National Child Development Study, a long-
term follow-up study of 16000 children born in Great
Britain in one week in March 1958. It includes those ascertained as physically and mentally handicapped as well as
some of those who, whilst not having received special
education, would have benefited from it in the opinion
of their teachers.

The study is looking at reasons for success as well as for
failure to get or keep a satisfying job, and is also examining
the effect of factors such as further education, training,
family circumstances and support, and the use of and
availability of other services.

Employment of Mentally Handicapped People

King's Fund Centre
126 Albert Street, London NW1 7NF
Tel: 01-267 6111

This is a report and discussion paper on the proceedings of
a two-day workshop held at the King's Fund Centre in
December 1974. The workshop tried to examine the facts
about employment for mentally handicapped people, and
to share the experiences of those responsible for training,
placing and employing them. Recent research findings
discussed at the seminar included statistics about the
employment prospects of people at adult training centres,
and discussions of the relationship between staff and
mentally handicapped individuals, which showed that the

potential for acquiring skills is often under-estimated. A list of fifteen very precise and practical recommendations was produced by the seminar members.

The report is available from the Centre – price 60p.

Registration

The Disabled Persons Register, kept by employment offices, is a register of people who are willing and capable of work, but are handicapped in finding it because of 'injury, disease or congenital deformity'. They must be over school-leaving age, permanent residents of the UK and the disability must be likely to last more than twelve months.

The aim is to identify people in need of help and certain statutory services are available only to people on the register – these include eligibility for the quota scheme, fares to work, designated employment (see **Open employment** below). It is, however, entirely voluntary, and you do not have to be registered in order to qualify for government-sponsored help in training.

You apply for registration to the disablement resettlement officer through the local employment office. He may accept your application himself, or if he is in doubt, he may refer it to the local disablement advisory committee. There are 227 of these, each of which has representatives of employers, workers, medical practitioners and others under an independent chairman.

Open employment

Once they have found a job, many handicapped people can hold their own in competition with able-bodied people. In order to help them find work the Disabled Persons (Employment) Acts provide that any employer of twenty or more workers must employ a quota of disabled people; that is to say, people on the Register of Disabled Persons. At present the quota is 3 per cent of the total. An employer below quota is not supposed to take on a worker who is not registered as disabled unless he has a permit to do so from the Secretary of State for Employment. If a permit is refused he can appeal to the local disablement advisory committee. Failure to employ 3 per cent is not in itself an offence and those campaigning for the handicapped person's right to work claim that very few employers pay much attention to this provision. In fact, when Mr Harold Walker, Employment Under-Secretary, was questioned in the House of Commons, in December 1975, about the quota scheme, he said that he had recently authorized two prosecutions – only to be described during the hearing of one case as 'a bureaucratic madman'.

The Acts also provide for the Secretary of State to designate occupations solely for disabled people. At present the only two occupations selected are car-park attendant and passenger-lift attendant. The Employment Service Agency has a limited loan scheme to provide special aids such as braille micrometers, special typewriters, etc. This enables people to take up a job when they cannot afford to provide tools themselves and the employer is unwilling to do so. They can also supply tools and machines to people unable to work away from home. The local office will be able to advise you whether these schemes are available locally.

Severely disabled people who are registered can be given help with fares to work if they are in ordinary employment and because of their disability have to meet high costs of travel such as taxi fares.

ASSOCIATION OF DISABLED PROFESSIONALS

Association of Disabled Professionals
The Stables, 73 Pound Road, Banstead, Surrey
Tel: Burgh Heath 52366

The Association is very keen to increase its student membership. Members include solicitors, engineers, computer programmers, dentists, actuaries, writers, librarians, social workers, economists, statisticians, doctors, university lecturers, psychologists, accountants, designers and civil servants. Some of the practising professionals in full-time employment are so severely disabled that they qualify for attendance allowance. They claim that you cannot be too disabled to work and that there are few professions that cannot be followed by disabled people no matter how severely disabled they may be. The Association says that its fundamental aim is that a battle fought successfully by one disabled person shall be a victory for all and that those who follow in the successful path of existing members shall encounter fewer obstacles and far more encouragement and help on the journey. The Association takes up issues with outside organizations on behalf of members. It will put young people contemplating a career in a certain profession in touch with a member already practising in the profession in spite of disability.

Despite Disability

Educational Explorers Ltd
40 Silver Street, Reading RG1 2SU
Tel: Reading (0734) 83103

This book about the career achievements of disabled people has a message of encouragement for any handicapped young man or woman who may feel daunted at the hurdles to be overcome. As the book shows, one of the worst of these is the attitude of the public and of officials towards them and their desire to be independent. The publishers hope that the book will be read not only by handicapped young people but also by others who are not themselves disabled, so that the message will get through that handicapped people can live a constructive life. The book tells eleven stories, written by people with a wide range of disability – including a deaf girl who is a fully qualified dentist, a blind man who is a staff reporter with the *Nottingham Evening Post*, several computer personnel, a solicitor who is confined to a wheelchair. What is immediately striking about them is that they share a great personal drive and ambition, whatever their handicap or final career, and they nearly all have parents who refused to give up hope for their children. The book is one of the 'My Life and Work' series edited by Rachael Bleackley, published by Educational Explorers Ltd, 1974, price £1.85. It should be available in bookshops but can be ordered direct from the publishers.

Sheltered work

Under the Disabled Persons (Employment) Act 1944 the Secretary of State for Employment can make arrangements for the provision of sheltered employment for severely disabled people, either by making grants to voluntary undertakings or local authorities, or by setting up non-profit-making public companies.

REMPLOY LTD

Remploy Ltd, 415 Edgware Road, London NW2
Tel: 01-452 8020

Remploy is the public company formed under this provision. Disabled people who want to work for Remploy must be on the Disabled Persons Register. The board of Remploy consists of seven full-time paid directors, plus ten part-time unpaid directors appointed by the Secretary of State for Employment from people with wide experience in industry and commerce and trade unions, together with an interest in disabled people. Some eighty-seven factories employ over 8000 severely disabled people. The company also has a consultancy and advisory service to workshops for the blind run by local authorities and charities. A few of the factories organize work at home for people who cannot get out to work. It is intended that not more than 15 per cent of the total work-force should be able-bodied or less severely disabled.

VOLUNTARY ORGANIZATIONS

There are twenty-eight workshops run by voluntary organizations aided by grants from the Department of Employment, providing employment and training for over 1000 handicapped people. Some cater for disabilities of all kinds, others for special groups of handicap. The local office of the Employment Service Agency would have information about any local organization of this kind.

Conditions of receiving the Department of Employment grant include the payment of satisfactory wages, a normal working week of forty hours and a reasonable level of output.

LOCAL AUTHORITY

Local authorities have been responsible since 1920 for providing sheltered work for blind people, either directly, or through the agency of a voluntary society. Since 1948 they have had powers to make similar provision for other seriously disabled people and are *required* to make provision for classes of severely disabled people designated by the Secretary of State for Employment.

ADULT TRAINING CENTRES FOR THE MENTALLY HANDICAPPED (ATCS)

Local authority social services departments are responsible for adult training centres for mentally handicapped people, usually those who live with their families or in residential homes and hostels, but sometimes also for hospital patients. In 1973 there were 31 000 places in England and Wales and 3200 in Scotland. Most of the centres organize workshop activities – simple process work – in conditions similar to normal employment. They are supposed to arrange programmes of social and educational training designed to help the trainee cope with everyday living.

In a recent seminar report by the King's Fund Centre, parents had serious criticisms of the way in which most centres operated. They felt that there was too much emphasis on production and work schedules, and too little on social and educational enrichment, a service that the best ATCs do provide. Many, they claimed, are not entitled to be called 'training' centres at all, they are 'day' centres where the mentally handicapped are kept occupied for a few hours a day on undemanding tasks with no educational content at all. The King's Fund report draws attention to the problems of the centres' management: they are expected to find work which is profitable (and often, therefore dull and repetitive jobs which no one else wants to do) and to keep to output schedules – particularly if work is contracted – and yet at the same time provide social enrichment and training on an individual basis (*Adult Education for Mentally Handicapped People*, Mental Handicap Papers 6, 1975, price 40p).

King's Fund Centre
126 Albert Street, London NW1 7NF
Tel: 01-267 6111

The *Survey of Scottish Adult Training Centres*, by Stephen Jackson and Margaret Struthers (published by the Scottish Society for Mentally Handicapped, price £1.25) gives an even more gloomy picture. It is unusual for mentally handicapped people to get open employment in Scotland and the ATCs (usually called senior occupational centres in Scotland) are usually the only day-care provision available. Out of the sixty-four local authority centres at the time of the survey, only eighteen were purpose-built and only half the staff employed had had any relevant training. There was little provision for reading and number training or social education. Support services were not readily available and there was little contact with parents. Yet waiting lists in some areas are long; in some cases parents may have to wait three years for their child to be admitted – with no alternative once school-leaving age is reached.

SSMH, 69 West Regent Street, Glasgow G2 2AN
Tel: 041-331 1551

A contrast to the gloomy picture presented in these reports is the account in *Special Education* (December 1974) of how one employer was able to integrate trainees from an adult training centre into open employment in his factory – to undertake tasks for which it was difficult to recruit staff. This shows how a sympathetic management, committed to confidence and trust in the ability of the handicapped to do a useful job, can help to achieve the aim of integrating handicapped people into the community. The manager of the ATC describes how people with stated IQs of 38 upwards, who had previously spent long periods in mental subnormality hospitals, could be helped by a social education programme organized at the ATC to obtain and hold down a job on equal terms with others in the factory.

ADVISORY SERVICE FOR RURAL TRAINING, EMPLOYMENT, OCCUPATION AND SETTLEMENT OF THE MENTALLY HANDICAPPED

David Carter (Director and Advisory Officer)
Lufton Manor, Lufton, Yeovil, Somerset
Tel: Yeovil (0935) 3124

Over the past eight years, the NSMHC has been running training courses for mentally handicapped young people in agriculture and horticulture. They have built up a fund of experience on every aspect of rural training and employment in gardening and farming for young people of IQs ranging from 40 to 70. They have been able to encourage them to carry out a wide range of jobs using modern commercial techniques. Because of the many inquiries about the work at Lufton Manor, the NSMHC have set up a National Advisory Service, with David Carter as Director, which can offer practical help and advice about setting up or improving schemes of rural employment and settlement for mentally handicapped people, and about the opportunities for open employment in agriculture and horticulture.

VILLAGE COMMUNITIES

All village communities offer one thing in common: residential care and a full and active working life within a supportive community.

Village communities may be run by the big national

societies. Others are run by charities set up for that purpose such as the Camphill Village Trust or the CARE villages (Cottage and Rural Enterprises). The essence of such communities is that the people live apart from the main stream of ordinary life in their own community. Some people see this as segregation, others as protection. Most village communities accept people when they leave school at sixteen although Ravenswood, a Jewish foundation, takes children from the age of six. Although they accept people referred by social services departments, disablement resettlement officers and so on, they may also accept private applications and may well have a waiting list. Any parent who is thinking of a village of this type for their child would do well to become a friend of the charity, offer help, subscribe to any newsletters and generally get to know what's going on long before their child is likely to go there.

SHARE COMMUNITY LTD

Share Community Ltd
170 Kingston Road, Merton Park, London SW19 3NX
Tel: 01-542 6241

Share is a community-based pioneering body. It does not provide a set range of services but, within its financial limitations, experiments and then re-evaluates to find what works and what doesn't. It is concerned, above all, with severely disabled people who are without work. It aims not so much to do things *for* disabled people as to give them an opportunity to help themselves, if they can provide their own spark of motivation. The Director, Tom Hood, says that the various experiments are intended to allow people to involve themselves in a situation in which *external* handicapping factors – access, transport, the attitudes of statutory authorities, employers, the public, the family – have been removed. He also recognizes that the handicap may stem as much from the 'inner person' as from the physical functional limitation which is the obvious disability. Lack of motivation and drive, lack of patience, lack of skills may each be a serious handicap when it comes to getting a job and making a go of it. Share tries to help solve these problems too. It offers an environment in which disabled people can come together on a friendly basis, sharing their joys and trying to find ways of meeting their difficulties. They have undertaken different types of personal counselling and can also refer people for help. Share was originally sponsored by the Quakers.

7   Fun and Friends

Social life, sports and hobbies

'Child's play' used to be a derogatory term to describe something which didn't really count although it might be tolerated. Nowadays children's play is seen as something which must be positively encouraged and has a serious function in their development. In the same way, hobbies, sports and all kinds of leisure activities can mean far more than fun and games in the life of someone who is handicapped or disabled. There are critical stages in the life of a young disabled person when, in the words of Dr John D. Kershaw (*The Handicapped Person in the Community*, edited by D. M. Boswell and J. M. Wingrove, Open University, 1974), these activities:

are particularly important socially and emotionally because they are based on common interests entered into of one's own free will and desire. They are among the very few parts of human activity where competition and cooperation go hand in hand, so that the expert is eager to welcome, help, encourage and train the beginner. . . . If before he leaves school, he has been initiated into the brotherhood of the swimmers, the model engineers, the stamp collectors, the bird watchers or any of a hundred others, he will have friends ready-made when the interruption of other relationships is imposed by leaving school.

The significance of recreation is recognized in one social services department at least. Four years ago the Royal Borough of Kensington and Chelsea appointed an education and recreation officer for the disabled. He wrote then:

In a nutshell I see my role as a catalyst and one who will help widen the disabled person's educational, cultural and leisure horizons and at the same time to educate the public as to the particular needs of the disabled in the confident hope that this will effect change.

We hope that in this chapter there is something for everyone whatever their inclinations or limitations.

General

DISABLED LIVING FOUNDATION

Disabled Living Foundation
346 Kensington High Street, London W14 8NS
Tel: 01-602 2491

> The information service produces comprehensive lists of organizations and aids concerned with leisure activities and hobbies – both indoor and outdoor – and physical recreation and sport. Practical research projects include gardening, music and physical recreation. Their publication, *Outdoor Pursuits for Disabled People* by Norman Croucher (1974), is full of encouraging stories – blind children learning to water-ski, competitive rowing for a boy with a caliper, spastic children tackling roped climbing. The foreword says 'the aim of this book is to produce results'. Where there is no organization specifically set up for handicapped people, the book suggests individuals who may be able to help. There is plenty of ammunition for fighting back when you get the answer 'it can't be done' by quoting examples where it has been. They have also produced what amounts to a film of the book called 'Not Just a Spectator'.

Town and Country Productions Ltd
21 Cheyne Row, London SW3 5HP
Tel: 01-352 7950

BRITISH ASSOCIATION FOR SPORTING AND RECREATIONAL ACTIVITIES OF THE BLIND (BASRAB)

Mr J. D. Benoy (Chairman), BASRAB
Pinebank, 5 Great Close, Chapel Brampton, Northampton
Tel: Northampton (0604) 842155

BASRAB was founded in November 1975. The committee are themselves blind and are aware of the outstanding needs of those who are newly blind and of visually handicapped children. They hope to work through schools and want to ensure that school-leavers are able to continue with their social and leisure interests when they find themselves back at home on their own. They plan to set up regional organizations with registers of all suitable groups in the area in order to offer an advisory service and also to identify needs and gaps. They intend to work with local authority leisure and amenity departments, encouraging them to include visually handicapped people in their ordinary activities and reassuring them if they are worried about the level of responsibility involved. They would try to act as intermediaries on behalf of visually handicapped people who were barred from any activities.

PINDER CENTRE

Pinder Centre
Old Coach House, Avington, Winchester, Hampshire
Tel: Itchen Abbas (096-278) 498

This therapeutic day centre was set up by Miss Margaret Pinder in honour of her parents who encouraged and supported her through her own childhood disablement. It is primarily for recreation for handicapped children. The building is a converted wing of an old coach house with fully accessible facilities for all medical, educational and social activities. There are forty acres of grounds for camping, riding and birdwatching. A nature trail is planned with rails and braille signs for the visually handicapped and a path with a surface suitable for wheelchairs. The indoor pool can be heated to the necessary temperature for hydrotherapy and has a jet stream for under-water massage. A physiotherapist and a state registered nurse are available for most sessions. Individuals and groups use the centre, some on a regular basis, others for a special outing. The first Sunday afternoon in the month is 'family day'. Check on booking arrangements before visiting.

Adventure playgrounds

There is a number of playgrounds especially for handicapped children in hospitals and special schools throughout the country. They are intended only for their own patients or pupils and no complete central register exists. They may vary from the most basic, unimaginative playground to properly designed, adventure playgrounds with a full-time playleader.

HANDICAPPED ADVENTURE PLAYGROUND ASSOCIATION

Handicapped Adventure Playground Association
3 Oakley Gardens, London SW3
Tel: 01-352 2321

The Association is an independent charity with the specific purpose of setting up adventure playgrounds for handicapped children. By the end of 1976 it will have four adventure playgrounds for handicapped children, all in the London area (Chelsea, Islington, Wandsworth and Fulham). The playgrounds are booked for groups of children throughout the year but during the school holidays some days are regularly left free for casual visits by individual handicapped children with their families and non-handicapped friends. Each playground has its own arrangements for this and it is vital to check up before planning a visit. They are all on the phone and details of addresses and numbers are available from the Association.

The Association feels that the paramount factor in designing the area should not be the handicaps but a child's sense of adventure. In fact, if all the children are comfortably familiar with the playground then it must be changed so that exploring it continues to be an adventure.

The Association does not intend to open any more playgrounds of its own at the moment. It has, therefore, for the first time, admitted as associate members other playgrounds whose standards of planning, staffing and philosophy are like their own. There are a total of about half a dozen affiliated playgrounds in the Midlands, the North and Surrey, all at different stages from hoping through planning to open and running. Details and plans from the Association.

Three playgrounds are the work of one architect, Stephen Gardiner, who has described his plans in a leaflet, *Adventure Playgrounds for Handicapped Children*, which is available from the Centre on Environment for the Handicapped (price 20p).

Centre on Environment for the Handicapped
126 Albert Street, London NW1 7NF
Tel: 01-267 6111

Angling

NATIONAL ANGLERS COUNCIL

National Anglers Council
17 Queen Street, Peterborough PE1 1PJ
Tel: Peterborough (0733) 54084

Fishing is an occupation which you can enjoy just as much from a wheelchair as from a fisherman's folding stool.

The National Anglers' Council held a conference in June 1975 on helping the disabled to go fishing and as a result has established a committee for disabled anglers to act as a national coordinating committee for all efforts to help handicapped people enjoy the sport. It hopes to appoint liaison officers in each region of Great Britain and is in the process of preparing a directory of clubs and individuals able and willing to help handicapped people. It hopes to promote research on special equipment and issue a special regular bulletin on angling for the disabled. The Council will certainly advise any parent with a handicapped child interested in fishing and put them in touch with any local group. One London society, for example, 'adopted' a group of handicapped children in a special school, provided them with tackle and took them to the canal and taught them how to fish. Another group persuaded its local park authority to provide a special fishing pool and exclusive fishing rights for disabled anglers.

SCOTTISH COMMITTEE FOR THE PROMOTION OF ANGLING FOR THE DISABLED

Mrs M. Taylor
Scottish Committee for the Promotion of Angling for the Disabled
18/19 Claremont Crescent, Edinburgh EH7 4QD
Tel: 031-556 3882

> The Committee works for the provision of facilities for disabled anglers, and training for people to accompany them where necessary. It helped to set up the Edinburgh and District Disabled Anglers Club, and hopes to form similar clubs in other parts of Scotland. Special equipment such as portable, purpose-built seats for use in boats, and a gantry to help severely disabled people into boats, has been designed and produced by members of the Committee. Some training classes in casting are held for disabled anglers.

Art and craft

TRUST FUND FOR THE TRAINING OF HANDICAPPED CHILDREN IN ARTS AND CRAFTS

Peter Spencer
Trust Fund for the Training of Handicapped Children in Arts and Crafts
94 Claremount Road, Wallasey, Merseyside L45 6UE
Tel: 051-638 1422

> The Trust Fund has been set up by the Association of Mouth and Foot Painting Artists (a cooperative association of severely disabled artists who earn their own living from their paintings) to encourage the art education of handicapped children. It gives practical and financial help; it may pay for extra materials and tuition for an individual child or support a specific art project in a school. For instance, it gave one school a new electric kiln for pottery.

LEISURE CENTRE

Janet Dalglish, Leisure Centre
30 Camberwell Road, London SE5

The Centre provides materials, encouragement, inspiration, expertise and training for anyone concerned with helping children and young people enjoy their free time creatively. It is concerned with all handicaps and likes brothers and sisters to be involved as well. The Centre will arrange sessions anywhere for any numbers at the request of organizations or individuals. Members can use the lending library of books, pictures, slides, records, charts, kits, craft samples, instructions for crafts in programmed-learning form, etc. As Miss Dalglish runs the whole project singlehanded, she can be elusive in the office, so it is often easier to write in the first place and she will make contact with you as soon as she can.

HAND CRAFTS ADVISORY ASSOCIATION FOR THE DISABLED

Hand Crafts Advisory Association for the Disabled
103 Brighton Road, Purley, Surrey CR2 4HD
Tel: 01-668 1411

The aim of the Association is to improve the standard of design and craftsmanship of disabled people so that they can be freed from the frustration of dependence on others. Many isolated and home-bound people are capable of producing excellent work but find it hard to keep up to date with new designs, materials and tastes. The Association believes that the best way to achieve this is to train specialist hand-craft teachers of the disabled. It runs up to thirty-five short two-day courses each year in nineteen different crafts including soft-toy making, rag dolls, paper sculpture and basic woodwork techniques. Membership is open to organizations or individuals, but priority on courses is given to people who are sponsored by member organizations.

Bird watching

ROYAL SOCIETY FOR THE PROTECTION OF BIRDS (RSPB)

RSPB, The Lodge, Sandy, Beds. SG19 2DL
Tel: Sandy (0767) 80551

> Over 50 000 people aged eighteen and under belong to the
> Young Ornithologists Club which has many local branches.
> The kinds of activities they run – bird-watching outings,
> nest-box schemes and so on – would often be particularly
> suitable for children who are not physically agile or
> mobile. A number of bird-watching hides are provided
> with ramps so that they can be reached in a wheelchair. All
> members of the YOC receive a bi-monthly magazine and
> a list of local groups.

> See also **Nature study**

Budgerigars

COMPANIONSHIP TRUST

Mr J. Kuttner, Companionship Trust
58 Broadwalk, South Woodford, London E18
Tel: 01-989 4130

> The Trust was set up to solve the enormous problem of
> loneliness – including the problem of handicapped children
> who are isolated socially or emotionally withdrawn – by
> making a gift of a budgerigar for a companion. Its dossier
> of case histories includes children with spina bifida and
> heart conditions who have become happier, and deaf or
> autistic children who have begun to communicate when
> they were given their own budgerigar. Anyone who wants
> a gift from the Trust can apply through any local welfare
> organization or the social services department. The local
> organization approaches the Trust for authorization to
> buy the bird and cage, a month's supply of food and an
> information leaflet about budgies. It sends the receipted
> account to the Trust which reimburses the whole cost.

A.H.F.P.—L

Canoeing

BRITISH CANOE UNION

British Canoe Union, 70 Brompton Road, London SW3 1DT
Tel: 01-584 9229

Disabled young people have successfully learnt canoeing.
The only rule which applies to every case is that they must
be happy in water – it is not necessary to be a swimmer.
In 1974, a party of girls from the Florence Treloar School
for physically handicapped girls gave a demonstration at
the Crystal Palace to a big audience from the British
Canoe Union. The headteacher said: 'They expected to see
the girls quietly paddling along. They were very surprised
when they capsized their canoes, performed Eskimo rolls
and took part in complicated rescue exercises.' The Union
can give guidelines on courses of canoeing for the disabled
and runs ordinary courses of its own.

Chess

Three national organizations should be able to tell you
about any local and specialist chess clubs and activities.

British Chess Federation
4 The Close, Norwich NR1 4DH
Tel: Norwich (0603) 612678

Scottish Chess Association
69 Inveroran Drive, Bearsden, Glasgow G61 2AT

Welsh Chess Union
Park House, Llangennech, Llanelli, Dyfed

BRAILLE CHESS ASSOCIATION

Braille Chess Association
128 Walm Lane, London NW2
Tel: 01-452 8336

Primarily an association for adults, it offers some services to children in conjunction with schools for the visually handicapped.

BRITISH CORRESPONDENCE CHESS ASSOCIATION

British Correspondence Chess Association
28 Canonbury Park North, London N1 2JT
Tel: 01-266 1026

Conducting a chess game through the post is suitable for anyone, however immobile. As well as organizing chess games, the Association teaches the game by correspondence.

BRITISH DEAF CHESS ASSOCIATION

G. D. Campbell, British Deaf Chess Association
4 Tanfield Avenue, Woodside, Aberdeen AB2 2AZ

A deaf child may join this Association, which is run entirely by deaf adults, when they are old enough to mix with adults. They have quite a few teenage members among their clubs. The Association organizes postal chess and a programme of tournaments for teams and individuals.

CHESS BY REMOTE CONTROL

Bill Bond, Medical Engineering Research Unit
Queen Mary's Hospital for Children
Carshalton, Surrey
Tel: 01-643 3300

The research unit of Queen Mary's Hospital has designed a remote control chess board on which the pieces are moved by a simple joy-stick. It can be used by people in bed or those with restricted arm movement. There is no mass production of these but Mr Bond can put parents in touch with small engineering firms who could undertake to make one to order. Although this would be expensive, the remote-control unit could be used for other purposes as well.

Clubs - Information services

NATIONAL YOUTH BUREAU

National Youth Bureau
17–23 Albion Street, Leicester LE1 6GD
Leicester (0533) 538811

> Set up to provide an information service for everyone
> concerned with the social education of young people, the
> Bureau has taken over the work of the Youth Service
> Information Centre. It runs a loan service of teaching
> materials and other documents and a personal inquiry
> service. It has published special reports on facilities for
> young people with a handicap.

SCOTTISH BOARD FOR INFORMATION ON YOUTH AND COMMUNITY SERVICE

Scottish Board for Information on Youth and Community Service
67 York Place, Edinburgh EH1 3JD
Tel: 031-556 8671

> This is an information/resource centre which offers training
> services, publications, advice and suggestions for develop-
> ment. It has a monthly newsletter about youth and com-
> munity education. In 1974 it carried out a survey on
> facilities and amenities offered to the disabled in Scotland
> by voluntary organizations. Although it does not offer a
> direct service to parents of handicapped children, it does
> keep information about facilities for the handicapped and
> has contacts with organizations for them.

YOUTH SERVICE

> The Youth Service is administered by the LEA and local
> voluntary organizations and may be able to offer valuable
> advice, financial and practical help to anyone wanting to
> run a club for handicapped children. It should also have
> information about clubs operating in your area. You
> should be able to contact the service through your local
> education office.

Clubs - Individual organizations

BRITISH ASSOCIATION OF THE HARD OF HEARING –
NATIONAL YOUNG PEOPLE'S COMMITTEE

Vincent Whalley, BAHOH
47 Yew Tree Drive, Bayston Hill, Shrewsbury, Salop

The British Association of the Hard of Hearing is the
national body of those who have lost all or part of their
hearing but have acquired the art of speech. The youth
section is concerned with people over school-leaving age.
Speech, lip-reading and writing are the usual means of
communication in their clubs; sign language, although
not actually banned, is not encouraged. Committee
members are drawn from young people's clubs in various
parts of the country. They are concerned with the personal
problems of hard-of-hearing young people. A lively
national newsletter describes their social activities: sports
of all kinds, holidays in Britain and abroad and social
weekends. Their members take part in international
rallies of young hard-of-hearing people from all over
Europe. They have sponsored youth leadership courses for
hard-of-hearing young people who want to run clubs and
organize activities. There is a postal membership scheme
for people who want to keep in touch but do not have a
club in their area.

CHALLENGE CLUBS

Chairman, Challenge Clubs
15 Huyton Hey Road, Huyton, Merseyside
Tel: 051-480 5963

The first Challenge Club was started in Liverpool in 1967,
launched with a £5 gift from the local muscular dystrophy
group. The name of Challenge has now spread throughout
Merseyside and Lancashire to Newcastle upon Tyne, with
six clubs all operating basically under the same constitution. Membership is limited to the age group eight to
eighteen and handicapped children with no local society

to help them. As blind and deaf children were well catered for they were excluded from the original club in Liverpool which has a full membership of 100 members and a waiting list of about twenty-five. On club nights an average of seventy-five children are occupied with swimming, wheel-chair games, board games and discussion groups. The club says: 'We are always impressed by the ability of a handicapped child to become the legs and arms of another disabled child. . . .' They have taken ten children on a special adventure holiday to Norway where they camped under the stars (without tents) and rounded off the holiday by staying with Norwegian families in their own homes. One of their older children who joined the club in the early years is now seventeen and has been chosen to compete in the Olympics for the Disabled in Toronto in 1976. Brian Speedy by name (and speedy by nature, according to the Chairman) is now looked up to by the other children and his success has become an exciting example for them all. The club says that it feels it is now in a position to advise anyone who wants to set up a club of this kind and that it would welcome inquiries.

DAVID LIVINGSTONE CLUB FOR HANDICAPPED YOUNG PEOPLE

David Livingstone Club
Livingstone House, London Road, Harlow
Tel: Harlow (0279) 20894

An outstanding example of what can be done by local voluntary effort, this club began in a church hall one night a week in 1959. It now has its own club house, to which it recently built a new extension and has also built a hostel attached to the club for eight full-time residents. The club caters for all handicaps and all ages and has about ninety members and twenty voluntary helpers – school pupils, students and older volunteers. Activities include hobbies, outings, dancing and swimming with a professional coach. Funds are raised by all kinds of local voluntary effort, large and small, and by a kiosk in the BP headquarters in Harlow selling confectionery, magazines, etc.

GATEWAY CLUBS

National Federation of Gateway Clubs
Pembridge Hall, 17 Pembridge Square, London W2 4EP
Tel: 01-229 8941

The Federation of Gateway Clubs is sponsored by the
National Society for Mentally Handicapped Children.
There are over 300 affiliated clubs offering leisure-time
activities specially adapted for the needs of the retarded.
They may take someone with a physical handicap in
addition to the mental handicap. Membership is usually
open to the teenage group, although there are some
junior clubs. They aim to provide all kinds of activities
such as painting, cookery, drama, games and so on.
The club is somewhere to relax and drink coffee with
friends. The clubs are run by volunteers trained by the
NSMHC and young people who are not handicapped are
encouraged to take part in the activities.

To give an extra dimension to the social and leisure
activities of the clubs, the Gateway Award Scheme
modelled on the Duke of Edinburgh's Award was launched
in 1973. It is designed to encourage and recognize progress
in carefully defined fields of personal achievement; each
candidate's target is assessed individually so that no one
is given an impossible goal. Most people enter through
their local Gateway Club, but the staff at headquarters
will try to make individual arrangements for anyone who
has no local club.

GIRL GUIDES ASSOCIATION

Programme Secretary, Girl Guides Association
17–19 Buckingham Palace Road, London SW1W 0PT
Tel: 01-834 6242

Extension units for handicapped girls, open to any girl
who is capable of understanding the Promise, are mainly
based in special schools and hospitals. A postal service is
available for any handicapped girl who is unable to get to a
unit. The guide handbook is available in braille and large

print. A leaflet, *Come Guiding with the Handicapped* (price 10p), has useful information for commissioners and guides.

NATIONAL ASSOCIATION OF BOYS' CLUBS

National Association of Boys' Clubs
17 Bedford Square, London WC1B 3JJ
Tel: 01-636 5357

Weekends for handicapped boys may sometimes be run by local members of the Association. The Association says that it will consider any suggestions for national schemes for the handicapped on the lines of its existing projects. They are planning to move at the end of 1977.

NATIONAL FEDERATION OF ST RAPHAEL CLUBS

National Organizer, National Federation of St Raphael Clubs
11 Thurlin Road, King's Lynn, Norfolk PE30 4QQ
Tel: King's Lynn (0553) 4584

The first St Raphael Club was founded in Norwich in 1946, and took its title from the patron saint of the disabled. The organizers want the name St Raphael to stand for the handicapped and disabled as St Dunstan does for the blind. The Federation now coordinates the efforts of the thirty-six clubs for the disabled, represents the interests of the disabled to national and local government and keeps people informed of the services which are or ought to be available. It also runs a well-established holiday scheme that organizes holidays for over 1200 disabled people and their families every year.

PHAB

PHAB, 42 Devonshire Street, London W1N 1LN
Tel: 01-580 4053

PHAB clubs arrange youth-club activities for Physically Handicapped and Able-Bodied young people to give them the opportunity to share common interests. There is a range of activities for all ages from thirteen years. A list of clubs is available from head office. Residential courses are also arranged for physically handicapped and able-bodied young people from different parts of Great Britain and abroad. Programmes include working together on art, music, drama and outdoor activities and sports.

SCOUT ASSOCIATION

Scout Association, Gilwell Park, Chingford, London E4 7QW
Tel: 01-524 5246

There are many scout groups in the country in which there are one or two members who have a physical disability or are slow learners and ordinary groups are positively encouraged by the Association to take in handicapped members. Any handicapped boy is able to join if he is capable of understanding the Promise and the Law. The Association publishes an advice leaflet on how training and activities may be safely adjusted to meet the needs of any specific handicap. In this way certain parts of the training programme and tests are made more suitable, absorbing and enjoyable for boys who are physically and mentally handicapped.

WOODCRAFT FOLK

Woodcraft Folk, 13 Ritherdon Road, London SW17 8QE
Tel: 01-672 6031

A co-educational movement with local groups throughout the country for anyone over six years. Adults work on a voluntary and equal basis with the children – a thoroughly democratic organization with everyone on Christian-name terms. Regular international exchanges and contacts are arranged with youth organizations in both Eastern and Western Europe. Activities at weekly meetings cover a wide range, including folk dancing, drama, singing, craft work, debates, etc. Regular weekend and summer camping for all age groups fosters a sense of community. No child would ever be excluded from a normal group because of a handicap but parents may occasionally need to be on hand to advise helpers.

Cooking

The Disabled Schoolchild and Kitchen Sense

This book, edited by Sydney Foott (published for the Disabled Living Foundation by Heinemann Health Books, 1976, price £1.75), was sponsored by the Disabled Living Foundation with help from Spillers Foods to encourage more schools to provide home economics teaching for handicapped children. There are contributions from a home economist who teaches in special schools, an occupational therapist and a housewife who suffers from arthritis. The book shows how even the most severely physically handicapped children can enjoy and benefit from the chance to shop and cook and contains very specific practical advice on organization of the work and syllabus, record keeping, equipment and layout of school kitchens and safety teaching. It is rather disappointing that no advice is given on how to help handicapped children in the kitchen at home.

Cycling

All the arguments in favour of cycling have additional force for a severely disabled child, for whom lack of mobility may be the greatest handicap. It is this, above all else, which makes it difficult for him to join in the activities of other children. So for a handicapped child, cycling in any form – bicycle, tricycle, go-kart, propelled by hand and/or feet – may mean more than an enjoyable hobby. It may be a vital step towards some form of independence. This whole subject is discussed in an admirable article and survey in the newsletter for Summer 1975 of the Toy Libraries Association (price 10p).

Toy Libraries Association
Sunley House, Gunthorpe Street, London E1
Tel: 01-247 1386

CYCLISTS TOURING CLUB (CTC)

CTC, Cotterell House, 69 Meadrow, Godalming, Surrey GU7 3HS
Tel: Godalming (048-68) 7217

Several regional groups of the club arrange tandem rides for handicapped children – where the handicapped child takes the rear position and is 'steered' by a capable and experienced rider. One member with a Down's Syndrome child writes: 'Cycling is an ideal family activity, providing fresh air and stimulation to all members, including the handicapped child.' Club members would be very willing to suggest and help with adaptations to standard bicycles for handicapped children to ride themselves. The Club headquarters can provide details of branches organizing tandem rides and a list of addresses of all regional groups.

DEPARTMENT OF HEALTH AND SOCIAL SECURITY

If it can be shown to be essential for a child's mobility, various types of invalid bicycles and tricycles can be supplied to handicapped children on a GP's or consultant's prescription. Details can be obtained from your local appliance centre (see chapter 3, **Aids**, page 104) or direct from the DHSS (leaflet NHS5). The Ministry prefers to supply machines which are on their lists but, if nothing suitable is listed, people have managed to persuade them to provide other machines on the market. The Toy Libraries Association advise that it is worth going to a great deal of trouble to get a cycle supplied by the Ministry because it will then maintain the vehicle.

DISABLED LIVING FOUNDATION

Disabled Living Foundation
346 Kensington High Street, London W14 8NS
Tel: 01-602 2491

The DLF has lists of specialist manufacturers of tricycles, cycles and go-karts for the handicapped and may be able to arrange for parents to view the ranges.

WINGFIELD RECOVERY CLUB

Miss B. J. Cook (General Secretary), Wingfield Recovery Club
24 Station Road, Epping, Essex
Tel: Epping 73229

The Club's slogan is 'Recovery must be fun'. The founder, Bert Lyon, invented the static quadrant energizer to provide a means of exercise for the paralysed. (This is now being produced by a workshop for the disabled.) He later developed this into a tricycle which gives children who would have been doomed to life in a wheelchair independent mobility from as young as two years. Eye sight, coordination and dexterity are improved. It looks like an ordinary tricycle with a larger seat and back-rest, but it works by quadrant propulsion – that is to say, it is driven by hands and feet pedalling together in a perfectly synchronized marching formation. Members of the club have been on a mini-marathon tricycle ride when each youngster covered four miles. Use of equipment at the club is free, but anyone can buy a tricycle made to measure for an individual child.

DEAF CYCLISTS

National Deaf Children's Society
31 Gloucester Place, London W1H 4EA
Tel: 01-486 3251

A bicycle sticker designed to warn that the rider is deaf (a drawing of an ear crossed by an X) is available from the National Deaf Children's Society.

Disco

MINI-HANDI-RECORD SESSION

Toc H, 1 Forest Close, Wendover, Aylesbury, Bucks
Tel: Wendover (0296-62) 3911

'Mini' means small and 'Handi' means handicapped. The idea of a disco for physically handicapped teenagers was thought up by Jimmy Savile. Toc H has been active in promoting the idea. An attractive and practical illustrated booklet explaining in detail how to organize a Mini-Handi has been published by them jointly with Jimmy Savile, and is available from Toc H publications department – send 15p in stamps.

Drama

SESAME

Sesame, George Bell House
8 Ayres Street, London SE1 1E7
Tel: 01-407 2159

A drama-therapy group which performs to and works with the sick and the handicapped, actively involving them in drama, mime, movement and music. Sesame arranges research and training programmes working through local authorities, hospitals and national organizations. Video-tapes and films have been made of some of their work and these are available on hire.

DRAMA WITH THE DISADVANTAGED

Betty Miller, National Drama Conference
26 Bedford Square, London WC1B 3HU
Tel: 01-636 4066

This group can give information on drama with the handi-capped, and has details of special courses for those who want to teach this. It keeps a useful reading list on every aspect of drama with disadvantaged children including speech, movement, dance, mime, improvisation and role-playing.

See also **Play,** PLAYSPACE, page 352

Drama for people with specific handicaps

BRITISH THEATRE OF THE DEAF

British Theatre of the Deaf, RNID
105 Gower Street, London W1E 6AH
Tel: 01-387 8033

The British Theatre of the Deaf developed from the RNID Mime Group, which was started in 1961 by a few individuals who believed in the ability of deaf people to act. Directed by Pat Keysell (a presenter of the BBC TV programme 'Vision On'), the company now works professionally and has performed at the Edinburgh Festival and on a national tour of theatres, schools and universities. Its aims are to demonstrate to the widest possible audience just how much can be achieved by deaf actors and actresses in their unique contribution to contemporary theatre. There are plans to form a theatre in education unit consisting of deaf and hearing actor/teachers who will visit schools, giving performances and holding special workshops for teachers.

DRAMA FOR BLIND PEOPLE

D. O. Mumford, Mobility Officer for the Blind
City of Coventry Social Services Department
New Council Offices, Coventry CV1 5RS
Tel: Coventry (0203) 25555 Ext. 2133

In 1975 David Mumford organized an experimental four-day residential drama course for the blind at the Belgrade Studio Theatre, Coventry. The aim was to explore the potential of practical theatre for the blind and to assess its feasibility and value for recreation and therapy. The course included sessions on movement, mime, improvisation, stagecraft, make-up, costume and script work, culminating in performances of scenes from plays ranging from *Macbeth* to Alan Bennett's *Forty Years On*. The project was supported by the Carnegie (UK) Trust. One student wrote after the course: 'I have come home with new ideas on teaching, have a keener appreciation of the theatre, an interest to join a sighted drama group and have discovered in movement and mime a new avenue of self-expression.' David Mumford feels that the weekend established its objectives by opening the door onto an excitingly new and as yet relatively unexplored horizon for blind people. He hopes that drama will not remain at an experimental level, but that it will be recognized as a medium with much to offer the visually handicapped.

DRAMA AND THE MENTALLY HANDICAPPED

Drama in Education, School of Education
The University,
St Thomas' Street, Newcastle upon Tyne NE1 7RU
Tel: Newcastle upon Tyne (0632) 28511 Ext: 2559

Dorothy Heathcote is a drama tutor who specializes in work with mentally handicapped children and adults. She creates an imaginary situation in which the mentally handicapped experience encounters with actual people. They have to be so unusual that it is impossible to ignore them and the problem they bring with them should be immediately understood on sight without any verbal explanation. The only way to convey the flavour of her work in writing is to describe an example of her own 'plots'.

The baby in the tree: There is a tree made of persons with their arms covered with leaves. High in the middle of them hangs a bright shawl with a baby doll in it. The 'tree' rocks gently and sings 'Rock a bye baby'. Then the mother tries to get the baby back. At the first touch the tree stops the lullaby and hisses. The children try to help the mother get the baby back, without annoying the tree so that it drops the baby.

Where will the birds go?: A lady measures the floor for her new house. In the corner is a man dressed as a tree. The children all hold the tape to help her to measure it. The lady says: 'We'll have to cut the tree down to put the kitchen there.' The man whispers to the children 'Where will the birds go if you cut me down?' The lady gets the saw to cut him down and the children try to stop her and get the birds to come back into the tree so she can't chop it down. One class of severely subnormal children whistled the birds back into the tree.

Part of the film 'Who's Handicapped?' shows Dorothy Heathcote at work.

Available from: Concord Films Council Ltd
201 Felixstowe Road, Ipswich, Suffolk
Tel: Ipswich (0473) 76012

Duke of Edinburgh's Award

Duke of Edinburgh's Award
5 Prince of Wales Terrace, London W8 5PG
Tel: 01-937 5205

This scheme offers young people aged fourteen to twenty-four the chance to develop existing interests or to take up something new in leisure, community service, sports, expeditions, etc. Success in it depends more on effort than on either brawn or brains. The leaflet, *No Handicap*, describes the special arrangements for both physically and mentally handicapped young people to take part. The programmes for the award scheme are controlled by the Trustees who license organizations which want to join in the scheme. A research project was started in 1975 to evaluate the scheme as undertaken by handicapped young people.

Gardening

Gardening is an occupation which disabled children can enjoy without being embarrassed by energetic competition from their able-bodied friends. Even severely disabled children are able to manage simple potting work or planting into small gardens. With indoor gardens, this can be done all the year round and, as it is not difficult to learn and shows quick results, it is very popular with young gardeners. Children confined to wheelchairs are able to garden at raised beds.

In the London area, there are two demonstration gardens laid out for handicapped people, including children. There are regular demonstrations given by gardening experts experienced in helping the disabled.

Gardening Centre, Syon Park, Brentford, Middlesex
Tel: 01-560 0882

This garden has raised beds, special provision for wheelchair access to greenhouse and potting shed and special equipment. A demonstration is given every Wednesday afternoon and Friday morning, though it would be advisable to telephone and check this. The garden is open from 10 a.m. daily to 6 p.m. in the summer, earlier in winter. There may be a small charge for admission.

Battersea Park Garden
East Drive, Battersea Park, London SW11

The GLC have provided a 2000 square foot area in the park and laid it out on lines suggested by the Disabled Living Foundation. There are raised flower beds, ideas for planting, specially designed equipment and a children's garden. The garden is situated near the Chelsea Bridge entrance and there is plenty of car-parking space nearby.

DISABLED LIVING FOUNDATION

DLF, 346 Kensington High Street, London W14 8NS
Tel: 01-602 2491

The information service has sets of leaflets on gardening – including lists of suitable tools and stockists and adaptations, diagrams for constructing raised plant beds, etc. It has published a book, *The Easy Path to Gardening* (1972, price £1.25), based on its research into gardening for the handicapped over the last ten years. It is planning another garden for the disabled at the Royal Horticultural Society Gardens at Wisley.

GARDENS FOR THE DISABLED TRUST

Mrs R. S. Kinsey, Gardens for the Disabled Trust
Headcorn Manor, Headcorn, Kent TN27 9NP
Tel: Headcorn (0622-890) 360

The Trust was founded to give practical help with gardening to disabled people of all ages. It makes grants to institutions to help with building special gardens with beds raised to a height suitable for working from a wheelchair or for a child wearing calipers, and provides special tools.

GARDEN CLUB

Mrs J. Cooper, Goddard's Green House, Benenden, Kent
Tel: Benenden (058-082) 521

In 1974 the Garden Club was founded as an off-shoot of the Gardens for the Disabled Trust to encourage individual handicapped people to take up gardening. There is a newsletter, and help and advice over gardening problems, a gardening lending library and a small fund to help with special gardening tools. The club aims to link up all handicapped people who have a common interest in gardening, wherever they live, in towns, cities or the depths of the country.

SCENTED GARDENS FOR THE BLIND

A number of local authorities are locating special gardens in their parks for blind and other handicapped people to enjoy and sometimes work in. These usually consist of raised flower beds filled with scented plants. Blind people can rub the leaves in their fingers to smell the scents and read the labels in braille. Suitable plants include rosemary, lavender, mint, marjoram, sweetbriar, blue rue and thyme. There may be specially recorded taped commentaries and descriptions to help the blind appreciate the plants and flowers.

Golf

GOLF FOUNDATION

Golf Foundation
Allington House, 136/142 Victoria Street, London SW1
Tel: 01-834 4688

The Foundation sponsors coaching for handicapped children through schools, youth clubs and voluntary societies, not individually. Any group may apply to join.

Holidays

See chapter 8

Libraries

BRITISH LIBRARY OF TAPE RECORDINGS FOR HOSPITAL PATIENTS

British Library of Tape Recordings for Hospital Patients
Pullman House, 91 Goswell Road, London EC1V 7ER
Tel: 01-253 1790

This organization was set up for patients in hospital unable to read for themselves – perhaps because they are temporarily blind or paralysed. Hospitals buy a special playback machine and tapes are provided by the library free of charge except for a nominal affiliation fee. Over 260 hospitals take part in the scheme and the library has recorded over 600 titles ranging from Westerns and historical novels to foreign-language books and archaeology. There is a children's book section with over sixty titles. The library is hoping to move in 1977 to 12 Lant Street, London SE1.

BRITISH TALKING BOOK SERVICE FOR THE BLIND

British Talking Book Service for the Blind
Mount Pleasant, Alperton, Wembley HA0 1RR
Tel: 01-903 6666

This is a library of books on tape, with a free postal service for tapes. The service, including the hire of the special playback machine, costs £4 a year (often paid by local councils). There is a student's library for O and A levels and Open University courses. Some twenty titles have been specially recorded for young children.

CALIBRE

Calibre, Wendover, Aylesbury, Bucks. HP22 6OP
Tel: Wendover (0296) 623119

A lending library of books on tape for anyone who cannot read a printed book. At present, books are available only for children and teenagers. One recent example is Peter Purves of Blue Peter reading *The White Horse Gang* by Nina Bawden. It is hoped to include adult books in 1976. Members have to provide their own cassette players (ordinary commercial ones) and pay postage both ways, unless they are blind, when postage is free. A doctor's certificate saying that you cannot read printed books is necessary for copyright reasons.

HOME LIBRARY FOR DEAF CHILDREN

Home Library for Deaf Children
23 Canning Street, Brighton BN2 2EF

This is a project sponsored by Breakthrough in order to try to help deaf children, who because of slow language development, lag behind in reading as they do in speech. The Library is producing simplified texts of popular children's books which are pasted into the original version, so that the format and illustrations remain unchanged. So far they have eighteen titles from the Bruna, Topsy and

Tim, Amelia-Anne and Giant Alexander stories. The Library depends on voluntary help and urgently needs funds to expand its work of helping young deaf and other handicapped children to get the same kind of pleasure from reading as their hearing contemporaries.

MURIEL BRADDICK FOUNDATION

Muriel Braddick Foundation
3c Clifford Close, Whipton, Exeter, Devon
Tel: Exeter (0392) 68407 (not after 6 p.m.)

The Foundation seeks to enrich the lives of homebound people by providing specially prepared tapes and cassettes on free loan specifically related to their own interests – documentaries, travel books, plays, poetry. Physically and mentally handicapped children use the service. Where necessary the Foundation can supply cassette players on loan although there is a waiting list. Most of the material is recorded at a specially equipped studio. Mrs Braddick herself is blind and confined to a wheelchair. Six groups, in addition to the original group in Exeter, are affiliated to the Foundation, which relies entirely on its own fund-raising to maintain *its* service. They issue a quarterly magazine. *Focus*, subscription 60p per year. One of their long-term objectives is to build up and maintain a large and comprehensive library of recorded material of all kinds which can be made available to handicapped people everywhere.

NATIONAL LIBRARY FOR THE BLIND

National Library for the Blind
35 Great Smith Street, London SW1 3BU
Tel: 01-222 2725/01-799 1782

This Library has books in braille, moon and large print, including children's books, which are provided free of charge mainly through a postal service. The Library is moving in 1977 to 15 Cromwell Road, Bredbury, Nr Stockport.

NATIONAL LISTENING LIBRARY

National Listening Library
49 Great Cumberland Place, London W1H 7LH
Tel: 01-723 5008

This charity, which was formed from a merger of the National Library of Talking Books for the Handicapped and the Listening Library, provides a talking book service for handicapped people who are unable to read books in the ordinary way. It is excluded from offering a service to blind or partially sighted people. A doctor's recommendation is needed for individuals. Hospitals, voluntary groups, schools for handicapped children can also take out membership. Members need to buy a special reproducer (cost about £40 in 1975) and pay an annual subscription of £12 of which £9 has to be spent on postage. These costs are usually paid by local authorities or voluntary organizations. Postage both ways is paid by the Library. The Library is building up its stock of titles for children of all ages, as it feels that books are very important to children who are restricted from joining in normal children's activities. They are limited, however, by lack of funds.

PUBLIC LIBRARY SERVICE

The Chronically Sick and Disabled Persons Act 1970 laid a duty on local authorities to provide library services for any handicapped person in their area. This adds to the obligation already made in the Public Libraries and Museum Act of 1964 to provide a comprehensive and efficient library service to everyone in the area who wants to use it. So your local library ought to be prepared to make special arrangements for the handicapped and disabled. Many do, in fact, run a mobile library service, bringing books and records to the housebound. You should be able to get details from any local library or the town hall.

A Library Service for the Mentally Handicapped

King's Fund Centre, 126 Albert Street, London NW1 7NF
Tel: 01-267 6111

A report based on a seminar on the subject held in 1973 is available from the Centre – price 25p. It contains much useful background information on library services as well as a series of recommendations on providing books for the mentally handicapped in hospital.

Movement

'In Touch'

Veronica Sherborne, 26 Hanbury Road, Bristol BS8 2EP
Tel: Bristol (0272) 33816

This film, distributed by Concord Films, 201 Felixstowe Road, Ipswich, shows the work of Veronica Sherborne who specializes in training students to use the medium of movement with severely subnormal children. Miss Sherborne is now working full time at Redland College, Bristol 6, where they have 120 students training to teach severely subnormal children. She is also involved locally with parents and their very young handicapped children.

Getting Into Rhythm

Training Section, Yorkshire RHA
Park Parade, Harrogate HG1 5AH
Tel: Harrogate (0423) 65061

This is a guide to organizing music and movement for the mentally handicapped in hospital, based on a great deal of first-hand experience. It is written by the director of rehabilitation at Fieldhead Hospital, Wakefield, who is qualified as a physiotherapist, a remedial gymnast and an occupational therapist. Although some of the points apply only to hospitals, the specimen programmes could be helpful to any one working with a group of mentally handicapped children. The details include not only the titles of the music but also the publisher and reference number for records. The booklet is free.

See also **Drama**, page 333, and **Play**, page 351

Museums and art galleries

GROUP FOR EDUCATIONAL SERVICES IN MUSEUMS

David Sorrell (Secretary)
Group for Educational Services in Museums
Leicestershire Museums, Art Galleries and Records Service
96 New Walk, Leicester LE1 6TD
Tel: Leicester (0533) 539111

For some time it has been felt nationally and internationally that more attention should be given to the needs of handicapped visitors to museums and art galleries; both children and adults, casual visitors or those following a planned course of study or making an organized group visit. The Group for Educational Services in Museums, which exists to promote and coordinate educational work in museums and art galleries, is now taking an active interest in this. It sponsored a weekend seminar in July 1976 on museums and the handicapped and has published a report, *Museums for the Handicapped*, which includes the specialist papers which were given there and summaries of the discussions. The report is illustrated and costs 80p, plus 25p postage per copy. The Group for Educational Services in Museums has a helpful list of museum education services, available on request, any of which could offer help in organizing museum visits for handicapped children or perhaps a loan service of specimens.

Music

DISABLED LIVING FOUNDATION

Disabled Living Foundation
346 Kensington High Street, London W14 8NS
Tel: 01-602 2491

The Music Panel of the Foundation has published a report on *Music and the Physically Handicapped* (1970, price £1.00, including postage). A project on access to music for the physically handicapped schoolchild and school-leaver was set up in September 1973. The Music Projects Officer has a series of leaflets on music and the handicapped, including one describing the project, available free (send stamped, addressed envelope, foolscap size), and can offer information and advice, visits and courses on many aspects of music for the disabled.

WINGFIELD MUSIC CLUBS

Miss B. J. Cook, 24 Station Road, Epping, Essex
Tel: Epping 73229

There are seven clubs in the London area and Essex. Weekly meetings consist of an hour's teaching and an hour of group playing. Once in two years all the clubs have a mass concert in the Royal Festival Hall. The guiding principle of the work has been that children who cannot normally take part in physical activities can be taught to play an instrument. The hope is that through the concentration and discipline needed for this and for playing together in an orchestra, they will learn to master their disabilities. One consultant wrote: 'I have seen the physical function of the handicapped child improve beyond the bounds of reasonable expectation – but even more impressive has been the achievement of self-confidence.'

MUSIC FOR SLOW LEARNERS PROJECT

Standing Conference for Amateur Music (SCAM)
26 Bedford Square, London WC1B 3HU
Tel: 01-636 4066

> The Music for Slow Learners Project has been completed
> and has produced a number of publications, such as *Sound
> Approaches for Slow Learners* by David Ward. SCAM
> has a full list.

SATURDAY MORNING MUSIC-MAKING FOR FAMILIES
WITH A HANDICAPPED CHILD

Morley College, 61 Westminster Bridge Road, London SE1 7HT
Tel: 01-928 8501

> Morley College is an adult education college which runs
> family classes on Saturdays. The 1975–6 academic year was
> the second series of music-making for families with a
> mentally handicapped child and their friends. Classes are
> run as a cooperative effort between the parents and the
> tutor. The morning is divided into two parts to reconcile
> the needs of those who are just beginning and those who
> are ready for more technical progress. It is not necessary
> for anyone to have any previous musical skills and musical
> instruments are provided.

TOBIN COLOUR MUSIC SYSTEM

Candida Tobin, Triad Regional Art Centre
Southmill Road, Bishop's Stortford, Herts
Tel: Bishop's Stortford (0279) 54322

> Learning to read music can present tremendous difficulties
> even to children who have no mental handicap. It may
> seem a daunting task to lead a mentally handicapped
> child on from the fun of improvising with musical instru-
> ments to reading music. The Tobin System expresses all
> musical theory in colour and pattern. Colour is also used

to identify notes on an instrument. The system is being used in a number of schools and enthusiasts claim that it is of particular interest to anyone wanting to teach educationally subnormal or handicapped children. It may be helpful to know that all the Tobin System material is available from ESA.

ESA Creative Learning Ltd
Pinnacles, Box 22, Harlow, Essex CM19 5AY

See also chapter 4, **Music therapy**, page 215

Nature study

There is a number of national organizations concerned with aspects of environmental studies. However, the distinctions between the interests of, say, the Field Studies Council with its conservation centres, the Countryside Commission with its country parks and the Nature Conservancy Council with its national nature reserves is unlikely to matter much to a parent whose child is interested in 'nature study' – to use an old-fashioned term which covers the lot of them. In most cases handicapped children will use the same facilities as everyone else. Anyone planning this sort of expedition with handicapped children is well advised to consult those in charge beforehand. Some special facilities have been set up for handicapped people where particular attention is given to avoiding the hazards which make ordinary facilities difficult to use. For instance, the Epping Forest Conservation Centre is particularly suitable for people in wheelchairs as it is built on one level, has a lecture theatre which can take several wheelchairs and the ground is even for some distance outside.

The Warden, Epping Forest Conservation Centre
High Beach, Loughton, Essex
Tel: 01-508 7714

There is information about the accessibility of buildings and surroundings in the following guides:

Access to Some Nature Reserves for Physically Handicapped People
Central Council for the Disabled
34 Eccleston Square, London SW1V 1PE
Tel: 01-821 1871

Nature Trails in Britain (published annually, 15p)
British Tourist Authority, 64 St James's Street, London SW1
Tel: 01-629 9191

CHURCHTOWN FARM FIELD STUDIES CENTRE

The Warden, Churchtown Farm, Lanlivery, Bodmin, Cornwall
Tel: Lostwithiel (0208) 872148

This Field Studies Centre has been specially designed for handicapped people by the Spastics Society. It offers residential courses for schools or for private individuals and there is purpose-built accommodation for twenty-four students and four visiting staff. There are three broad categories of activities:

1 Natural sciences based on a nature reserve next to the Centre and trips further afield.
2 Rural studies using the Centre's own small market garden, greenhouses and domestic animals.
3 Adventure pursuits including camping, pony-trekking, canoeing, sailing or angling.

Most courses can be adapted to all ages and types of handicap but the course on 'Discovering the Countryside' is particularly suitable for younger children or those with a young mental age.

TRENT PARK NATURE TRAIL FOR THE BLIND

Park Manager, The Rookery, Trent Park, Cockfosters, Herts
Tel: 01-449 8706

This trail is arranged so that visually handicapped people

who make their way to Cockfosters station on the underground can get to the park and the nature trail on their own by following the directions on a braille leaflet. The trail is three-quarters of a mile long. It has braille notices – the position of these is indicated by a change of ground surface – describing points of interest. Cassette information tapes are also being prepared.

See also **Bird watching**, page 32

Outward Bound

OUTWARD BOUND TRUST

Outward Bound Trust, 14 Oxford Street, London W1
Tel: 01-637 4951

The philosophy of the Trust is summed up in a quotation from one of the founders, Kurt Hahn: 'It is wrong to coerce young people into opinions, but it is a duty to impel them into experiences.' No special physical ability is needed to attend their courses and at least one Outward Bound school has encouraged youngsters with a handicap. They say that there is an excellent record of achievement with deaf, partially sighted and physically handicapped young people. Local Outward Bound Associations are willing to help young people in their area and have funds to deal with local needs including paying the fees in some cases.

Pen-friends

FRIENDS BY POST

Friends by Post
6 Bollin Court, Macclesfield Road, Wilmslow, Cheshire SK9 2AP
Tel: Wilmslow (099-64) 27044

Mrs Ilse Salomon runs a voluntary scheme for arranging regular correspondence for lonely people. She takes great care to match the interests of pen-friends and would be glad to help parents and handicapped children. Each correspondent is offered a partner to write to once a week. She suggests: 'You might want to talk about an article in the paper, something you heard or saw, some everyday happenings – jotted down as they occur, they are lively and express the feeling of the moment.' There is no charge for the service, but please send a stamped, addressed envelope when writing to her.

JIM'S PEOPLE

JIM's People, White Rails
86 Turnpike Road, Aughton, Ormskirk, Lancs
Tel: Aughton Green (0695) 422005

Anyone can join the 'Joint Involvement Mutual Society – Friendship of the Air'. Their introductory letter explains: 'If you need a friend to help you, whether you are sick or well, young or old, housebound or active, we aim to help you in every way we can.' Locally, JIMS communicate by phone or through the local radio programme; further afield by letters and tapes. JIMS encourages people to set up local groups as well as providing a regular magazine and newsletter which is also recorded on tape and transcribed into braille. It is international and interdenominational. The minimum subscription is 50p a year. There is a special Junior JIMS section for young people.

WIDER HORIZONS

Miss Vera Dench
12 Birchwood Road, London SW17 9VQ
Tel: 01-677 0545

An organization for encouraging wider interests among handicapped people who are cut off from activities they previously enjoyed or were never able to lead active lives. It runs a correspondence scheme, which includes an exchange of tapes, a handcraft competition covering a wide range of skills, and a regular (six times a year) magazine containing members' work. Most of the organizers are themselves disabled.

Photography

PHOTOGRAPHY FOR THE DISABLED

Photography for the Disabled
190 Secrett House, Ham Close, Ham, Richmond, Surrey TW10 7PE
Tel: 01-948 2342

> The committee is composed of amateur photographers who take a special interest in the problems of disabled people who would like to take up photography. They design special equipment for individual needs to enable severely physically handicapped people to operate a camera. They have supplied one school for physically handicapped girls with a complete darkroom – built by members of the committee in their spare time – and equipped with cameras with specially designed supports and other adaptations. They do not always have funds for expensive projects and cannot necessarily afford to supply equipment free of charge. However, they will always offer advice and help.

Play

MAKE CHILDREN HAPPY

Make Children Happy
16/20 Strutton Ground, London SW1
Tel: 01-222 0261

> Make Children Happy runs a local groups project to involve parents of handicapped children, the children themselves, and other local volunteers in the sharing of play and leisure activities during leisure time. Full-time staff are employed to promote and support the development of local groups, although from the outset each group is expected to take considerable responsibility for its own organization. The project is funded by an annual grant from the Department of Health and Social Security.

PLAYSPACE

Short Course Unit, Polytechnic of Central London
309 Regent Street, London W1
Tel: 01-580 2020

Playspace is an educational trust established in 1971 by a voluntary group of students, teachers, artists and community workers to promote the enjoyment of creative work in different situations through every kind of medium. Although the trust has worked with schools and institutions of all kinds, its particular emphasis is on small groups and work with families. The trust organizes different kinds of activities. As well as undertaking research, Playspace runs training courses for people in the helping and learning professions. These are mainly based at the Polytechnic but can be set up anywhere else on demand.

'The Magic Box of Performing Arts' takes theatre to people who can't go to the theatre themselves. For a token fee they will go along and stage a performance in a local hall. Bookings must be made two months in advance because every performance is specifically designed to involve the particular audience – both children and adults.

Playspace also functions as a freelance agency for group workers, artists, playleaders, advisers, therapists and voluntary workers, so that organizations can ask for lectures, demonstrations, conferences, advice and consultation on all forms of play and creative work. They have organized 'Playdays' for parents and handicapped children. These can be one-off events or longer courses according to need.

Play – information

FAIR PLAY FOR CHILDREN CAMPAIGN

Fair Play for Children
237 Pentonville Road, London N1
Tel: 01-278 5314

The Campaign is a coming together of over 300 voluntary

bodies of every size who combine forces to campaign for better facilities for children's play. They range from the National Playing Fields Association to the Cramlington Summer Playscheme in Northumberland. One part of its activities is to encourage members to share resources so as to avoid duplication of effort. The development officer has helped to set up about sixty district play councils. The Campaign acts as a clearing house for information on all matters relating to play. It will try to help individual parents in search of any kind of play, from holiday playschemes to toy libraries. If a parent with a handicapped child found that difficulties were being made about the child joining in a local playscheme, the Campaign would be prepared to step in and try to sort out any misunderstandings.

NATIONAL PLAYING FIELDS ASSOCIATION (NPFA)

NPFA, 25 Ovington Square, London SW3
Tel: 01-584 6445

The Association is very concerned about the play and recreation needs of handicapped children. The Information Centre keeps a file of pamphlets, journal articles and press cuttings on the subject. The Children and Youth and Technical Departments are available to give help and advice on such subjects as adventure play, play provision, play leadership, layout of playgrounds and surfacing. It is possible that in some cases limited funds may be available from the Association. The NPFA's regional play advisors in various parts of the country can give on-the-spot help. The Association has produced several inexpensive pamphlets on various aspects of play for the handicapped. The Information Centre is open weekdays from 9.30 a.m. to 5.30 p.m.

The NPFA is fully involved in the Fair Play for Children Campaign.

Play for Physically and Mentally Handicapped People (1976)

Centre on Environment for the Handicapped
126 Albert Street, London NW1 7NF
Tel: 01-267 6111

> This bibliography and information sheet, compiled by
> Janet Hyde, contains many references to articles and
> publications which are not easily obtainable. Some of
> these are available as reprints and in every case they are
> in the CEH library which offers photocopying facilities.
> (Price 25p including postage.)

Printing

BRITISH PRINTING SOCIETY

British Printing Society
Alan F. Turner, Assistant Secretary (Disabled Printers)
38 North Drive, Orpington, Kent BR6 9PG
Tel: Orpington 53846

> Many hospitals can provide printing in their occupational
> therapy departments where they use the activities as a
> means of exercising limbs. In most cases machines and
> equipment can be adapted to suit a particular disability;
> for instance, hand machines may be foot-operated. The
> British Printing Society suggest that anyone with a dis-
> ability who wants to take up printing ought to ask his
> family doctor to put him in touch with a hospital with a
> print shop so that he can see if it is possible to try his hand
> on a hospital machine before buying one of his own. The
> Assistant Secretary of the Society – who is hemiplegic
> following a stroke – says: 'I started this way myself, being
> first taken daily to work in the neighbourhood ambulance
> for a couple of hours each morning. Having got the
> printing bug I then did much of my typesetting at home,
> using the machine at the hospital. Some time after I
> acquired a machine of my own, the hospital decided I
> didn't need to come any more!'
>   Membership of the British Printing Society is open to all

who are interested in printing and includes day centres, schools and clubs as well as individuals. Its objects are: to unite full-time, part-time and hobby printers in friendly association; to improve the standard of craftsmanship of its members in printing and allied crafts; to encourage printing as a hobby. The Society publishes a monthly magazine, *Small Printer*, which plays an important part in the life of the Society and reaches all members, whether they are able to join in the activities of a local branch or have little chance of contact with other printers. *Basic Letterpress*, a booklet published by the Society, is a primer on what one needs to know to become a printer, including a chapter on the approach to printing by someone with a disability.

Puppets

PUPPET CENTRE

Puppet Centre Trust, Battersea Town Hall
Lavender Hill, London SW11 5TJ
Tel: 01-223 5356
Open 2–6 p.m. Monday to Friday and at other times by appointment

The Puppet Centre Trust is a registered charity formed to serve the needs of anyone engaged in or interested in any branch of amateur, professional or educational puppetry. This includes the use of puppets in therapy where the case histories show that they can be particularly effective in work with handicapped children. A report in *New Psychiatry* said: 'Those who are too shy or inhibited to express themselves in acting roles, can often manage well through the indirect medium of puppetry. For the disabled or handicapped, puppets offer a substitute theatre where quick movements, dancing and fighting are represented on a more abstract level.' They hold regular day, evening and week-end courses – subjects include 'Puppets in Special Education' – and can arrange special courses on request. They can also arrange practical workshop sessions for groups and private individuals in addition to their own workshops. Lectures and demonstrations can be provided at the centre or elsewhere. There is a free reference library and an information and advisory service. Public performances of amateur and professional puppeteers are held. Other plans include a travelling exhibition.

Reading

BOOKS FOR CHILDREN

One encouraging sign of growing sensitivity to the needs of handicapped children is that several publishers now produce books for children about handicapped children. An outstanding example is *Mark's Wheelchair Adventures* by Camilla Jessel (published by Methuen, price £1.95). With the help of the Nuffield Foundation and the Community Development Trust, Camilla Jessel was able to carry out a pioneering study of relationships between handicapped and sound children. She has used this material, and her own photographs of the children involved, to present a simple unsentimental account of Mark, a handicapped child, and his adventures with other children on the estate, including a spastic girl. The book manages to draw attention to the common social problems of handicapped children without obtrusive comment. The author says that one of her main purposes in writing the book was 'to suggest to children that they can get to know each other'.

A less ambitious book, published by the Bodley Head in association with the Disabled Living Foundation, is *Rachel*, a picture story book for younger children (price £1.45). Written by Elizabeth Fanshawe, who is in charge of the Aids centre at the DLF, and illustrated by Michael Charlton, it describes Rachel and her everyday adventures and shows that although she is in a wheelchair, she is very much like any other child and enjoys the same games and amusements.

Another book for younger children, *Don't Forget Tom* by Hanne Larsen, translated from the Danish by Peggy Blakeley, is published by A. and C. Black Ltd (1974, price £1.35). This describes a mentally handicapped boy's life with his family in a realistic and sensible way that young children can understand and appreciate. It avoids the pitfall of excessive sympathy and sentimentality, both in the text and the photographic illustrations. *Sally Can't See* (1976) by Palle Peterson is in a similar style, also based on a Danish publication. *Claire and Emma* (1976) is written by an English mother, Diana Peters, about her own deaf daughters. A. and C. Black say that if someone comes to them with an idea for a new book about a handicapped child, and they can find a suitable family to use, they will consider publishing it.

LARGE-PRINT BOOKS

Cedric Chivers Ltd, Book Sales Division
93–100 Locksbrook Road, Bath BA1 3EN
Tel: Bath (0225) 28685

Cedric Chivers claim that their large-print section now covers every large-print book available in this country, including the former Franklin Watts list, with the exception of the Ulverscroft range. Their adult list includes classical and modern novels, romances, crime novels, a variety of non-fiction and a large first dictionary and ten-volume encyclopedia. They are expanding their children's titles with a new series of books, in addition to old favourites like *Black Beauty* and *Little Women*. The first titles are three 'Nurse Matilda' stories by Christianna Brand, illustrated by Edward Ardizzone, at £2.00 each.

Ulverscroft Large-Print Books Ltd
The Green, Bradgate Road, Anstey, Leicester LE7 7FW
Tel: Anstey (053-721) 4325

Ulverscroft books are printed under the auspices of the Ulverscroft Foundation, a registered charity in aid of people who have difficulty in reading normal print. They provide the kind of 'entertaining, escapist reading that many people require' from mysteries and romances to light non-fiction. They have been disappointed in the support for their list for boys and girls aged eleven to fifteen and have had to discontinue new titles, but the fourteen titles in print include *Little House in the Big Woods, Caverns of the Moon* by Patrick Moore and *A First Dictionary*. They have also produced a series of 'Trigger Books' intended to supplement first reading schemes for older slow readers. One book, for example, tells the story of a multi-racial pop group who want to make their own gramophone record. 'Trigger Books' are distributed by William Collins Sons & Co. Ltd.

W. Collins Sons & Co. Ltd
144 Cathedral Street, Glasgow G4 0NB

Riding

RIDING FOR THE DISABLED ASSOCIATION

Riding for the Disabled Association
Avenue 'R', National Agricultural Centre, Kenilworth
Warks. CV8 2LY
Tel: Coventry (0203) 56107

'When a disabled person is mounted on a horse the two weak legs are replaced by four good strong legs.' There are over 260 organizations throughout the country arranging riding for disabled people (list available) including the first purpose-built riding centre for the disabled in the world. Pupils suffer from conditions such as cerebral palsy, polio, loss of limbs and blindness. The aim is to provide a new incentive, greater independence, enjoyment, physical recreation and a sense of achievement, as well as making a link with the able-bodied world. The Association also organizes trekking and riding holidays for disabled people.

WOMEN'S ROYAL VOLUNTARY SERVICE

WRVS, Head Office, 17 Old Park Lane, London W1Y 4AJ
Tel: 01-499 6040

The WRVS also has a number of special facilities for teaching riding to handicapped children. Some of these are run in conjunction with the Riding for the Disabled Association, others are run independently. They do not exclude children with severe physical or mental handicaps who will never be able to ride without support.

Rowing

See **Water sports**

Sailing

CHRISTIAN SAILING CENTRE

Christian Sailing Centre
Dodnor Creek, Newport, Isle of Wight PO30 5TE
Tel: Newport (098-381) 2195

The Centre is run as a Christian home as well as a sailing school and some time is given each day to examining Christian beliefs. The Centre can take up to sixty people in a modern building with single, double and four-berth rooms. They cannot normally accept bookings for unaccompanied children of fourteen and under. They have had children with spina bifida and mentally handicapped children and would make every effort to help groups or individuals with a handicap.

PRINCE OF WALES COMMITTEE

Group Administrator, Prince of Wales Committee
9 Marine Parade, Penarth, Glam.
Tel: Penarth (0222) 708318

The Prince of Wales Commmittee, the Inland Waterways Association, the Variety Club of Great Britain and other groups have combined in a project to restore a stretch of the Montgomery canal and establish a pilot scheme of special boats on which handicapped and disadvantaged children can enjoy outings and holidays. The 70-foot boats will travel at 2 to 3 mph to give the children an opportunity to enjoy the remote countryside and its wild life. They have specially designed toilet and sleeping facilities, ramp boarding, extra headroom and will be able to take wheelchairs and stretcher cases. Trips are entirely free and are expected to run all through the winter. Groups are planning schemes for other areas, including a Scottish project for canals between Glasgow and Edinburgh.

RYA SEAMANSHIP FOUNDATION

RYA Seamanship Foundation
Victoria Way, Woking, Surrey GU21 1EQ
Tel: Woking (048-62) 5022

The Seamanship Foundation is an independent charity set up in association with the Royal Yachting Association. It aims to create new opportunities to improve their seamanship for all who use water for fun. It has no formal timetable of courses for those who are handicapped but has worked successfully with people who are blind, deaf or physically handicapped (although not every physically handicapped person will be able to learn to sail). It can offer all kinds of practical help and support, including training aids. The British Association for Sporting and Recreational Activities of the Blind is enthusiastic about the activities of the Foundation. It says it has found it eager to find ways of helping, very open-minded, with no hang-ups about disability, and prepared to have a go at anything to see if it will work out.

SPARKLE

Central Council for the Disabled
34 Eccleston Square, London SW1V 1PE
Tel: 01-821 1871

Sparkle is a specially designed day boat for disabled would-be sailors. She was built by SPARKS (Sportsmen Pledged to Aid Research into Crippling), and is completely financed by that organization. She can take ten people in wheelchairs, three who are ambulant and two able-bodied helpers. It is possible for a third helper to be accommodated if one of the disabled passengers needs constant attendance. *Sparkle* operates from a number of resorts during the May to September season. Bookings can be accepted for day or half-day trips excluding Mondays and Tuesdays. Individual disabled people and groups are invited to write for details and application forms.

YOUTH AFLOAT

Youth Afloat
96 High Street, Pensnett, Brierley Hill, West Midlands
Tel: Brierley Hill (0384) 77691

Youth Afloat is a sailing club for teenagers at Pensnett, with a centre at Brightlingsea. Children from all over the West Midlands can learn to sail first on tiny Optimist dinghies, progressing eventually to salt-water sailing in cruising or racing yachts. The centre was formed by the Johnnie Johnson Adventure Trust. It claims that the adventurous spirit among many disadvantaged children has found an outlet with it. Blind, deaf, spastic and autistic children all benefit and can learn. Handicapped children are given an introduction to sailing in a dry sailing session: the boat and its gear, safety drill, rigging and first rules of where to sit, and so on, are taught on dry land. The centre would like to expand its work with the handicapped but need contacts fairly close to the centre because of transport costs. Like most other voluntary groups, shortage of funds prevents it from doing all it would like to do.

Skiing

BRITISH SKI CLUB FOR THE DISABLED

David Adams, British Ski Club for the Disabled
38 Mountside, Stanmore, Middlesex
Tel: 01-863 5852

The Club was formed in October 1974 and is now a registered charity. It was able to take a visually handicapped fourteen-year-old boy on a skiing course in Switzerland. Handicapped children use the artificial ski-slopes at the National Mountaineering Centre, Plas y Brenin in North Wales. The chairman writes: 'Given some financial assistance and a bit of time we should be able to help handicapped children and we will take our lead from the various organizations on the continent who have already been working in this field for some time.' A newsletter is available in braille.

Sports

BRITISH SPORTS ASSOCIATION FOR THE DISABLED (BSAD)

BSAD, Stoke Mandeville Stadium
Harvey Road, Aylesbury, Bucks
Tel: Aylesbury (0296) 84848

The coordinating body for organizations including schools and clubs who are in any way concerned with sport for the disabled. Individuals may join as supporting members. It has regional committees which work with the regions of the Sports Council and with local authorities to organize meetings and courses and to form clubs. Organizations affiliated to BSAD may take part in the Junior Multi-Disabled Games held at Stoke Mandeville every summer. About 400 children aged between ten and sixteen, with every kind of disability, compete in all kinds of sports and track events, indoor and outdoor. Whatever kind of sport a disabled person is interested in, BSAD ought to know the most suitable and convenient place to do it.

SCOTTISH SPORTS ASSOCIATION FOR THE DISABLED

Scottish Sports Association for the Disabled
Claremont House, 18/19 Claremont Crescent, Edinburgh EH7 4QD
Tel: 031-556 3882

This Association promotes the development of sport amongst disabled people and coordinates activities of member organizations, arranges sports meetings, coaching, and help in the provision of necessary facilities.

WELSH SPORTS ASSOCIATION FOR THE DISABLED

Welsh Sports Association for the Disabled
Crescent Road, Caerphilly, Mid Glamorgan
Tel: Caerphilly (0222) 869224

The Association organizes sport and physical recreational events of all kinds for disabled people and encourages sport centres and organizations to provide access and facilities for them. Its main annual events are the Welsh National Multi-Disabled Games and a national swimming gala. Other activities range from rifle shooting to wheelchair dancing.

CENTRAL COUNCIL OF PHYSICAL RECREATION (CCPR)

CCPR, 70 Brompton Road, London SW3 1HE
Tel: 01-584 6651/2

The CCPR represents the views of the voluntary bodies and clubs concerned with sport, both in negotiating with the government and local authorities, and in dealing with the media, sponsorship and international events. It has encouraged all its member organizations to appoint at least one officer to deal specially with the needs of disabled people. Although it has now surrendered many of its former functions to the Sports Council, it remains as 'a forum for debate and springboard for action', for all voluntary organizations concerned with sport.

SPORTS COUNCIL

Sports Council, 70 Brompton Road, London SW3 1EX
Tel: 01-589 3411

This body, under the chairmanship of Sir Roger Bannister, is independent by statute but its members are appointed by the government. It was set up to encourage all kinds of physical recreation and outdoor activities and to channel government grants for sport. When it was established in 1972 it took over many of the functions, assets and staff of the CCPR and now runs all the national sports centres such as Crystal Palace and Holme Pierrepont National Water Sports Centre. It has a particular interest in encouraging sport for the disabled. One of the council members is himself a disabled sportsman. The Information Centre acts as a clearing house for information about all kinds of sports provision, including nature conservation and study centres. There are separate councils for Scotland and Wales, responsible for local sport in their areas under the aegis of the Sports Council. The Scottish Sports Council has organized swimming classes, activity evenings and outdoor pursuit courses for physically handicapped people with the assistance of voluntary groups and schools.

Scottish Sports Council
1 St Colme Street, Edinburgh EH3 6AA
Tel: 031-225 8411

Sports Council for Wales, National Sports Centre for Wales
Sophia Gardens, Cardiff
Tel: Cardiff (0222) 397571

Swimming

ASSOCIATION OF SWIMMING THERAPY

Mr and Mrs J. McMillan, Association of Swimming Therapy
24 Arnos Road, London N11
Tel: 01-368 3251

Mr McMillan pioneered the Halliwick method of teaching swimming to people of all ages with every kind of disability. There are clubs throughout Great Britain and in many countries abroad. Send a stamped, addressed envelope to the Association for the details of the regional or national organizer who will put you in touch with local clubs. All the instructors are volunteers; members and instructors are on first-name terms so that there is no feeling of 'them and us'. The Association runs intensive weekend lecture and training courses but as there is such a demand it has to plan ahead and try to cover the country over the course of a year.

AMATEUR SWIMMING ASSOCIATION (ASA)

Miss L. V. Cook, Amateur Swimming Association
12 Kings Avenue, Woodford Green, Essex IG8 0JB
Tel: 01-504 9361

The Association gives awards for proficiency in personal survival. There are special conditions laid down for handicapped persons entering for these awards. There is also a scheme of joint swimming awards for the physically handicapped granted by the ASA in association with the English Schools' Swimming Association. Candidates for these awards are those who have any degree of physical handicap and there is allowance made for the use of a buoyancy aid in extreme cases, where the examiner thinks it desirable.

NATIONAL ASSOCIATION OF SWIMMING CLUBS FOR THE HANDICAPPED

National Association of Swimming Clubs for the Handicapped
4 Hillside Gardens, Northwood, Middlesex
Tel: Northwood 27784

The purpose of the Association is to encourage, develop and promote swimming for the handicapped, because of its immense value in the physical and psychological development of the individual. It is compiling a register of all clubs for the handicapped and can put people in touch with their nearest clubs. It recommends teaching methods and organizes galas on a team handicap system, with rules that allow for different types of physical and mental disability.

SPORTS COUNCIL COORDINATING COMMITTEE ON SWIMMING FOR THE DISABLED

Miss Elizabeth Dendy
Coordinating Committee on Swimming for the Disabled
Sports Council, 70 Brompton Road, London SW3 1EX
Tel: 01-589 3411

> The committee has been set up to draw together all those concerned with swimming for the handicapped including medical specialists, representatives of local councils and swimming organizations. Its functions are to collect and disseminate information, and to encourage the provision of facilities for the handicapped. It is promoting conferences and courses about this and is producing a series of leaflets on specific aspects of the sport.

JOHN GROOMS ASSOCIATION FOR THE DISABLED

John Grooms Association for the Disabled
Edgware Way, Edgware, Middlesex
Tel: 01-959 3292

> The Association has a purpose-built swimming pool in Edgware built exclusively for the use of disabled bathers, with easy wheelchair access to toilets, changing rooms, showers and footbath. Wheelchairs have access up to the pool itself, where a hoist is available to transfer the bather right into the water. There is a social centre where swimmers can meet friends and helpers. The pool cost over £70 000 which had to be raised by voluntary efforts. Disabled children and adults who are members of organized groups can use the pool. Write for bookings to the Principal.

Guidelines for Teaching the Disabled to Swim

> This booklet costs 20p from the Swimming Teachers' Association.

Swimming Teachers' Association
1 Birmingham Road, West Bromwich, West Midlands
Tel: 021-553 5828

Toys

TOY LIBRARIES ASSOCIATION

Toy Libraries Association
Sunley House, 10 Gunthorpe Street, London E1 7RW
Tel: 01-247 1386

Toy libraries are centres where families can borrow the best toys for handicapped children – sometimes toys specially designed for them. An invaluable meeting place which is a source of advice and support for parents as well as children. They cater for children with any kind of handicap, however young they are, because the right play material can do so much to stimulate and encourage handicapped children. One or two groups have organized mobile toy libraries to visit remote areas and people who can't get into town centres. The Association prides itself on the friendly, informal contacts and communication between parents and professionals that arise from their involvement in their local group.

The Association works nationally with therapists, psychologists, teachers and research workers; with manufacturers, art colleges and toy designers. There is a regular newsletter and many helpful leaflets which manage to be friendly, informative and encouraging without being patronizing or hearty, on all aspects of toys for the handicapped. A display of toys ranging from a tricycle worked by hand controls to a foam-rubber see-saw has been assembled at its headquarters, and can be visited by appointment.

NOTTINGHAM UNIVERSITY TOY LIBRARY

Nottingham University Toy Library, Psychology Department
University Park, Nottingham NG7 2RD
Tel: Nottingham (0602) 56101 Ext. 3198

The Toy Library is run by the Psychology Department as a support service to parents as well as to help with the training and research of educational psychologists. The aim is to help parents by discussing in detail the use of particular toys, and by suggesting games and activities for parents to use in encouraging the child to develop. Information sheets are available free of charge, although donations are welcome because all toys, equipment and books are paid for out of voluntary contributions. Two audio tapes are available for hire on the work of the Toy Library. They consist of tape reels or cassettes together with a set of fifty to sixty slides, all designed for use on ordinary domestic equipment. They are suitable for viewing by audiences or individuals.

Medical Recording Service Foundation
PO Box 99, Chelmsford CM1 5HL

TOY LIBRARY TRAINING PACK

King's Fund Centre, 126 Albert Street, London NW1 7NF
Tel: 01-267 6111

The King's Fund Centre has put together a training pack for people thinking of starting a toy library. It consists of tapes, slides and useful background material. The cost of hiring is £6 for fourteen days – the hirer is able to keep most of the literature.

Play Specials

ESA Creative Learning Ltd
Pinnacles, PO Box 22, Harlow, Essex CM19 5AY
Tel: Harlow (0279) 27464

Although many manufacturers produce suitable toys, ESA is the only commercial firm which has a toy catalogue featuring toys specially selected for their play value for handicapped children. Many of these toys are from standard ranges, others are Extra Specials designed to overcome some particular handicap, for example a hand-driven cart for a child unable to walk or feely toys for visually handicapped children. ESA offers a 20 per cent discount to help schools, playgroups, toy libraries or other charities or voluntary organizations who have to raise their own funds to pay for the toys. The catalogue covers all toys for all children because it has found that good toys are enjoyed by ordinary and handicapped children alike, whoever they were originally designed for, and it hopes that toys can play an important part in bridging the gap between normal and handicapped children within the community.

Water sports

ADVISORY PANEL ON WATER SPORTS FOR DISABLED PEOPLE

Sports Council, 70 Brompton Road, London SW3 1EX
Tel: 01-589 3411

The Council has set up a steering committee to promote water sports for disabled people. Sports covered include canoeing, sailing, fishing, rowing, water-skiing, sub-aqua diving. Information on all these sports should be available from this committee. In November 1975 they published *Water Recreation Areas – Access for Disabled People*.

Wheelchair dancing

WHEELCHAIR DANCE ASSOCIATION

Wheelchair Dance Association, Physical Education Adviser
Spastics Society, 8 Starvecrow Close, Shipbourne Road
Tonbridge, Kent
Tel: Tonbridge (0732) 352877

Wheelchair dancing was started by chance at one of the Spastic Society's schools. It grew out of lessons devised to help new wheelchair users to manoeuvre their chairs. Over the course of several years the emphasis changed from dancing being a therapy to it being an enjoyable activity in its own right. An annual dance festival has been held for several years. At the 1975 festival eighteen teams were present and the highlight of the occasion was the final free dancing session with as many as a hundred dancers on the floor.

In 1974 the Wheelchair Dance Association was formed, which issues a quarterly bulletin, and promotes wheelchair dancing in every way. It encourages cooperation between member clubs and as well as offering them advice and help, it aims to run courses to instruct wheelchair users and other people in the teaching of wheelchair dancing.

See also **Disco,** page 333

8　Holidays

The larger voluntary societies listed in chapter 2 usually arrange holidays for their members. Many of them have cottages and caravans for family holidays. This chapter has information about other organizations providing holidays for handicapped children, with or without their families. They aim to give children a good time as distinct from simply looking after them to give the family a break.

Social services departments should be able to arrange or advise on free or low-cost holidays for handicapped children. They may make their own arrangements or combine with voluntary organizations. They may be able to help with the cost of a holiday. The education welfare service, if there is one, or a child's school may be able to arrange recuperative holidays for handicapped children of school age. When it is the family rather than the child which really needs a break, it may be possible for short-term care to be arranged (see chapter 3, **Residential care,** page 165. If you are planning a holiday with or for a handicapped child you will find useful information under **Travel,** page 183, and **Medical treatment away from home,** page 234.

The National Society for Mentally Handicapped Children warn that some overseas countries do not allow mentally handicapped people to go there on holiday. They suggest that parents should check with the High Commission or Embassy concerned before they make any arrangements.

Information

AUTOMOBILE ASSOCIATION
AA, Fanum House, Stanmore, Middlesex
Tel: 01-954 7373 or any AA office

The AA's *Guide for the Disabled* (price 15p) is free to
members. It includes general information, a gazetteer of
special accommodation, advice on motoring and a list of
organizations on the Continent which give travel advice to
handicapped visitors. The AA's manager in the Reading
area, himself disabled, takes a special interest in the mobility problems of handicapped people.

AA, Fanum House, 45 Oxford Road, Reading RG1 7QL
Tel: Reading (0734) 581122

BRITISH TOURIST AUTHORITY

British Tourist Authority
64 St James's Street, London SW1
Tel: 01-629 9191

The Authority has a leaflet of advice and information about
travel in Britain for the handicapped, available free. It can
also supply a free list prepared by the Scottish Tourist
Board of hotels and accommodation in Scotland suitable
for disabled people.

CENTRAL COUNCIL FOR THE DISABLED (CCD)

CCD, 34 Eccleston Square, London SW1V 1PE
Tel: 01-821 1871

The Council runs a holiday information service for
physically handicapped people. It publishes an annual
guidebook, *Holidays for the Physically Handicapped* (65p,
plus 50p postage; also available from W. H. Smith).
This lists by counties private accommodation and voluntary organizations offering holidays. There is also a section
on holidays abroad. The Council issues a list of publications on holidays and access guides to a number of
resorts.

CHILDREN'S HOLIDAY INFORMATION CENTRE (CHIC)

CHIC, 41 Water Street, Birmingham B3 1HP
Tel: 021-233 2030

> This Birmingham centre offers help and advice on any aspect of children's play, including play facilities for handicapped children, and cooperates with the local education department in offering training for volunteers who want to help on play schemes. It publishes a directory of holiday playschemes and residential holidays available to 'Brum' children with details of those catering in any way for handicapped children. The directory includes notes about resources for anyone wanting to set up his own scheme. (Price 20p in 1976.)

CHILDREN AND YOUTH ACTION GROUP (CYAG)

CYAG, Victoria Chambers
16-20 Strutton Ground, London SW1
Tel: 01-222 0261

> The Group produces an annual directory of residential holidays for children on their own – including handicapped children – called *Where to Stay* (price 50p, plus postage).

EDINBURGH COUNCIL OF SOCIAL SERVICE

Edinburgh Council of Social Service
11 St Colme Street, Edinburgh EH3 6AG
Tel: 031-225 4606/8

> The Edinburgh Council of Social Service has published a booklet called *Individual and Group Holiday Provision* for individuals and organizations, both statutory and voluntary, who arrange holidays for the disadvantaged. It gives information on accommodation available to groups and to individuals and details of cost, recreational facilities, and extent of care and supervision provided, as well as indicating whether the accommodation is suitable for young or old, disabled or fit. It hopes to produce a completely revised edition in 1977.

NATIONAL SOCIETY FOR MENTALLY HANDICAPPED CHILDREN (NSMHC)

Holidays Officer, NSMHC
Pembridge Hall, 17 Pembridge Square, London W2 4EP
Tel: 01-229 8941/01-727 0536

As well as holidays organized by the Society (including special care holidays) the Society publishes an annual list of more than 100 hotels and guest houses willing to accept a mentally handicapped holidaymaker. Available free.

HOLIDAY LIST

Coldeast Hospital School
Sarisbury Green, Nr Southampton SO3 6ZD
Tel: Locks Heath (048-95) 4241 Ext. 259

Through the medium of newspapers and magazines Marjorie Murphy publicized a need for information from those in the holiday trade who were ready and willing to accept mentally handicapped children for holidays accompanied by their parents. She then compiled a list which has been published as a non-profit-making venture by Coldeast Hospital School. The list does not specifically recommend any of the accommodation. Anyone who wants a copy should send a stamped, addressed, foolscap envelope to the school, plus 20p to cover printing costs.

Camping

FOREST SCHOOL CAMPS

The Secretary, Forest School Camps
3 Pine View, Fairmile Park Road, Cobham, Surrey KT11 2PG
Tel: Cobham 2920

A registered charity which organizes camping holidays for more than a thousand children each year. It runs some camps for mentally handicapped children where experienced and new campers are both welcome. In 1975 these special camps were for boys and girls from eight to eighteen years. There is a very high staff-to-child ratio so that each child gets the care and encouragement he needs to enjoy new experiences with confidence. In addition, it is willing to consider offering places in some of its other camps to experienced campers with a handicap. It often has some children with mild physical handicaps in its camps and can offer places to a few active children with more severe handicaps. It will give advice as to which camps might suit an individual child. Severely handicapped children in camp may need one staff member each. This would increase the costs were they not offset by charitable donations. The Forest School Camps says that if parents think their handicapped child would enjoy camping they should not let the cost – £20 plus fares for 10 days in 1975 – deter them from applying because it may be possible to arrange financial help.

DISABLED CAMPERS CLUB

Frank J. Strong (Secretary), Disabled Campers Club
28 Coote Road, Bexleyheath, Kent DA7 4PR
Tel: 01-303 0753

Although membership of the club is restricted to handicapped and able-bodied people of eighteen and over, there are members' children at camp meets and a parent or other adult can join the club in order to bring along a physically handicapped child. This is a new club for people who do not want an organized communal holiday. Each group is self-catering and independent but the club plans to acquire special equipment such as a portable toilet with handrails and a tent large enough to take the toilet, a wheelchair and a helper. There is a discount scheme for members to buy equipment at reduced cost. The quarterly bulletin includes reports on commercial camp sites.

WOODLARKS CAMP

Mrs V. G. Palmer (Hon. Secretary), Woodlarks Camp Site Trust
Kathleen Marshall House, Woodlarks Camp, Tilford Road
Farnham, Surrey GU10 3RN
Tel: Farnham (025-13) 6279

Founded in 1930 to provide camping holidays for severely
handicapped men, women and children. Woodlarks Camp
consists of twelve acres of grassland, heather and woodland.
The camp buildings include a large brick dining room, a
sixteen-bed dormitory for those not allowed to sleep in
tents, and a toilet block with wash cubicles, bathrooms,
showers and lavatories. Tents, bedding and cutlery are
provided. Each morning prayers are said in an open-air
chapel and services are held there on Sundays. There is a
heated swimming pool and a wide range of other activities.
Each camp is organized by a camp leader who accepts as
many handicapped people as the helpers can manage. The
committee of the Trust act as liaison between would-be
campers and helpers as well as maintaining the site and its
facilities. Many of the campers are in wheelchairs and each
has one helper – the two becoming partners for the
duration of the camp. The helpers are voluntary and there
is a particularly close link with the scout and guide movements. Camps for children which are run as guide or scout
camps are not necessarily limited to children who are
members of the movement.

Holiday schemes

BARROWS GREEN

Assistant Children's Officer (Residential)
Dr Barnardo's, North-West Divisional Office
248 Upper Parliament Street, Liverpool L8 7QE
Tel: 051-709 6291/2

Barrows Green is a holiday centre for up to sixteen
mentally handicapped children (including those with

additional handicaps) between the ages of twelve and sixteen. It is a large and lovely house with almost fourteen acres of ground, on the edge of the Lake District about three miles from Kendal. Barnardo's say that their objectives are two-fold: to provide short-term relief from the inevitable pressures on the families of mentally handicapped children, and also to provide new and stimulating experiences for the children. At the holiday centre staff are allocated to individual children for the whole of their stay and friendships formed with the staff can be renewed on other holidays. All members of staff are encouraged to carry out observations of the children and report any progress made; this is passed on to parents wherever appropriate. During 1975 the charge was £31.50 a week and most holidays were expected to last for nine days.

BREAK – HOLIDAYS FOR HANDICAPPED AND DEPRIVED CHILDREN

Break, 20 Hooks Hill Road
Sheringham, Norfolk
Tel: Sheringham (0263) 823170

Break has three centres on the North Norfolk coast – the Sandcastle at Hunstanton, the Rainbow and the Wigwam at Sheringham. These are open all the year and will accept children with mental, physical or emotional handicaps. Brothers and sisters, and occasionally the whole family, may be accepted. Ages up to sixteen, including preschool children, but older ages will always receive sympathetic consideration. Break can provide a home-base during holidays for handicapped children at boarding school. Parties of handicapped children from schools, or parents' groups, with or without accompanying staff, are welcome. Escorts can be arranged from Liverpool Street station in London to each centre for the cost of fares and expenses.

BRITISH RED CROSS SOCIETY

British Red Cross Society
9 Grosvenor Crescent, London SW1X 7EJ
Tel: 01-235 5454

Many of the Society's branches arrange special holidays for handicapped people, including children. At least one branch has its own permanent holiday home. The County of London branch, for instance, organizes a holiday once a year for twenty physically handicapped children in wheelchairs who live in London or go to school there. The children go to Wargrave for a week in August where each child is looked after by a Red Cross cadet. Activities include riding and swimming.

BUCKETS AND SPADES

Mr L. Silverman, Buckets and Spades
20 Mersham Drive, London NW9 9PM
Tel: 01-204 7414

This is a holiday home at St Leonards-on-Sea run by a Jewish organization which takes children of all races and religions. It will accept children with all mental and emotional handicaps, including those associated with physical handicaps. Priority is given to children living at home. It is open all the year, but from January to March it is available for adults only. The home has three acres of grounds, a children's playground and a large playroom. Ages: boys under thirteen, girls under sixteen.

ELIZABETH FITZROY HOMES

Welfare Department, Elizabeth Fitzroy Homes
Coach House, Whitegates, Liss, Hants
Tel: Liss (073-082) 3577

This Catholic charity, which caters for mentally and multiply handicapped children irrespective of religion, has four small family homes offering all kinds of residential care. Many children return there for holidays year after year. One mother wrote: 'There are never any tears when she is left at Donec because she knows she is amongst friends who love and care for her.' The Trust also organizes special holidays every year for severely physically handicapped young people. These holiday weeks are held in schools and a great deal of effort goes into creating a holiday atmosphere. Reports in the journal, *Trust*, on the three holidays held in 1975 include a canal trip arranged by the parish priest which was paid for by the parish and an evening barbecue with a scout group who were camping in the school grounds at the same time, arranged by the headmaster of the host school and his family.

ELLERSLIE COURT

Ellerslie Court, 38 Westcliffe Road, Birkdale, Southport
Tel: Southport (0704) 68545

Ellerslie Court was opened by the Southport, Formby and District Spastics Society to provide holidays for spastic and other handicapped people and their families from all parts of the country. It is close to the beach and looks and is run exactly like a normal modern private hotel except for the extra facilities. Guests can be met at railway and bus stations by ambulance if necessary. They hope more and more to take spastics unaccompanied on repeat visits to give their families a break. From April 1977 the charges per week are £45 for an adult and half for children.

INTER-SCHOOL CHRISTIAN FELLOWSHIP

Activities Secretary, Inter-School Christian Fellowship
47 Marylebone Lane, London W1M 6AX
Tel: 01-486 2561

The Fellowship organizes ten days' holiday in August for (a) blind and sighted girls, (b) deaf and hearing girls, (c) physically handicapped and fit boys and girls. Ages fourteen plus. It is hoped that the holidays will provide an opportunity to make new friends and share an enjoyable holiday with people of the same age, some of whom are handicapped, some not. There are informal prayers every day or discussions about the Christian faith and its application to everyday life.

JANE HODGE HOLIDAY CENTRE

Jane Hodge Holiday Centre, Cowbridge, Glamorgan
Tel: Cowbridge (044-63) 2608

The Centre provides two-week holidays for physically handicapped children with a wide range of handicaps – spastic, spina bifida, muscular dystrophy, thalidomide. It is a specially designed and equipped building in a seven-and-a-half acre site with a boating lake, playroom, music and television room. There is a hydrotherapy swimming pool with an aqua roundabout. The staff is fully qualified. A coach supplied by the Variety Club takes the children on outings. The Centre is supported by voluntary contributions and makes no charge to parents. Financial difficulties, however, have made it consider taking more children sponsored by local authorities and other organizations who can afford the economic cost of £120 for a twelve-day holiday.

KIDS

Director, Kids Holiday Centre
Easton Maudit, Nr Wellingbrough, Northants

This is a registered charity with its own holiday centre which is open throughout the year for twelve-day holidays, starting on Mondays. It takes twelve children from pre-school up to the age of fifteen. All physically handicapped and deprived children are eligible; severely mentally handicapped children are also accepted. Normal brothers and sisters may go along on holiday with them. Activities include riding, swimming, roller skating, tennis, billiards, plays and concerts, woodwork and crafts. The staff are qualified and special diets can be coped with. Families may apply direct and it is 'first come, first served' for the vacancies. The full cost is £40.61, including VAT, for children whose fees are paid by a local authority, but Kids will try to help any family who has to pay the cost themselves. An escort can be arranged to and from St Pancras, London, to the Centre.

NENTHOLME

Mr and Mrs V. Hefter
Nentholme, Alston, Cumbria CA9 3JQ
Tel: Alston (049-83) 525

Mr and Mrs Hefter run a small family holiday home for mentally handicapped children. They can take up to six children at one time and are open throughout the year, although school holidays are usually fully booked by 'regulars'. They have plenty of land and animals to go with it, including three donkeys. They take the children on walks and picnics and outings by the lakes and sea. They are both professionally qualified and the home is registered with Cumbria County Council. In 1976 the weekly charge was £25.

OPPORTUNITY HOLIDAY TRUST

Opportunity House, Lamington, By Biggar, Lanarkshire
Tel: Lamington 636

The Trust runs two houses which are available for holidays for disabled people. Opportunity House can provide facilities from May to September at a cost per head of £3 a week for organizations supplying their own staff and food. Applications can also be considered from individual handicapped people aged over sixteen from March to December, excluding August. The cost for these is £15 a week. There is also a smaller house for eight people in Argyll which may be used by organizations during April and offers holidays for individuals from May to July and in September.

WINGED FELLOWSHIP TRUST

Winged Fellowship Trust
79/80 Petty France, London SW1H 9HB
Tel: 01-222 3589

The Trust was established to provide centres specially designed, equipped and furnished for even the most severely handicapped person to have an enjoyable holiday. It aims also to provide an after-care service, in cooperation with other agencies. The holidays give volunteers the opportunity of working together to help handicapped people. At present it has two holiday centres, at Grange Farm, Essex, and Crabhill House, Surrey. It has a special youth fortnight at Grange Farm and has arranged exchange holiday schemes for young handicapped people from Britain and the Continent. It also has a site at the National Water Sports Centre at Holme Pierrepont. Mrs J. Brander, one of the founders of the Trust, has given a great deal of thought to the problems of holidays for severely handicapped people. Writing in *Social Services* (14 September 1975) she said: 'One should never forget that a holiday centre is not a "home" in the sense that it is providing somewhere where heavily disabled people can sleep and eat and be cared for until they can rejoin their relations once more. It is not a hospital or a nursing home environment which gives a holiday, it is the atmosphere and range of activities which count.' To arrange this for severely handicapped visitors needs a staff ratio of at least one to one, including volunteers.

YOUNG DISABLED ON HOLIDAY (YDH)

Chairman, YDH
25 Belvedere Road, London SE19
Tel: 01-771 1367

Young Disabled on Holiday is a charity arranging holidays for young physically handicapped people between the ages of sixteen and thirty. This age limit also applies to the voluntary helpers – of whom there is at least one for each disabled person. They comment that 'helpers do not require any special skills and do not have to be especially fit, strong, sober. . . .' It is their policy where possible to accept any disabled person regardless of the degree of disability. The more popular pursuits include discotheques, pop concerts, barbecues, pub outings, car rallying, folk singing, wheelchair sports, riding, swimming and so on. YDH runs five or more different holidays a year including continental or camping holidays as well as one-week holidays based at Worth Abbey in Sussex. An annual reunion is held at Christmas. YDH is run by a committee of disabled and able-bodied young people. They comment that 'the most remarkable feature of YDH is the tremendous atmosphere of friendship and spirit which has grown up amongst those who have been involved with the holidays.' YDH began in 1970 as an off-shoot of Holidays for the Disabled which caters for older age groups.

Pilgrimage

ACROSS TRUST

Across Trust, Crown House, Morden, Surrey SM4 5EW Tel: 01-540 3897

Since 1972 the Trust has raised the money to build and equip three 'jumbulances' which can take sick and handicapped people in comfort across the Channel to Lourdes where the Trust has its own chalet. They also go on tours of Britain and Europe. Each bus carries a 'family' of twenty-two passengers, half of them qualified volunteer helpers who pay all their own expenses, the others people who are severely handicapped or chronically sick. All the arrangements are made by the Trust.

The jumbulances are also available for hire to societies who want to arrange their own tours.

HANDICAPPED CHILDREN'S PILGRIMAGE TRUST

Handicapped Children's Pilgrimage Trust
95 Carshalton Road, Sutton, Surrey
Tel: 01-643 4431

> The Trust takes more than 900 handicapped children and
> the same number of voluntary helpers to Lourdes every
> Easter holidays. Children of every creed or denomination
> are accepted. The Trust hopes that regional development
> will enable even more groups to go. The children enjoy a
> real holiday with outings, excursions and entertainments
> as well as their daily visit to the Grotto. They are split into
> groups of ten children and ten helpers which include a
> group leader, a doctor or qualified nurse and a chaplain.
> The children stay in hotels, not in hospitals. Local fund-
> raising groups support this voluntary Trust which needs
> more than £50 000 a year, even though the helpers pay all
> their own expenses. The Trust has a friendly newsletter.

Playschemes

CHEYNE HOLIDAY CLUB FOR HANDICAPPED CHILDREN

Mrs V. Dill-Russell
Cheyne Holiday Club for Handicapped Children
Office: 61 Cheyne Walk, London SW3
Tel: (home) 01-946 6935; (office) 01-352 8434

> These clubs for physically handicapped children aged
> seven to sixteen years meet from 10 to 3.30 on two days a
> week in school holidays. The programme of activities
> includes whole day outings. The clubs meet at four
> different 'links' in London – Chelsea, Islington, Wands-
> worth and Tulse Hill – and transport can be arranged.
> It is best to talk to the organizer at her home before
> applying. Correspondence should be addressed to the
> office.

NATIONAL PLAYING FIELDS ASSOCIATION (NPFA)

NPFA, 25 Ovington Square, London SW3
Tel: 01-584 6445

> The Association compiles a *Summer Holiday Playscheme Register*. Playschemes for handicapped children are included in the register, which is arranged by county. Anyone may send for free details of schemes in their own and neighbouring counties (send a stamped addressed envelope). In order to make the register as comprehensive as possible, anyone planning to run a holiday playscheme should contact the Information Centre of the NPFA with details at the earliest possible date (the register is normally published at the end of June). In addition the NPFA has a free fact sheet and a booklet (15p, plus 10p postage) about holiday playschemes to help anyone who feels he would like to run a holiday playscheme but doesn't know where to begin.

> See also chapter 7, **Play – information**, FAIR PLAY FOR CHILDREN CAMPAIGN, page 352

Visits and exchanges

CHIVE AND DIVE

CHIVE and DIVE
c/o Central Bureau for Educational Visits and Exchanges
43 Dorset Street, London W1N 3FN
Tel: 01-486 5101

> CHIVE stands for Committee for Hearing-Impaired Visits and Exchanges. DIVE stands for Disabled International Visits and Exchanges. Most of their work – serviced by the Central Bureau – is with the sixteen to thirty age group and although younger people are not excluded there are fewer opportunities for them. As well as individuals, a wide range of organizations are members of CHIVE and DIVE. The basic aim of CHIVE and DIVE is a pooling of information, expertise and contacts. They are the base for an international clearing house of information on visits and exchanges and can often help

A.H.F.P.—N

disabled people with a particular interest in arts, sports or anything else. They can also advise anyone who is planning a visit or exchange on travel methods, accommodation, grants and how to apply for them, insurance and reciprocal emergency health cover. They act as international go-betweens for groups wanting to find exchanges and they help individuals to organize visits for themselves and provide them with contacts. There is a step by step CHIVE and DIVE pamphlet, *Guidelines for Arranging a Project*. Most groups involve able-bodied as well as disabled people and the long-term aim is for handicapped people to be able to join in with normal youth clubs and youth exchanges. CHIVE and DIVE arrange some visits themselves as well as helping other organizations.

HANDIHOLS

Handihols, The Cottage, The Chase
Ashingdon, Rochford, Essex
Tel: Hockley (037-04) 3503/2481

There are a number of holiday home-exchange schemes for able-bodied people; Handihols is a new register and agency for homes adapted for disabled people. Anyone who would like to exchange his specially adapted home for holidays pays an annual registration fee of £3 to cover costs. He may arrange as many exchanges as he wishes for this. The organizers – both themselves disabled – hope that the scheme will make it possible for disabled people to see the whole UK and, in time, have holidays abroad as well, with only travel costs to pay in addition to normal living expenses.

HOME LINKING

Kay Duncalfe, Principal, New Forest International Youth Centre
Staddlestones, North Gorley, Fordingbridge, Hants.
Tel: Fordingbridge (0425) 54433

Kay Duncalfe has been working informally for the past few years on a scheme for providing paying-guest or exchange holidays for young handicapped visitors from abroad as an extension of her work in arranging educational visits and exchanges for able-bodied young people. She has, for example, arranged for a German girl with spina bifida to stay with an English family whose two daughters were severely handicapped and confined to wheelchairs. One of the English girls then went to stay with the other family in Germany. It is hoped to establish a more formal international committee to promote and extend these activities. She would like to find more homes anywhere in this country where a handicapped holiday visitor would be welcome.

Work camps

FRIENDS SERVICE COUNCIL (QUAKERS)

Friends House, Euston Road, London NW1 2BJ
Tel: 01-387 3601

Quaker work camps are held in the UK every year during July and August. They are projects designed to help others, and are open to all irrespective of race or religious affiliations. Some of the schemes are involved in helping handicapped people, but, more important, they have often recruited handicapped volunteers and any handicapped young person over sixteen is welcome to apply. In some years they also organize 'handicamps' where at least half the volunteers are physically handicapped. One year, for example, this was a playscheme for physically handicapped children in Waltham Forest. British volunteers are asked to contribute £3 a week towards the cost of food wherever possible. All volunteers must pay their own fares and pocket money.

9 How to Make Your Own Local Guide

This *Handbook for Parents with a Handicapped Child* is intended to help parents anywhere in England, Scotland or Wales. So we could not always give you chapter and verse: we have told you that you apply to your local social security office for the attendance allowance, but couldn't possibly give all the addresses of the local offices or the opening hours; a local guide should do that. Some of our lists consist of types – types of school, types of residential care and so on. A guide to local services can fill in all the details. Discretionary services are another example – we have said what the local authority *may* do; it is up to a local guide to say what they actually do.

We have written a local guide ourselves – covering the London Borough of Camden – and have seen a number of others. Our comments in this chapter are therefore based partly on first-hand, partly on second-hand experience.

Deciding who is to do it

There are two ways of producing a local guide – official sponsorship and do-it-yourself. Our own guide – like the *Health and Welfare Services in the New Sunderland Area* – was published officially. In our case by the social services department, in Sunderland by the social services department jointly with the council of social service. The other guides have mostly been produced by parents' groups concerned with handicapped children.

Official sponsorship has some advantages:

1 You don't have to worry about raising money for the publication costs and ought to be covered for other

expenses so there will be no need to charge for the guide.

2 In theory, you ought to be able to get all the official information you need without a hassle or having recourse to unseemly stratagems. You will have a 'passport' in dealing with other organizations so you shouldn't have to worry about explaining and justifying who you are, what you are doing and what right you have to do it. When we were doing our guide the director of social services supplied us with an official letter vouching for our *bona fides* in asking for information.

3 An official publication could be distributed through doctors' surgeries, family health centres, assessment centres, special schools, libraries and so on. It may be difficult for a voluntary group to reach such a wide potential readership.

Set against these advantages there are a number of disadvantages:

1 A guide to services written or published by the local authority is like *Which* written by the manufacturers instead of by the Consumers' Association. A guide written by the consumers can combine accurate information about existing services with campaigning for better ones. Here is a tactful example from one parents' guide on getting free plastic pants, disposable nappies and so on: 'Parents have advised us that a persistent attitude is required.'

Parents with a handicapped child are often diffident about using services. The really helpful suggestion from other parents could make all the difference. A parent who reads: 'This clinic is run by Dr Andlaw who takes a special interest in the dental care of mentally handicapped children' is much more likely to see that his child goes to the dentist.

2 You may lose editorial control over selection of items, production processes, pricing, publicity and distribution.

Sponsorship may not be the issue; the question 'Who is to do it?' may simply mean looking round your members and naming 'You, you and you' as volunteers. Few people could manage a project like this single-handed, but there must always be one coordinator/progress chaser. It will be up to the chaser to see that no organization is contacted fifteen times on fifteen different aspects of its work and he will have to carry the can if, on the day appointed for putting the sections of the guide together, one whole chapter is missing because no one knew that an unexpected family crisis had put one worker out of action.

How to pay for it

Even if you are not officially sponsored, you may be able to get some financial help. In order to apply for a grant from any source you need to have a credible budget. Printing costs are the major item for this kind of guide. Volunteers may do all the clerical work free but don't forget to allow for out-of-pocket expenses for stationery, postage and telephone. We found that every entry involved at least one letter and one phone call and a substantial number took more.

OFFICIAL GRANTS

Local authority social services departments and the education departments have both been given specific powers under Acts of Parliament by which they could give a grant towards the cost of producing this type of guide; for instance, the social services department helped towards the production costs of the Peterborough guide. In addition, Section 137 of the Local Government Act 1972 gave local authorities the power to use the product of a 2p rate for 'a purpose which is, in the Council's opinion, in the interests of the area and its inhabitants'. Some councils have a special grants committee to administer applications for grants. It may help to find out which councillors have a say in deciding about grants and whether they have any special interest in handicapped children so that you can involve them personally in the idea before it comes up to the committee officially.

The same kind of organizations – such as the Round Table, the Lions – which often help local good causes may be prepared to help a project of this kind; the Cambridge guide had a grant from a prominent local industry, the Southwark guide had a grant from the Variety Club. In addition to their grant from social services and some help from the Development Corporation, voluntary groups concerned with handicapped children chipped in with contributions towards the Peterborough guide. If you cannot get the money, you may be able to get help in kind such as free loan of a duplicator. This sort of equipment is to be found in the offices of schools, colleges, students' unions, flourishing clubs and societies.

Production

PRINTING

When you choose your printing method and format, the deciding factors will be how much money you have and what is available locally. But there are other criteria which should be kept in mind for a local guide of this type. It will rapidly get out of date. The more professionally produced the publication, the more difficult it is to revise. In the first place any alteration is expensive, in the second place a 'proper' book has a permanent look about it which discourages the idea of scrapping it and beginning again. So the Camden book was published in January 1974, attractively produced as a bound book with a glossy paper cover showing paintings done by children at local special schools. Two years later, with many of the addresses out of date, there were no plans for bringing out a revised edition. In contrast, *Mental Handicap in Bristol – a Review*, published in the same month, was cheaply printed and stapled together. By March 1975 – just over a year later – a second edition was already available. If you duplicate your guide you can staple a few sets at a time and can easily replace single sheets. Alternatively the Sunderland guide is bound in a slide binder so that single sheets can be added or removed. It is worth costing cheap card loose-leaf folders. It is important not to economize at the expense of legibility and even if you are getting them free, don't hesitate to check on the quality of stencils and duplicating before you gratefully accept.

Print: How You Can do it Yourself tells any amateur group turning publisher or printer absolutely all it needs to know. There are separate sections explaining and advising on how every type of duplicating and method of printing works. There is a national address list of non-professional print shops and larger commercial printers and typesetters. The section on paper gives the measurements of all standard sizes; a glossary explains everything from 'bleeding' and 'justification' to 'knock up' and 'scum'. Our objective critical comment is that it is absolutely smashing. It costs £1, plus 15p for each copy for postage. Please send cash with order to Inter-Action Trust Ltd.

Inter-Action Trust Ltd
Wilkin Street, London NW5

FORMAT

For a book to be simple to use there must be a logical, consistent and obvious system of reference, e.g. listing organizations under the name of the handicap they cater for, not the name of the organization. To see what we mean, try to find the society which deals with autism without knowing if it is British, English, National, Royal: the Association, Society, Council or Group for.

There must also be page numbers and an index. Don't let anyone convince you that these are added complications which make the guide more difficult to use. Without them, you have to read the whole book from cover to cover each time you want to look up disposable nappies and can't remember whether it is under disposable nappies, incon-

tinence aids, nappies, pants and pads, services provided
by the Area Health Authority, services provided by the
social services department.

Amateur publishers make some common errors. They
forget to print the publication date – especially important
where rates of benefits or grants are quoted. They are so
busy publicizing the other organizations that they frequently forget to identify themselves and say where to find
them. Another oversight is cross references. The typist
can't give an exact page reference until he or she has
finished. So the script is typed with 'see page ?', and more
often than not printed like that because no one remembers
to go back and fill it in.

What to call it

Nearly all the local guides include a reference to handicap
in the title. So when you give parents a copy of your
handbook/guide/review/survey you are implicitly saying
that their child is handicapped. A parent of a child with
spina bifida can't avoid knowing this; you may cause deep
offence to the parents of an educationally subnormal or
maladjusted child or one with coeliac disease, however
helpful the information in your book could be to that
family. Some general bland heading such as 'Services for
children with special difficulties' may lack the impact of
Cardiff's cover banner 'If you have a mentally handicapped child you need this book', but may make it acceptable
to parents who would shy away from the label 'handicapped'.

Content

A local guide should enable readers to arrive at the right
address at the right time. For every service described there
must also be details of how to apply or be referred and
what support is needed for your application. The information must be direct; that is to say, it must enable you to go
straight to the source without needing to refer anywhere
else for further details. Don't, for example, say that the

address of the social security office is in the post office; give details yourself of addresses, which office serves which area, hours of opening, how to get an appointment.

EXCHANGE AND MART

There has been a free exchange and mart of information between the local guides which we have seen. Borrowing (with permission and an acknowledgement we hope) is a useful way of getting started. But remember that other people's material is protected by copyright. We, personally, are happy to give permission for people to use the material in this book provided that they ask us first (which also makes it possible for us to warn them if the section they want to quote is already out of date) and *as long as they give a full acknowledgement to the source.* Never quote anything without checking that the information is still current. One entry of ours described a project which was entirely dependent on one keen and committed individual. We were very sorry three years later to receive a letter from his wife telling us that he had died. Unfortunately, at least two other publications, without contacting us first, later 'borrowed' this entry and suggested that people should get in touch with him.

FINDING OUT

The obvious method may seem to be a standard questionnaire, but when we have tried this it hasn't worked out. The reason may be that you can write a successful questionnaire only if you already know what the answers will be. Otherwise, the answers people want to write won't fit the questions you've asked. People can be floored by the layout and instructions as well as the content of a questionnaire. So if you do decide to use a questionnaire, it is essential to try it out on a pilot run.

For this book we simply wrote a letter explaining what we hoped to do and the criteria we would use for assessing the information. We asked people to tell us about their activities and send us any newsletters, annual reports and so on. We found that we received more of the right kind of information first time round than we did on the two occasions when we sent a questionnaire.

VOLUNTARY ORGANIZATIONS

All the national organizations listed in this book ought to be able to give you the address of any local group in or near your area. You should also check with citizens advice bureaux, councils of social service and community councils. Local libraries sometimes produce a guide to leisure activities in the area and the youth service should keep a list of local youth clubs. The superintendent in charge of the swimming baths should know of any clubs for handicapped people which make bookings. Voluntary organizations are always happy to talk about their activities or to send you any information. But for many of them the office is a corner of the dining room table and the stamps come out of the housekeeping money. The less work involved in replying to you, the sooner you'll hear from them. Explain that if they are sending you leaflets and reports about their group, they don't need to write a covering letter – as long as you have an address and phone number where you can reach them.

STATUTORY SERVICES

Professional and statutory services are far more difficult to pin down. There is an in-built reluctance of anyone in public service to give information to members of the public without pointed inquiries about who you are and why you want to know. They are puzzled as to why you should want to tell the public about their rights or what services are available since the professionals are always happy to tell them whatever it is good for them to know. What is more, in a large department, such as the social services department, it is very difficult for the left hand to know what the right hand is doing. So the reason they can't give you the information you want or else get it wrong is quite likely that they don't know themselves.

The answer is not to ask anyone – not even the director – 'What services does the social services department provide for handicapped children?' Or at any rate to regard the answer to such a question as an interesting hypothesis until it has been thoroughly tested and proved to be fact.

This applies equally to the largest social services department of all – the Department of Health and Social Security. In conversation with their exceptionally friendly and helpful information department, an officer of one of the largest voluntary societies for handicapped children said that she would love a guided tour round all the sections of the department to find out who did what. The response was enthusiastic: 'What a splendid idea – and when it's arranged we'd like to come along too.'

You will do better to ask: 'Where can I get transport to take a handicapped child to a social club?' and then ask the people actually running the service for precise details of what is provided and when and where and how to get it. The list of services in chapter 3 will give you a good idea of the questions to start on.

Distribution

Ideally your book would go to every member of every local group to whose interests it is relevant and to parents of all pupils in special schools; to councillors and local MPs; to social workers, doctors, health visitors; to citizens advice bureaux and every other local advice centre; to headteachers of all schools, special or otherwise. It would be freely available in clinics, doctors' surgeries and libraries. This needs money, petrol, energy and shoe leather, but you can take a few short-cuts. Many public organizations have some internal post or messenger system: from education office to schools, from central library to branches and so on. With goodwill and cooperation they can take on some of the distribution for you. One parcel of books to the town hall with a covering letter to the members' lobby should ensure that every councillor gets a copy.

The local press and radio will normally give publicity to an effort like this; if they do, make sure they explain where to get it.

Any local guide ought to be given away free to the families for whom it was written if possible. But there is often a national demand from professionals and parents interested in the services described or in acquiring useful hints and information for similar publications of their own. There's no reason why they shouldn't pay for a copy.

Making a local guide can be an instructive process. In the first place, you gain first-hand experience and insight (if you didn't already have it) of the frustrations and difficulties in store for anyone who wants to know what services are available and how to get them. Secondly, you become painfully conscious of the gaps. If you start with a list taken from any of the chapters in this book, in some areas of the country you will find that service after service does not exist. One group wrote to us to say: 'We are trying to compile a local guide but we are struggling to find copy to fill the second page.' When their excellent guide appeared, they had included the gaps as well as the facts. This was their heartfelt entry under the heading 'Baby-sitting Circle': 'It's about time somebody organized a babysitting circle among parents of handicapped children. Then there would be one!! Any volunteers?'

So a local guide for parents with a handicapped child will do at least two things at once: it will tell people all about what is available and it will give them the right ammunition for complaining and campaigning about all the things which are not available and should be.

What are you waiting for?

Local guides we have seen

Mental Handicap in Bristol – a Review (March 1975) Bristol Campaign for the Mentally Handicapped and their Parents, 24 Walsingham Road, Bristol

A Guide to Services for the Mentally Handicapped and their Parents (August 1975)
Cambridge Society for Mentally Handicapped Children, Mr John Sharp, 16 Leyburn Close, Cherry Hinton, Cambridge

A Review of the Services for the Mentally Handicapped in Cardiff (1975)
CMH Cardiff Universities Social Services, Joint Students Union, Park Place, Cardiff

Health and Welfare Services in the New Sunderland Area (March 1973)
Sunderland Social Services and Council of Social Service, Social Services Department, Civic Centre, Sunderland

Services for Handicapped Young People in Southwark (1972)
Southwark Council of Social Services, 53 Chatham Street, London SE1 (25p, plus postage)

Camden Handbook for Parents with a Handicapped Child (January 1974)
Cost 55p for non-Camden residents, plus 14p postage. Public Relations Department, London Borough of Camden, Room 402, Great Northern House, 79–81 Euston Road, London NW1

Peterborough Handbook for Parents of Handicapped Children (November 1975)
Carol Peel, 36 Ramsey Road, Whittlesey, Peterborough PE7 1DR

Appendix

A number of organizations which do not help parents of handi-capped children directly help in an indirect way through the professional commitment of their members. We have listed here some of those organizations which do not have a full descriptive entry in the book.

ASSOCIATION OF CHILD PSYCHOTHERAPISTS
Burgh House, New End Square, London NW3

ASSOCIATION OF EDUCATIONAL PSYCHOLOGISTS
Mrs J. Currie, 10 Manor House, Shincliffe, Durham DH1 2NS
Tel: Durham (0385) 62883

ASSOCIATION FOR THERAPEUTIC EDUCATION
Mrs Doris Holden
The Cottage, Heathlands, 56 Parkside, London SW19
Tel: 01-947 7373

ASSOCIATION OF WORKERS FOR MALADJUSTED CHILDREN
John Cross, New Barns School, Church Lane, Toddington, Glos.
Tel: Toddington (024-269) 200

BRITISH ASSOCIATION FOR THE RETARDED
17 Pembridge Square, London W2
Tel: 01-229 1855

BRITISH ASSOCIATION OF SOCIAL WORKERS
16 Kent Street, Birmingham B5 6RD
Tel: 021-622 3911

BRITISH ASSOCIATION OF SOCIAL WORKERS
Scottish Office
Dennis Gower, 50 Queen Street, Edinburgh EH2 3NS
Tel: 031-226 4526

BRITISH ASSOCIATION OF TEACHERS OF THE DEAF
Mr Arnold Bates
Thomasson Memorial School, Devonshire Road, Bolton
Tel: Bolton (0204) 43063

BRITISH DIETETIC ASSOCIATION
305 Daimler House, Paradise Street, Birmingham B1 2BJ
Tel: 021-643 5483

BRITISH PSYCHOLOGICAL SOCIETY
St Andrews House, 48 Princess Road East, Leicester LE1 7DR
Tel: Leicester (0533) 549568
> The Society has a division of educational and child psychology and a Scottish division of educational and child psychology.

COLLEGE OF TEACHERS OF THE BLIND
B. Hechle, Royal School for the Blind
Church Road North, Wavertree, Liverpool L15 6TQ
Tel: 051-733 4117

EDUCATION WELFARE OFFICERS NATIONAL ASSOCIATION
Mrs Joyce Burton
Kendall, Green Lane, Tivetshall, Norwich NR15 2BJ
Tel: Tivetshall (037-977) 310

JOINT COUNCIL FOR THE EDUCATION OF HANDICAPPED CHILDREN
Roy Bushell, 4 Old Croft Road, Walton-on-the-Hill, Stafford ST17 0LS
Tel: Stafford (0785) 61108

NATIONAL ASSOCIATION FOR THE EDUCATION OF THE PARTIALLY SIGHTED
c/o Joseph Clarke School, Vincent Road, Highams Park, London E4 9PP
Tel: 01-527 8818

NATIONAL ASSOCIATION OF INSPECTORS AND EDUCATIONAL ADVISERS
R. C. Jelley, 19 Whitby Avenue, South Bents, Sunderland
Tel: Whitburn (078-329) 3283

NATIONAL ASSOCIATION FOR MULTI-RACIAL EDUCATION
Mr M. Blakeley, 23 Doles Lane, Findern, Derby, DE6 6AX
Tel: Repton (028-389) 2848

NATIONAL ASSOCIATION OF ORIENTATION AND MOBILITY INSTRUCTORS
(of the visually handicapped)
Mrs A. Klemz, 31 Tennyson Road, Hutton, Brentwood, Essex
Tel: Brentwood (0277) 221635

NATIONAL ASSOCIATION FOR REMEDIAL EDUCATION
Roy Cooper, 77 Chignall Road, Chelmsford, Essex CM1 2JA
Tel: Chelmsford (0245) 50086

NATIONAL ASSOCIATION OF TEACHERS OF THE MENTALLY HANDICAPPED
Mrs Edna Hughes, 1 Beechfield Avenue, Urmston, Manchester M31 3RT
Tel: 061-748 2123

NATIONAL COUNCIL FOR SPECIAL EDUCATION
1 Wood Street, Stratford-upon-Avon, Warwickshire
Tel: Stratford (0789) 5332

NATIONAL UNION OF TEACHERS
Advisory Committee for Special Education
Hamilton House, Mabledon Place, London WC1H 9BD
Tel: 01-387 2442

RESIDENTIAL CARE ASSOCIATION
Fairfield Hall, Station Road, Ossett, Nr Wakefield, WF5 0JE
Tel: Ossett (0924) 271758

ROYAL COLLEGE OF PSYCHIATRISTS
7 Belgrave Square, London SW1
Tel: 01-235 2351

Index

Figures in italics have been used to show the main reference for an entry

FOR THE LOVE OF ANN

The true story of an autistic child

by James Copeland
based on a diary by Jack Hodges

'The doctor cleared his throat and spoke very quietly. "I am so sorry to have to tell you this, but I'm afraid that our tests show that it is extremely unlikely that your daughter will ever be educated, or for that matter, that she will ever be able to recognize you as her parents".'

This was in 1958 and Ann Hodges was six years and eight months old. Today the same girl is in her twenties. Full of charm. Devoted to her parents and her brother, and excitedly taking in the world and its challenges.

Between these two dates lies a remarkable story. A love story born out of hopelessness and ignorance and nurtured in years of tears and joy. . . .

ALL FOR THE LOVE OF ANN

WHAT TO DO WHEN 'THERE'S NOTHING TO DO'

Boston Children's Medical Center and Elizabeth M. Gregg

Outside: rain
Inside: mother – very busy, tired
       child – very bored, inactive

An all too familiar situation.

Needed: ideas. Ideas that are cheap. Ideas that do not require either undivided attention or artistic genius from the mother. Quickly, easily organized ideas.

Here are over 600 such ideas.

They have been collected by the staff of the Boston Children's Hospital Family Health Unit and nursery school teacher Elizabeth M. Gregg.

Simple household objects are used: clothes pegs, cotton reels, pots, pans.

With a foreword by Dr Philip Evans, Senior Physician at the Hospital for Sick Children, and amusingly illustrated by Marc Simont, the book is divided into six age groups. Here is the practical answer to the problem 'What to do when 'There's nothing to do'.

'A boon for fed up mothers' *Liverpool Daily Post*

MAGPIE MAKE AND DO

Eileen Deacon

Published jointly by Arrow and Look-In Books

Make your own pebble people . . . magazine trees . . . collage pictures . . . Maggie Magpie

Every day will be fun with this book, which brings you exciting things to 'make and do' that have been featured in Thames Television's popular *Magpie* programme, plus other original ideas and crafts to try. Clear instructions and diagrams show how you can turn everyday ordinary materials into an amazing variety of bright pictures, ornaments, gifts and toys.

Eileen Deacon is the author of many handicraft books and a regular contributor to Thames Television's *Magpie* series.

THE ROLF HARRIS QUIZ BOOK:
Animals of the British Isles

Roy Harris

Published jointly by Arrow and Look-In Books

How do mice eat frozen meat?
How do hedgehogs catch live birds and animals?
What happens when two shrews meet?

These and over 300 other intriguing questions are posed and answered in this fascinating book covering all the animals found in the British Isles. The question/answer technique provides a unique method for children to gather information on their native animals without even realizing they are learning! And the book also describes how children can observe the animals in their natural habitat making it a complete guide to wild animals.

Television personality, Rolf Harris, well-known for his interest in the conservation of wildlife has written a general introduction to the book and also an introduction to each group of animals. Roy Harris (no relation!) has devised the questions and the book is delightfully illustrated with nineteen full-page drawings by one of Britain's leading animal artists – Tony Morris.

FLOCKTON FLYER

Peter Whitbread

Published jointly by Arrow and Look-In Books

Three entertainers lost in a thick fog . . . sheep stranded in the snow . . . a ruthless kidnapper . . . a blazing circus wagon! And it's THE FLOCKTON FLYER to the rescue in this book of exciting new stories.

The Flockton Flyer is a 1932 steam locomotive lovingly restored to run on the Flockton–Lane End line in rural Somerset. When Bob and Kathy Carter, and their children Jimmy, Jan and Jessica go to live the disused Flockton station and try to set up a regular train service, they face local opposition and lack of money. This book tells of the family's adventures as, with the help of friends like Commander Frost and Bill Jelly, their hard work and ingenuity win through.

RUNAROUND QUIZ BOOK

Compiled by Robin May

Published jointly by Arrow and Look-In Books

What is a gecko? . . . Who shot Billy the Kid? . . . When was the first walk in space? . . . How long is a killer whale? . . . When were trousers introduced?

This RUNAROUND QUIZ BOOK brings you the answers to hundreds of fascinating questions like these. Test your knowledge on a wide range of subjects – from famous people, places and events to favourite books, animals, sports and science. Taken from Southern Television's popular *Runaround* series – the hectic and unusual ITV quiz game in which contestants literally race each other round the studio to answer – every question in this book has a choice of three possible answers.

Give your friends the runaround by quizzing them!

GROWING UP
A practical guide to adolescence for parents and children

Catherine Storr

Adolescence – parents look forward to it with dread; children see it as the start of growing up. For both it means adapting to unavoidable and sometimes painful change.

Despite his or her growing independence, your child will often need your support and reassurance. Will you know when – and how – to give it?

This book, by an experienced psychiatrist, takes a look at the real-life problems of growing up and offers parents and children – practical suggestions on how to cope.

THE HEBRIDEAN QUINTET

Five hilarious accounts of Miss Beckwith's life among the Hebrideans

WHAT THE CRITICS SAID:

THE HILLS IS LONELY

'A bouquet for Miss Beckwith. . . . She is a gallant woman, and has written with brio and delight, a book that will be deeply appreciated by those who value an imaginative understanding of far places' Eric Linklater

THE SEA FOR BREAKFAST

'Hilarious . . . I haven't laughed so much since *Whisky Galore*' Stanley Jackson, *Evening News*

THE LOUD HALO

'A sparkling book which could well become a Scottish humorous classic' *Weekly Scotsman*

A ROPE – IN CASE

'As delightfully and unsentimentally drawn as ever' *The Sunday Times*

LIGHTLY POACHED

'. . . one of the best writers on escape to the country' George Thaw, *Daily Mirror*